INTERNATIONAL DEVELOPMENT IN FOCUS

Connecting to Thrive

Challenges and Opportunities of Transport Integration in Eastern South Asia

MATÍAS HERRERA DAPPE AND CHARLES KUNAKA, EDITORS

WORLD BANK GROUP

1 2 3 4 23 22 21 20

Books in this series are published to communicate the results of Bank research, analysis, and operational experience with the least possible delay. The extent of language editing varies from book to book.

ISBN: 978-1-4648-1635-2

DOI: 10.1596/978-1-4648-1635-2

Cover design: Debra Naylor / Naylor Design Inc.

Contents

Boxes

Figures

Maps

Tables

Foreword

Intraregional trade accounts for barely 5 percent of South Asia's total trade—just a fraction of the 25 percent for the Association of Southeast Asian Nations (ASEAN) region. Bilateral trade between Bangladesh and India, the two largest economies in eastern South Asia, represents about 10 percent of Bangladesh's trade and 1 percent of India's trade.

Transport and trade challenges in South Asia mean that it is about 15–20 percent less expensive for a company in India to trade with a company in Brazil or Germany than with a company in Bangladesh. Several factors account for the high cost of trade between Bangladesh and India. They include inadequate transport infrastructure, protective tariffs and nontariff barriers, and a broad trust deficit throughout the region. In the case of Bangladesh and India, the low level of trust is reflected in the fact that vehicles from one country are banned from plying the roads of the other. Removing these constraints and integrating South Asia have the potential of delivering significant economic gains.

The World Bank is helping governments in the region improve highways, inland waterways, border posts, and ports along key regional corridors, as well as related logistics services. Even more important than these efforts are activities that support dialogue to build consensus toward one integrated and prosperous South Asia. The World Bank works with a number of partners to provide analyses and technical assistance to strengthen transport and trade links.

This publication is one such initiative, with financial support from Australia's Department of Foreign Affairs and Trade through the South Asia Regional Trade Facilitation Program. It presents innovative analyses of some of the building blocks for effective seamless regional connectivity. The report analyzes the Bangladesh-Bhutan-India-Nepal Motor Vehicles Agreement (MVA) and compares it with international best practices to identify its strength as well as areas where improvements would lead to seamless regional connectivity. It is the first such analysis of the MVA. The report shows that if it is strengthened, the agreement could transform regional transportation in eastern South Asia and bring significant economic gains to Bangladesh and India. The report discusses regional policy actions countries could take to strengthen the MVA and identifies infrastructure investments that could help countries realize its benefits.

Bringing economic opportunities to rural communities along the regional corridors the MVA will open, particularly to women in those communities, requires more than opening the transport network to vehicles from a neighboring country. Unleashing income gains in rural areas requires that farmers and agricultural enterprises have access to the corridors, to transport, to logistics services, and to know-how and technologies to increase production and sales and move up agricultural value chains. The report shows that interventions to remove gender-related challenges at the macro, meso, and household level are needed to improve women's participation in export-oriented agricultural value chains, which would increase inclusive development.

The analysis presented in this report should help policy makers in South Asia create an environment that is conducive to seamless regional connectivity. Such connectivity would allow deeper integration of regional markets, which would increase prosperity in South Asia.

Cecile Fruman
Director for South Asia Regional
Integration and Engagement
World Bank

Guangzhe Chen
Regional Director South Asia Infrastructure
World Bank

Acknowledgments

This report was prepared by a team led by Matías Herrera Dappe and Charles Kunaka, which included Megersa Abate, Muneeza Mehmood Alam, Yashar Araghi, Ursula Casabonne, Barbara Coello, Gerard de Jong, Gijs van Eck, Gaia Hatzfeldt, Marco Kouwenhoven, Mathilde Lebrand, Rachit Mittal, Mayank Pratap, Manish Sharma, Niklas Sieber, Roman Constantin Skorzus, and Diana Van Patten. The Bangladesh Center for Communication Programs prepared background work on gender and agriculture value chains. Tateishi Eigo provided mapping support. Tema Alawari Kio-Michael provided administrative support. Barbara Karni edited the report.

The report was prepared under the guidance of Hans Timmer, Shomik Mehndiratta, and Martin Rama. Peer reviewers Karla Dominguez Gonzalez Somik Lall, Tesfamichael Nahusenay, Antonio Nunez, Gerald Olivier, Mark Roberts, and Sebastian Saez provided insightful and constructive comments on the draft report.

The team thanks the following colleagues for their helpful contributions, comments, and suggestions: Arnab Bandyopadhyay, Valerie Mercer Blackman, Cecile Fruman, Virgilio Galdo, Henrike Hers, Mandakini Kaul, Richard Martin Humphreys, Erik Nora, Rajesh Rohatgi, and Siddharth Sharma.

This work would not have been possible without financial support from the South Asia Regional Trade Facilitation Program administered by the World Bank, with a financial contribution from Australia's Department of Foreign Affairs and Trade.

About the Editors and Authors

EDITORS

Matías Herrera Dappe is a Senior Economist in the Infrastructure Practice Group of the World Bank, where he leads policy research programs on infrastructure. He has published extensively on the links between transport and trade and transport and economic development, the efficiency of ports and logistics, infrastructure investment needs and access, private participation in infrastructure, competition, and auctions. Before joining the World Bank, he worked for consulting firms and think tanks, advising governments and companies in Latin America, North America, and Europe. He holds a PhD in economics from the University of Maryland, College Park.

Charles Kunaka is a Lead Private Sector Specialist and Global Product Specialist on Connectivity and Logistics at the World Bank, where he leads several investment operations and projects on logistics and connectivity in East Asia, South Asia, and Africa. He has published extensively on a variety of connectivity and logistics topics, including trade and transport corridors, the Belt and Road Initiative, road transport services, and logistics. He has served as joint Secretary of the Global Infrastructure Connectivity Alliance, a G20 initiative to share knowledge and experience in order to promote an integrated and coherent connectivity agenda across the world. He holds a PhD in transport from University College London.

AUTHORS

Megersa Abate is a Transport Economist at the World Bank. An expert on sustainable transport, air transport regulation, and transport modeling, he has published in leading journals in the field such as Economics of Transportation, Journal of Transport Economics and Policy, Transportation Research Part A and E. Before joining the Bank, he was a researcher at VTI in Sweden and at the VU University of Amsterdam. He holds a PhD in transport economics from the Technical University of Denmark and was a visiting student in the Institute of Transport Studies at the University of Leeds.

Muneeza Mehmood Alam is an Economist in the Transport Global Practice of the World Bank, where she works on transport and economic policy, particularly economic corridors and regional connectivity, urban transport, logistics, gender, and electric mobility. She has a keen interest in understanding the mechanisms through which the economic and social benefits of transport investments can be maximized and more equitably distributed. Before joining the World Bank, she worked in economic consulting. She holds a PhD in economics from Yale University.

Yashar Araghi is a Project Manager at the Netherlands Organisation for Applied Scientific Research (TNO). Before joining TNO, he was a Researcher at Significance BV. He holds a PhD in civil engineering from the Delft University of Technology.

Ursula Casabonne is a Senior Social Development Consultant at the World Bank, where she works on qualitative research on gender equality, and social inclusion in Latin America, Europe and Central Asia, and South Asia. She holds an MA in public policy from Georgetown University.

Barbara Coello is a Lead Rural Economist who has been consulting for the World Bank and other international institutions for more than a decade. Her work focuses on food systems, particularly the nexus of agriculture, food security, and gender. She holds a PhD in development economics from the Paris School of Economics–Paris 1 La Sorbonne.

Gerard de Jong is Director of Significance BV and Research Professor at the Institute for Transport Studies at the University of Leeds. He led projects on national freight models for Denmark, Norway, and Sweden and helped develop national and regional freight models in Belgium, in the Netherlands, and at the European scale. He has coordinated several studies on project appraisal and worked on stated preference studies on passenger and freight transport in Austria, Belgium, Denmark, France, Germany, the Netherlands, and the United Kingdom. He holds a PhD in econometrics from the University of Amsterdam.

Gaia Hatzfeldt is a Gender and Social Inclusion Consultant at the World Bank, where she works on operationalizing and generating knowledge and capacity building on social inclusion in the water sector. Her passion is designing and conducting qualitative research. She holds a PhD in social anthropology from the University of Edinburgh.

Marco Kouwenhoven is Research Leader at Significance and a Researcher in the Transport and Logistics Group of the Delft University of Technology. He has worked on stated preference studies in freight transport in five countries, working on both survey design and model estimation, and value of time and value of reliability studies in the Netherlands, Norway, and Paris. He holds a PhD in astrophysics from Utrecht University.

Mathilde Lebrand is an Economist in the World Bank's Infrastructure Chief Economist Office, where she works on the Belt and Road Initiative, economic corridor development, and connectivity. Her research focuses on economic geography, transport, international trade, networks, and political economy. She has taught at the University of Montreal and worked at the World Trade Organization. She is a Research Fellow at the Center for Economic Studies ifo Institute (CESifo). She holds a PhD in economics from the European University Institute.

Rachit Mittal is a Manager at PricewaterhouseCoopers Pvt. Ltd. He has worked extensively in the port and logistics sector in South Asia and the Middle East, managing sectoral policy reviews; roadmaps for infrastructure and services improvement; and projects on process improvement, commercial due diligence, market and financial feasibility, and business plan formulation. He has worked with government and private port operators, multilateral agencies, central government ministries, and other private logistics players. He holds a post-graduate diploma in Management from the Indian Institute of Management, Indore.

Mayank Pratap is a Manager with PricewaterhouseCoopers Pvt. Ltd. where he has worked on port and logistics advisory in India and Bangladesh. His has worked on sectoral policy reviews, roadmaps for infrastructure and services improvement, process improvement, due diligence, market and financial feasibility, and business plan formulation with government and private port operators, multilateral agencies, central government ministries, and other private logistics players. He holds a post-graduate diploma in Management from the Indian Institute of Management, Ahmedabad.

Manish Sharma is a Partner with PricewaterhouseCoopers Pvt. Ltd. in India, where he leads the Capital Project and Infrastructure practice. He works on transport and logistics, including ports and shipping, roads, railways, airports, and industrial corridors. His area of expertise include policy and regulatory advice, sector reform and planning, economic and financial analysis, performance improvement, business planning, transactions, and public-private partnerships. In addition to his work on India, he has consulted in Bangladesh, Bhutan, Indonesia, Kuwait, Maldives, Saudi Arabia, South Africa, Sri Lanka, and the United Arab Emirates. He is an active participant in various industry forums and has published numerous articles on transport, logistics, and private participation in transport infrastructure. He holds an MBA from the Faculty of Management Studies, Udaipur.

Niklas Sieber is a consultant on transport economics and regional planning with 30 years of experience in transport economics and evaluation and the environmental and social design of sustainable transportation. His specialization is transport impact assessments on economic development and poverty alleviation in developing countries. He is the author of numerous scientific publications on transport planning, management of transport systems, rural transport, and environmental economics. He holds a PhD in transport economics from Karlshure Institute of Technology.

Roman Constantin Skorzus is a consultant to the World Bank's Urban South Asia team on local governance development in Sri Lanka and to the Energy East Asia and Pacific team on hydropower development in the Solomon Islands. He is also a consultant for the International Rice Research Institute in the Philippines, covering digital development and corporate strategy. His expertise is in geospatial analysis, data science, and monitoring and evaluation. He holds a master's degree in public policy from the Lee Kuan Yew School of Public Policy in Singapore and a master's degree in geoinformatics from the Friedrich-Schiller-University Jena.

Gijs van Eck is researcher at Significance, where he works on the estimation and application of national and regional model systems in passenger and freight transport. He holds a master's degree in civil engineering from the Delft University of Technology.

Diana Van Patten is a Postdoctoral Associate at the International Economics Section in the Department of Economics at Princeton University. Her research lies at the intersection of macroeconomic development, international trade, and economic geography. As a consultant to the World Bank, she contributed to several studies on South America and South Asia. She holds a PhD in economics from the University of California, Los Angeles.

Abbreviations

3PL	third-party logistics service provider
ACS	Agreement on Coastal Shipping
ASEAN	Association of South East Asian Nations
BBIN	Bangladesh, Bhutan, India, and Nepal
CBTA	Cross Border Transport Agreement
ECMT	European Conference of Ministers of Transport
EXIM	export-import
FMCG	fast-moving consumer goods
GATT	General Agreement on Tariffs and Trade
IMT	intermediate means of transport
IT	information technology
IWT	inland waterway transport
MNL	multinomial logit model
MVA	Motor Vehicles Agreement
OSM	OpenStreetMap
PIWTT	Protocol on Inland Water Transit and Trade
QUASAR	Quantitative Air Services Agreement Review
Rs	Indian rupee
RP	revealed preference
SATCC	Southern African Transport and Communication Commission
SME	small and medium-size enterprise
SP	stated preference
TIR	Transports Internationaux Routiers
WTO	World Trade Organization

Overview

MATÍAS HERRERA DAPPE AND CHARLES KUNAKA

The Bangladesh–India border is the fifth-longest border in the world, and it is a thick border. It is more costly for Bangladesh and India to trade with each other than for either of them to trade with Germany (figure O.1). As a result of the thick border, bilateral trade represents about 10 percent of Bangladesh's trade and 1 percent of India's trade. These figures compare poorly with East Asian and Sub-Saharan African economies, where intraregional trade accounts for 50 percent and 22 percent of total trade, respectively.

High tariffs, paratariffs, and nontariff barriers are part of the problem. Simple average tariffs in Bangladesh and India are more than twice the world average. And in Bangladesh the average tariff almost doubles if paratariffs—taxes levied on imports but not on domestic output—are taken into account (Kathuria 2018). Complicated and nontransparent nontariff measures—that is, policy measures other than tariffs that affect the free flow of goods and services across borders—add to the high trade costs.

Lack of transport integration is another important contributor to the thickness of the border. Trucks are not allowed to cross borders. As a result, cargo must be transloaded, adding to transport and trade costs. On average, crossing the India–Bangladesh border at Petrapole–Benapole, the most important border post between the two countries, takes 138 hours, including 28 hours spent transloading cargo. In contrast, the time to cross borders handling similar volumes of traffic in other regions of the world, including East Africa, is less than six hours. Cargo transported by rail also has to be transloaded at the border, because of restrictions on the use of freight wagons on foreign railways. Cargo shipped between Bangladesh and India in seagoing vessels has to be transshipped in Colombo or ports in East Asia, such as Singapore and Port Klang. Deficits also exist in transport and trade infrastructure, but the main drivers of the high costs are policy and regulatory barriers.

Lack of transport integration between Bangladesh and India also means that Indian trucks are not allowed to transit through Bangladesh. As a result, India's northeast states are connected with the rest of India only through the Siliguri corridor, a 27-kilometer wide tract of land commonly known as the "chicken's neck" (map O.1). The transit restriction leads to long and costly routes between northeast India and the rest of India and the world. Goods from Agartala, for

FIGURE O.1

Average trade costs between Bangladesh and India, and between each country and Germany in 2010–17

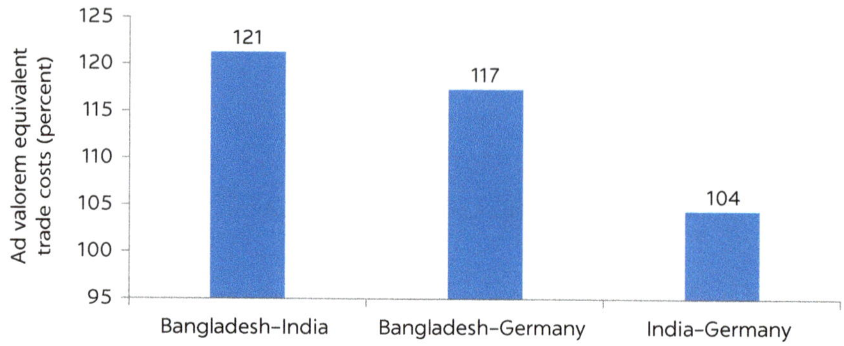

Source: Based on data from http://www.unescap.org/resources/escap-world-bank-trade-cost-database.
Note: Average trade costs are simple averages for 2010–17.

MAP O.1

Connectivity network in northeast India

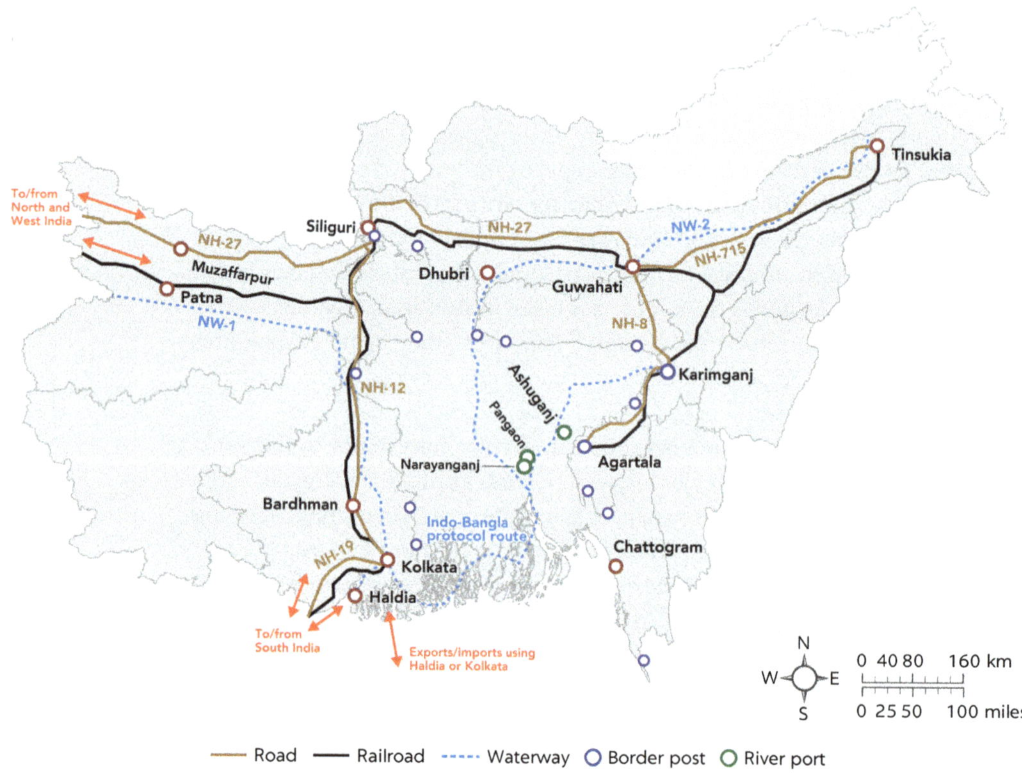

Source: World Bank.

example, travel 1,600 kilometers through the Siliguri corridor to reach Kolkata Port instead of 450 kilometers through Bangladesh. If the border were open to Indian trucks, goods from Agartala would have to travel just 200 kilometers to the Chattogram Port in Bangladesh, and the transport costs to the port would be 80 percent lower.

Northeast India lags behind the rest of India. The seven northeast Indian states contribute only 2.8 percent to India's GDP and about 1.5 percent of the

GDP contributed by manufacturing activities. The distribution within the region is highly skewed, with Assam contributing about 61 percent of the region's GDP, followed by Tripura (9 percent) and Meghalaya (7 percent) (Reserve Bank of India 2019).

Nighttime light intensity per capita—a proxy for income per capita—shows that Guwahati, in Assam, is the main economic center in northeast India, with the rest of the northeast lagging significantly behind (map O.2). But even in Guwahati, nighttime light intensity per capita is markedly lower than in all major economic centers in India, such as Delhi, Mumbai, Bangalore, and Kolkata. Poverty in northeast India is higher than in India as a whole or in other mountain states, and the rate of poverty reduction has been lower in the northeast—a fifth of the rate for India as a whole over 2005–12 (Srinivasan 2020).

Northeast Indian states lag behind other states partly because of the long distances to the rest of India and the world. Because of increasing returns to scale and transport costs, firms have an incentive to concentrate production close to large markets, which results in greater production and higher wages and prices

MAP O.2

Nighttime light intensity per capita in India and Bangladesh

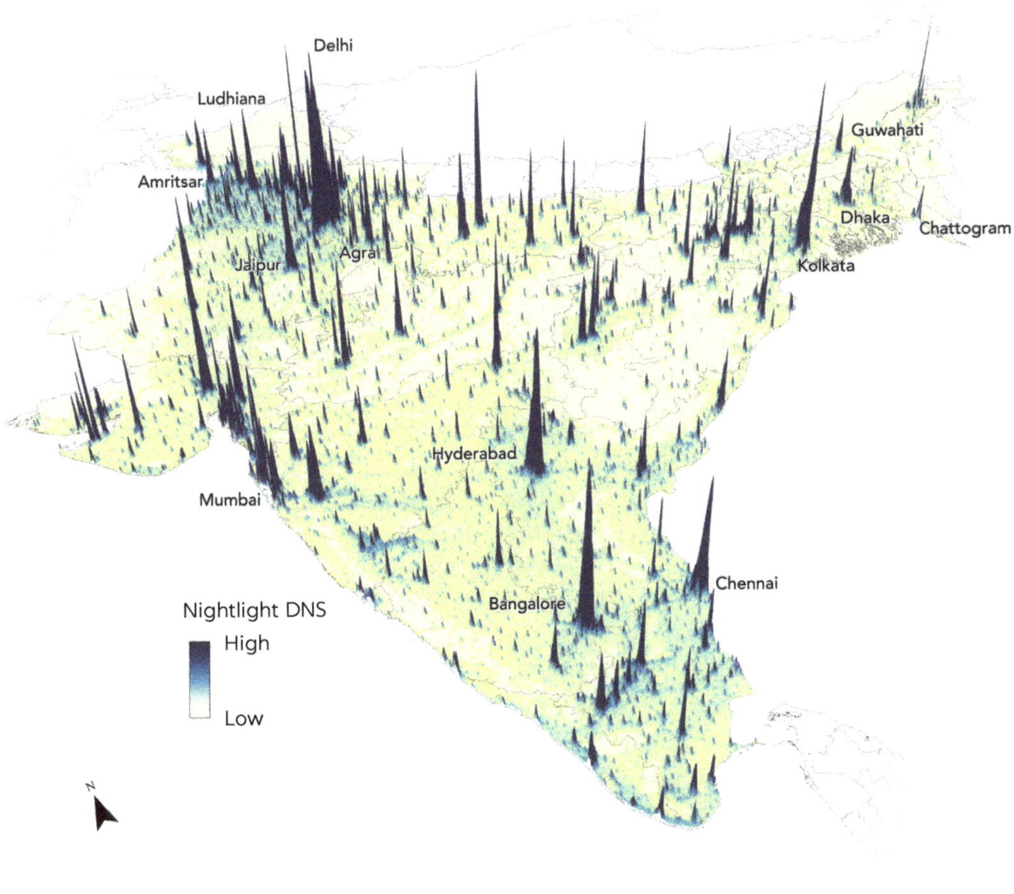

Source: Bird and others 2018.

of production factors (Redding and Venables 2004; Hanson 2005; Breinlich 2006; Head and Mayer 2006; Mayer 2008; Redding 2010; Donaldson and Hornbeck 2016). Market access is strongly correlated with income in India (Alder, Roberts, and Tewari 2018), and northeast states tend to have more limited access to markets than other states, because of their remoteness (Roberts 2016).

Economic activity in Bangladesh is concentrated in Dhaka and Chattogram; border and poorly connected districts lag behind. Nighttime light intensity per capita across the country highlights the concentration of economic activity around the capital (see map O.2). Traditionally, the districts between the western border with India and the Jamuna River have lagged the eastern part of the country, largely because of their limited connectivity and, hence, limited market access. On one side, because of the Jamuna River, which is crossable via only a single bridge, the western districts are far away from the capital city of Dhaka and the main seaport (Chattogram). On the other side, because of the thick border with India, the western districts' access to Indian markets is very limited, even though they are only a short distance from Kolkata. As a result, poverty in southwest Bangladesh is higher than in most eastern districts.

Limited connectivity leads to inefficient allocation of production inputs across sectors, firms, and regions. Misallocation of resources across firms is one of the main sources of differences in productivity and economic activity across countries. Differences between the marginal products of factors caused by misallocation may account for up to 60 percent of the total factor productivity gap between India and the United States (Hsieh and Klenow 2009). The highway investment along the Golden Quadrilateral in India led to real income gains of 2.7 percent, with the better allocation of factors accounting for 7.4 percent of those gains (Asturias, García-Santana, and Ramos Magdaleno 2018). High transport costs prevent firms from choosing optimal locations and keep production factors from being optimally allocated across sectors and regions.

MAKING THE BORDER IRRELEVANT CAN DELIVER SIGNIFICANT GAINS

The Bangladesh–India border could be made irrelevant from a trade perspective by removing trade barriers. De, Raihan, and Kathuria (2012) estimate that Bangladesh's exports to India could increase by 182 percent and India's exports to Bangladesh by 126 percent if the countries signed a free trade agreement. Improving transport connectivity between the two countries could increase exports even further, yielding a 297 percent increase in Bangladesh's exports to India and a 172 percent increase in India's exports to Bangladesh.

Removing all border frictions to the movement of trucks between Bangladesh and India could deliver significant economic benefits to both countries. Full transport integration between the two countries would allow trucks from each country to transit through the other, delivering exports and picking up imports, using any border post. Under full integration, exports and imports would be cleared at the destination, obviating the need even to stop at the border. Under full integration, income would increase by 16.6 percent in Bangladesh and 7.6 percent in India, as chapter 3 of this report shows.

The effects of full integration would differ across regions in each country, with some regions gaining more than others—and some potentially losing out—because of differences in the nature of the economic shocks on India and Bangladesh. Indian states experience both a decrease in trade costs to reach markets in other Indian states and an improvement in access to Bangladeshi markets. Bangladeshi districts benefit only from improved access to Indian markets; domestic transport costs do not change in Bangladesh. Reductions in transport costs and therefore prices increase the competitiveness of some regions. Workers and economic activities move toward the regions that gain more from integration.

The overall benefit from the opening of new transit routes for Indian trucks and improved connectivity for bilateral trade would be distributed across India. The main driver of the benefits for Indian states would be improved access to Bangladesh. The states seeing the largest increases in real income would be just west of Bangladesh, such as West Bengal, Uttar Pradesh, and Maharashtra (map O.3). West Bengal would benefit from its prime location. Uttar Pradesh would also benefit from its relatively short distance to Bangladesh but particularly from its large labor force and low wages. Maharashtra would

MAP O.3

Predicted percentage changes in real income in Bangladeshi districts and Indian states under full transport integration

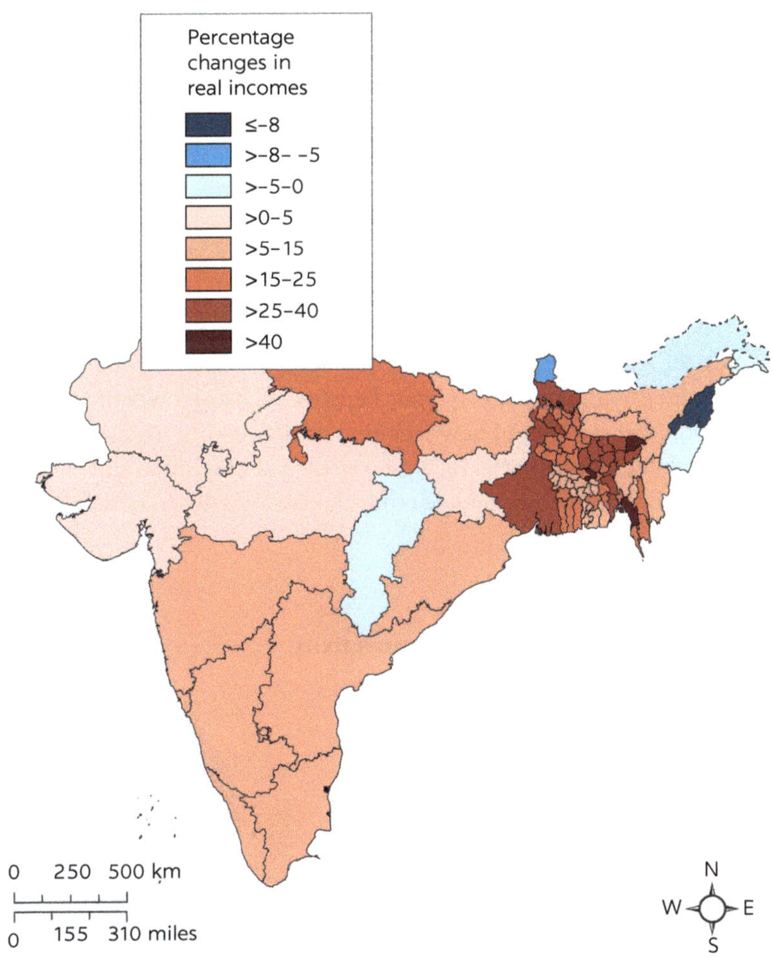

Source: World Bank analysis.

leverage its comparative advantage as India's leading industrial state. In northeast India, the overall benefits from integration would be greatest in Assam, Meghalaya, Mizoram, and Tripura, largely because of their proximity to Bangladesh. As easternmost states experience greater competition from western states and Bangladesh, some of their economic activity would move to more competitive states.

All districts in Bangladesh would benefit from integration, with the eastern districts enjoying larger gains in real income. Bangladeshi districts would see reductions in the prices of goods and inputs from India and receive higher prices, net of transport costs, for their exports, becoming more competitive. The eastern districts would benefit the most, because of their comparative advantage, which would lead workers in southwest Bangladesh to migrate to the north and east of the country, where real wages would increase by as much as 37 percent.

REGIONAL AND DOMESTIC BUILDING BLOCKS ARE NEEDED TO ACHIEVE EFFECTIVE SEAMLESS REGIONAL CONNECTIVITY

Achieving seamless regional freight connectivity and reaping its benefits requires a set of regional and domestic building blocks (figure O.2). Effective regional integration agreements are the foundation of seamless connectivity. Policies that ensure that transport service markets are competitive are also important. Agreements can remove policy constraints for the integration of transport service markets, but non-policy-related entry barriers and market distortions may also preclude the provision of cost-effective and high-quality regional transport services. Seamless regional connectivity requires an integrated transport network capable of handling demand efficiently. It requires road, rail, and inland water corridors and land, river, and seaports that can handle current and future freight volumes in a timely and cost-effective manner.

Transport integration agreements can increase the use—and hence the potential—of existing regional corridors and open new regional corridors. Corridors can generate wider economic benefits, such as growth of income and consumption, the creation of new jobs, and greater equity. The impacts work through agglomeration effects, increased trade and migration, and changes in the local economic structure, among other channels (ADB and others 2018).

FIGURE O.2

Building blocks for effective seamless regional connectivity

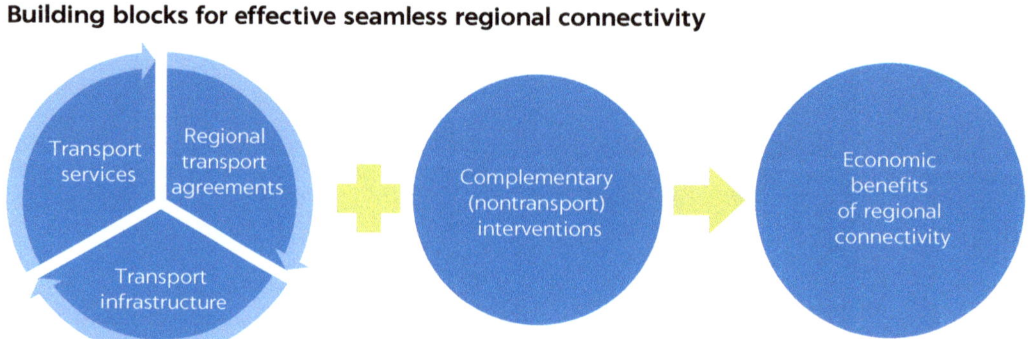

Source: World Bank.

Unleashing wider economic benefits at the local level requires that economic agents located along or near corridors have access to the corridors and to transport and logistics services to reach local, regional, and global markets. Such access is limited in rural areas, where transport infrastructure tends to be neglected and agricultural enterprises tend to suffer from inefficiencies, because of their small scale. Hence, policies that improve rural connectivity and access to logistics services are important to leverage the improved connectivity provided by regional corridors.

Wider economic benefits can be heterogeneous, with some regions or population groups gaining more than others—and some even losing. Wider economic benefits could be amplified and more fairly distributed with the help of complementary interventions that remove the most binding constraints, which can be caused by market imperfections, institutional failures, and socioreligious norms. Complementary interventions could aim to improve education and access to finance, increase women's empowerment, and remove land use constraints, among other goals.

This report presents innovative analyses of selected policy-relevant aspects of the building blocks for effective seamless regional connectivity. The report does not provide an exhaustive analysis of all policy areas needed to achieve effective seamless regional connectivity. It presents a collection of in-depth and innovative technical analyses that fill key knowledge gaps in areas that are important for taking forward the policy discussion on regional connectivity in South Asia, particularly between Bangladesh and India.

EXPERIENCE WITH TRANSPORT INTEGRATION AGREEMENTS YIELDS VALUABLE LESSONS

International transport agreements are concluded to achieve various objectives, some political, others economic. Politically, transport agreements can be used to signal the closeness of the relationship between a pair or group of countries. Even when the objective is political, however, the justification for an agreement is often economic. The main economic motivation is typically to facilitate trade in goods and services between the participating countries. Agreements can also help unlock latent demand that can be used to underpin large-scale infrastructure improvements.

International experience

As infrastructure has improved across most of the developing world, attention has shifted to the need to make sure that regulatory and procedural environments are conducive to efficient transport and logistics operations. International, regional, and bilateral agreements on transport are the main tools used to reduce if not eliminate regulatory and procedural constraints on the cross-border movement of traffic.

Most multilateral international legal instruments on transport and trade facilitation are concluded under global organizations or their specialized agencies (the United Nations, the World Trade Organization, the World Customs Organization, and the International Maritime Organization, among others). Some of the major international legal instruments on road transport include the following, to mention only a few:

- the Convention on the General Agreement on Tariffs and Trade (GATT)
- the General Agreement on Trade in Services (GATS)
- the Contract for the International Carriage of Goods by Road (CMR)
- the Convention on International Transport of Goods under Cover of TIR (Transports Internationaux Routiers) Carnets (the TIR Convention)
- the Vienna Convention on road traffic
- the Agreement on the International Carriage of Perishable Foodstuffs and on the Special Equipment to be Used for Such Carriage (ATP).

Agreements and treaties at the global level typically set the minimum provisions that are acceptable to all members of a particular organization, irrespective of their level of development or geographic location. It is then up to pairs or groups of countries to define more specific requirements, which they usually do through bilateral or regional treaties and in some cases domestic legislation. Some agreements can be self-executing, in that they do not need to be adapted through national legislation but become legally enforceable as soon as the agreement is ratified by a participating country.

In most regions of the world, groups of countries have signed road transport agreements (table O.1). Three prominent examples include the following:

- the Cross-Border Transport Agreement (CBTA) signed by the Lao People's Democratic Republic, Thailand, and Vietnam for the facilitation of the cross-border transport of goods and people
- the original tripartite agreement on road transport signed by Kenya, Tanzania, and Uganda, which has since been opened to all member countries of the East African Community (currently six countries in total)
- the Agreement on International Land Transport (Latin American Integration Association [ALADI]), signed by Argentina, Bolivia, Brazil, Chile, Paraguay, Peru, and Uruguay, for the facilitation of the cross-border transport of goods and people.

Regional agreements tend to reflect more explicitly the operating environment of the group of participating countries and offer more pragmatic provisions for those countries than do international agreements. Modern regional agreements on road transport emphasize the importance of focusing on the quality, not the quantity, of services (see, for example, Kunaka and others 2013), because quantity restrictions tend to limit supply, raise prices, and encourage suboptimal operations.

Where regional agreements are not signed, it is common for groups of countries to adopt template agreements that pairs of countries can sign. The idea is that as more and more pairs sign similar agreements, progress toward regional convergence in practices will occur. Examples of template agreements include the model bilateral agreement adopted under the European Conference of Ministers of Transport (ECMT) and the SATCC, which was part of the Southern African Development Community. Template agreements offer sets of provisions that can be accepted by most countries; they do not necessarily need to be best practice. In terms of promoting regional convergence, the ECMT is indirectly supported by a progressive multilateral permit and quota system that allows free access to bilateral, transit, and third-country transport market segments for transport operators in the territory of other ECMT participating states. Evidence abounds that the ECMT system has been successful in developing an efficient European road transport environment that is contested, though with some persisting restrictions (Kunaka and Carruthers 2014).

TABLE O.1 **Examples of regional agreements or templates on road transport**

REGION	AGREEMENT AND MODEL TITLE	NUMBER OF PARTICIPATING COUNTRIES
Africa	Memorandum of Understanding on Road Transportation in the Common Customs Area Pursuant to the Customs Union Agreement between the Governments of Botswana, Lesotho, South Africa, and Swaziland	4
	Southern African Transport and Communication Commission (SATCC) Model Bilateral Agreement on the Regulation of Cross-Border Freight Road Transport	15
	Tripartite Agreement on Road Transport (Uganda, Kenya, Tanzania)	3[a]
Black Sea Region	Memorandum of Understanding on the Facilitation of Road Transport of Goods in the Black Sea Economic Cooperation Region and the Agreement on Multilateral Transit Permits	7
Europe (including Caucasus)	Recommended Model Bilateral Agreement on Road Transport between European Conference of Ministers of Transport (ECMT) member countries	45[b]
	South-East European Cooperation Initiative (SECI) Memorandum of Understanding on the Facilitation of International Road Transport of Goods	10
South America	Agreement on International Land Transport (Latin American Integration Association [ALADI])	7
South Asia	Motor Vehicles Agreement (MVA) for the Regulation of Passenger, Personal, and Cargo Vehicular Traffic between Bangladesh, Bhutan, India, and Nepal	4[c]
South-East Asia	Agreement between and among the governments of the Lao People's Democratic Republic, the Kingdom of Thailand, and the Socialist Republic of Vietnam for Facilitation of Cross-Border Transport of Goods and People (Cross-Border Transport Agreement [CBTA])	3

Source: Based on Kunaka and others 2013.

a. The provisions of the agreement have since been incorporated in a wider agreement for members of the East African Community.

b. The model has been used by several pairs of countries. The exact number and the extent to which it has been followed is difficult to determine.

c. Four countries signed the MVA (Bangladesh, Bhutan, India, and Nepal). Bhutan pulled out after its parliament failed to ratify it.

Experience in South Asia

For several years, South Asian countries attempted to reach multilateral agreements to create integrated and modern transit systems across the region. These attempts failed, largely because of tensions between India and Pakistan. In response, the eastern South Asian countries—Bangladesh, Bhutan, India, and Nepal—signed multilateral and bilateral agreements.

The Motor Vehicles Agreement (MVA) between Bangladesh, Bhutan, India, and Nepal (known as the BBIN countries), signed in 2015, seeks to facilitate the unrestricted cross-border movement of cargo, passenger, and personal vehicles between BBIN countries. Under the agreement, trucks carrying export-import or transit cargo can move inside the territories of other countries without trans-shipping to local trucks at border land ports.

Implementation of the MVA has been delayed as the countries work to clarify some of the provisions that are supposed to be elaborated in protocols. The MVA is a framework agreement; legal instruments and operating procedures still need to be agreed upon by the countries. Some of the countries, particularly India and Bangladesh, have taken some steps toward implementation. Trial runs have taken place, in which Bangladeshi trucks have delivered exports in the Indian hinterland and Indian trucks and vessels have plied Bangladeshi roads and rivers.

The countries have signed other transport agreements on coastal shipping and inland waterways. In 2015 Bangladesh and India signed the Agreement on Coastal Shipping, which seeks to facilitate the coastal movement of cargo through river-sea vessels directly from ports in India to ports in Bangladesh. Limited direct shipping between the seaports of both countries is taking place, albeit with a restriction on vessel size of 6,000 gross tonnage.[1] Both governments are planning to allow the use of larger vessels in a revision of the agreement scheduled to be signed in 2020. In 2018 the two countries signed an agreement for the use of the Chattogram and Mongla ports for the movement of goods to and from India. It stipulates specific routes to connect both ports with northeast India.

Both Bangladesh and India have extensive networks of navigable rivers that provide an environmentally friendly transport alternative for landlocked northeast India and Bhutan. Consequently, they have signed bilateral agreements to increase use of their inland waterways for regional trade. The Protocol on Inland Water Transit and Trade (PIWTT), signed by India and Bangladesh in 2009 and subsequently amended to add new routes and ports, seeks to facilitate transit cargo movement through Bangladesh's vast inland waterway network. In 2019 Bangladesh and Bhutan signed the standard operating procedure that operationalizes the memorandum of understanding signed in 2017 for bilateral and transit cargo to be transported on inland waterways.

THE MOTOR VEHICLES AGREEMENT IS AN IMPORTANT FIRST STEP THAT CAN BE IMPROVED

The agreement has both strengths and gaps

The MVA was signed in Bhutan on June 15, 2015. It has since been ratified by Bangladesh, India, and Nepal. In 2017 the legislature of Bhutan declined to ratify the agreement, citing gaps and conflicts between the agreement and the national concerns over such areas as immigration, routes and infrastructure, ability to compete, and environmental impacts, among other concerns. Technically, it is possible for Bhutan to ratify the agreement at any moment.

Given the absence of bilateral agreements on road transport between some South Asian countries, the MVA fills a critical void. It addresses many of the essential items that are part of regulating international road transport services. Road transport agreements such as the MVA can enhance operational efficiency, signal the strength of economic and political relations, or achieve other objectives. As such, the MVA is as important for what it covers as for what it excludes.

The MVA includes many important features considered necessary for international agreements of movement on road transport (chapter 1 describes the main features of such agreements). It allows countries to access all territories of the parties and does not limit distance. It allows equal sharing of operator permits by parties. However, permits can be issued for only one year at a time, with a set time limit for authorization by the neighboring country, to avoid delays in approvals. The MVA offers clarity on the types of traffic the agreement regulates and the way in which taxes are treated in foreign territories. It allows most regular types of traffic to ply on designated routes.

Like similar agreements, the MVA provides for nondiscriminatory treatment of commercial charges on highways. Where fees are payable, the agreement provides that they shall be collected at the point of entry. It explicitly provides that no additional fees shall be payable on the way, especially fees levied by municipal authorities. The agreement also provides for the temporary admission of vehicles free of customs duty. These measures are progressive, consistent with some of the more open agreements.

The agreement has some critical gaps, which could hamper the emergence of a regional integrated and contested market for road transport. Chief among them are the lack of standards for the design of infrastructure on which services are permitted, the absence of rules on the training and issuance of driver's licenses, and the omission of general principles for transit movements. The MVA does not permit triangular traffic movements, which could offer flexibility to operators in how they route trucks across the region. Triangular operations can be important, given the geography of trade flows across the region and the prevalence of unidirectional traffic flows in some corridors. The agreement also provides for operations only on specified routes and through designated border-crossing points, which can be a constraint as trade interactions become more intense and complex. In addition, the agreement places an onerous regulatory burden on truck operators, mandating at least 10 documents that must be carried on each passenger vehicle and 9 on each goods vehicle. The lack of regulation of driver working hours is another important gap in the MVA—one that could compromise safety. The agreement allows participating states to resort to national law in cases of gaps or conflict between regional and domestic requirements—a possible source of uncertainty for operators, as it opens the possibility of countries using their domestic requirements to limit regionally integrated services. These more technical elements can prevent the full realization of the benefits of the liberalization of services that the agreement entails. The BBIN countries clearly recognize the importance of addressing some of the above gaps, and indeed are already working on several of them. However, the point remains valid that unless the various issues are all tackled, then the benefits of the MVA will not be maximized.

Despite gaps, the MVA represents a significant step toward the creation of a cross-border integrated road transport market among BBIN countries. If the agreement is to live up to its promise, the BBIN countries need to negotiate protocols to address some of the missing features. Priority should be placed on the technical aspects of transport services, requirements for goods carriage, and driver qualifications and licensing.

Routes and modes that are not based on the preferences of shippers and carriers can lead to inefficiencies

Ideally, countries should not prescribe the routes and modes to be used for freight transport, leaving that decision to shippers and carriers unless there are important safety, security, or environmental reasons to limit the volume of traffic in certain areas. If countries do prescribe the routes and border posts to be used, as the MVA does, the selection should be based on shippers' and carriers' preferences. If they are not, integration agreements could lead to limited or no changes in transport costs, patterns, and volumes. Shippers and carriers decide on the routes and modes they use to transport freight based on the level of service of different routes and modes—that is, the time, costs, reliability, probability of cargo damage and theft, number of handlings and transshipments, and efficiency of border crossing along the routes and modes.

A stated-preference analysis of shippers and carriers in Bangladesh and India operating along corridors in eastern South Asia shows that unrestricted transport integration would significantly change freight patterns between northeast India and the rest of India and the world and between Bangladesh and India. The analysis, presented in chapter 2, shows that carriers and shippers in the region have a strong preference for road corridors through Bangladesh and that carriers and shippers engaged in bilateral trade between Bangladesh and India would also make significant use of coastal shipping.

Almost all road-based freight movements between northeast India and the rest of India are expected to go through Bangladesh if the restrictions to free movement of freight are removed. A significant share of freight currently moving on rail through the Siliguri corridor is expected to shift to the road corridors through Bangladesh (map O.4). Even some freight currently traveling between northeast India and the rest of India on inland waterways through Ashuganj is

MAP O.4

Predicted freight traffic between northeast India and rest of India in 2025 under integration

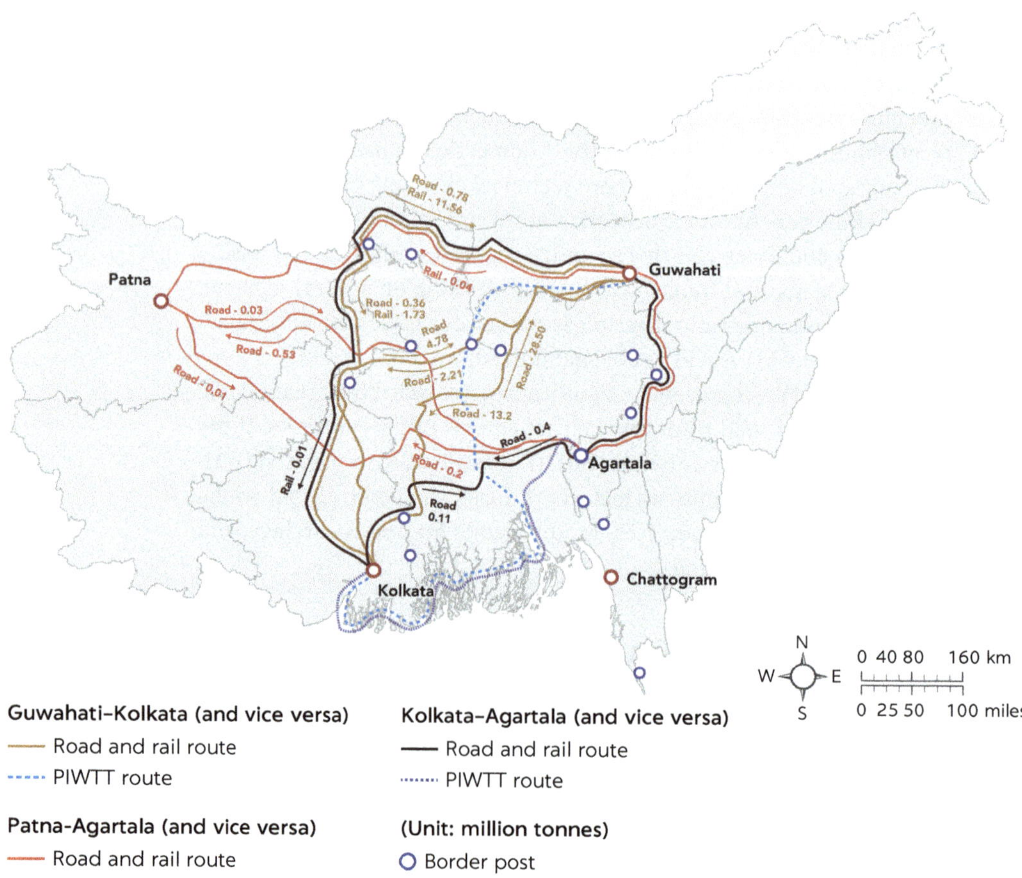

Source: World Bank.

expected to shift to road corridors once they are open to Indian trucks. Changes in freight flows are driven by significant reductions in transport time and costs. For example, the transport time and costs on the route between Agartala and Kolkata through Bangladesh is one-third that of traveling through the Siliguri corridor. The transport time and costs between Agartala and Patna via Hili in the northwest of Bangladesh are 40–50 percent lower than through the Siliguri corridor. For freight traveling between Guwahati and Kolkata, the routes through Bangladesh are about 20–25 percent faster and less costly than the routes through the Siliguri corridor.

Given the choice, shippers in northeast India trading with the rest of the world would prefer Chattogram Port over the Kolkata and Haldia ports. Currently, 95 percent of exports from Assam, Meghalaya, Manipur, Nagaland, and Arunachal Pradesh are transported to the Kolkata and Haldia ports on the road through the Siliguri corridor; the remaining 5 percent moves by rail through the same corridor. Once restrictions on the movement of Indian cargo through Bangladesh are lifted, 93 percent of exports from northeast India are projected to use the Chattogram Port, with almost all freight going by road (map O.5). The preference of Chattogram over Kolkata and Haldia reflects the lower time and costs to reach Chattogram. The Guwahati to Chattogram road

MAP O.5

Predicted freight traffic of exports from and imports to northeast India in 2025 under integration

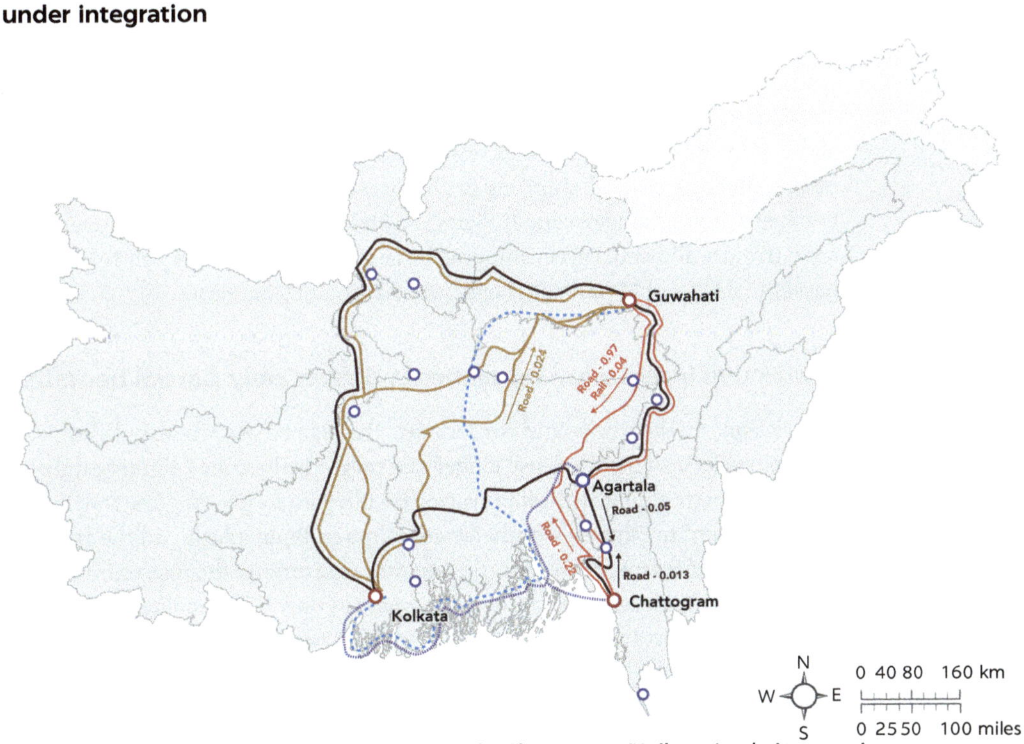

Guwahati–Kolkata (and vice versa)
- Road and rail route
- PIWTT route

Guwahati–Chattogram (and vice versa)
- Road and rail route

Agartala–Chattogram/Kolkata (and vice versa)
- Road and rail route
- PIWTT route

(Unit: million tonnes)
- Border post

Source: World Bank.

route is about 40 percent faster and cheaper than the current Guwahati to Kolkata route through Siliguri corridor. Reaching Chattogram from Agartala by road takes only 30 percent of the time it takes to reach Kolkata through Siliguri and costs 80 percent less.

The optimal routes connecting Guwahati and its catchment area with Kolkata and the rest of India through Bangladesh do not use the Sylhet–Benapole corridor. Shippers and carriers prefer either using the Gasuapara–Benapole corridor through the Bangabandhu Bridge or entering Bangladesh through Mahendraganj and leaving through Hili. For the latter route to be a viable option, a bridge over the Jamuna River in the Rangpur division and its approach roads need to be built. Crossing Bangladesh between Mahendraganj and Hili ranks high among Indian shippers' and carriers' choices, because it is the route with the shortest length and time in Bangladesh. Similarly, some of the optimal routes connecting Agartala with Patna and north India go from Akahura in the east of Bangladesh to Hili and Darshana in the west. None of these routes is among the routes mentioned in public documents as being considered for the implementation of the MVA. The routes usually mentioned are the southwest–northeast and northwest–southeast corridors.

Once direct shipping between seaports using larger vessels is allowed between both countries, coastal shipping will become more prominent in bilateral trade between Bangladesh and India. Currently, the road route through Petrapole-Benapole accounts for 77 percent of bilateral trade between the two countries; inland water transport captures 17 percent, followed by rail and coastal shipping, which account for 4 percent and 2 percent respectively. When the agreements are in place, the road routes through the Petrapole-Benapole land port will remain the key route facilitating freight movement (map O.6). The shares of road transport and coastal shipping are projected to increase to about 87 percent and 11 percent, respectively. The main reason for the increase in the share of coastal shipping is the presence of direct shipping services between Chattogram Port and Kolkata and Haldia ports using larger vessels than are currently allowed. Direct shipping by large seagoing vessels will be about 50 percent faster and 75 percent cheaper than through Colombo.

Restrictive integration agreements deliver only partial benefits

Restrictions on the routes and border posts that can be used by Bangladeshi and Indian trucks lead trucks to use longer and more costly routes, limiting the benefits of the agreement. If Indian trucks are allowed to ply only the northeast-southwest and northwest–southeast corridors in Bangladesh and the frictions that affect trucks from both countries are removed only on the main border posts along these corridors, real income will increase by only 11.3 percent in Bangladesh and 5.6 percent in India. These gains are 68–74 percent of the gains under full integration, where trucks can ply any road and use any border post along the Bangladesh–India border.

Limiting the routes and border posts that can be used affects the spatial distribution of the gains from integration. Under both full integration and the MVA, Dhaka district will enjoy the largest gains in real income and real wages, followed by Chattogram district. Under just the MVA, gains in real income in Dhaka and Chattogram will be 67 percent and 59 percent, respectively, of the gains under full integration; for the median district, the gains in real income under the

MAP O.6

Predicted bilateral freight traffic in 2025 under integration

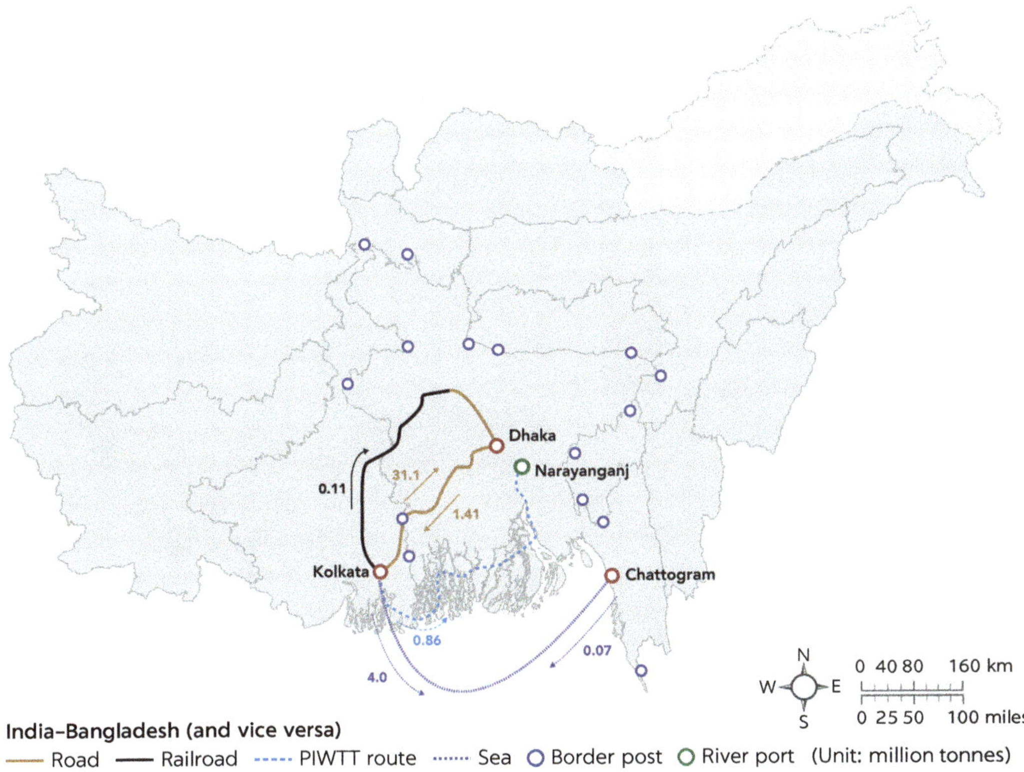

Source: World Bank.

MVA will be 44 percent of the gains under full integration (map O.7 and figure O.3). Indian states will enjoy smaller gains with the MVA than with full integration, with states closer to Bangladesh gaining less, relative to the gains under full integration, than more distant states.

Regional policy actions can strengthen the Motor Vehicles Agreement

Accommodating differences in infrastructure is costly in terms of both time and money. Less costly to change are constraints imposed by different countries' policy choices. This sub section discusses key regional policy actions the countries should take to strengthen the MVA.

Harmonizing driver's licensing and visa regimes

It is important for the MVA countries to negotiate and implement complementary reforms, especially standardization of road signage, driver training, insurance, and related dimensions. The MVA requires vehicle crews to carry passports and be issued multiple-entry visas valid for at least one year. However, the agreement does not state where the visas should be issued. In some regions, agreements explicitly state that visas may be obtained at the border, which saves crews the burden of having to travel to the capital for consular services. Bhutan cited the MVA provision on visas as one of the reasons for not ratifying the MVA.

MAP O.7

Predicted percentage changes in real income in Bangladesh and India from the Motor Vehicles Agreement

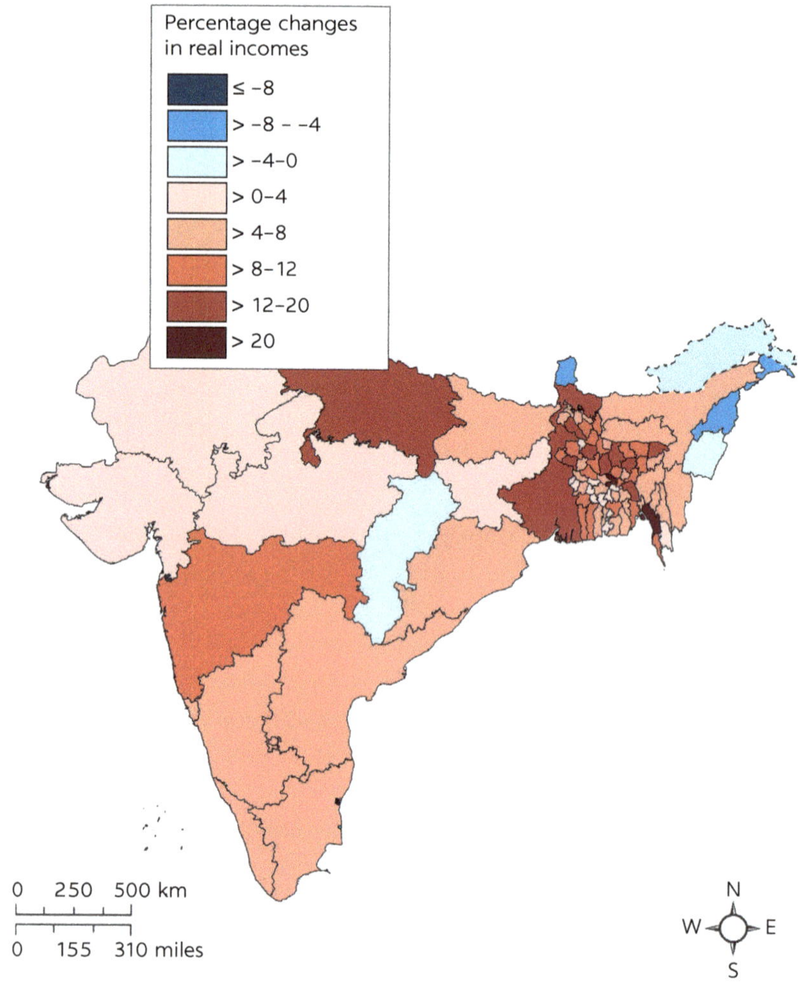

Source: World Bank analysis.

Establishing an efficient regional transit regime

A well-functioning transit regime is a prerequisite for efficient cross-border road transport operations. The MVA does not provide much detail on transit, other than acknowledging that the agreement covers transit movements. The absence of integrated and modern transit regimes has long been an impediment to transit traffic across South Asia. Ongoing and planned improvements in intra- and interregional connectivity are adding to the urgency of developing such a regime, especially given the geography of the region, where transit across a foreign territory is often unavoidable. Policy makers can borrow from several international practices and exploit the new capabilities offered by information technology (IT) in data sharing and cargo tracking by customs administrations.

Two considerations are critical to introduce an efficient transit regime. First, a functional transit procedure through Bangladesh is needed that allows the seamless movement of goods between West Bengal and the northeastern states of India and through India for traffic between Bangladesh and Bhutan and Nepal with no significant waiting time at the border or en route because of inspections

FIGURE O.3

Correlation between real income gains in Bangladesh and India under full integration and the Motor Vehicles Agreement, by district and state

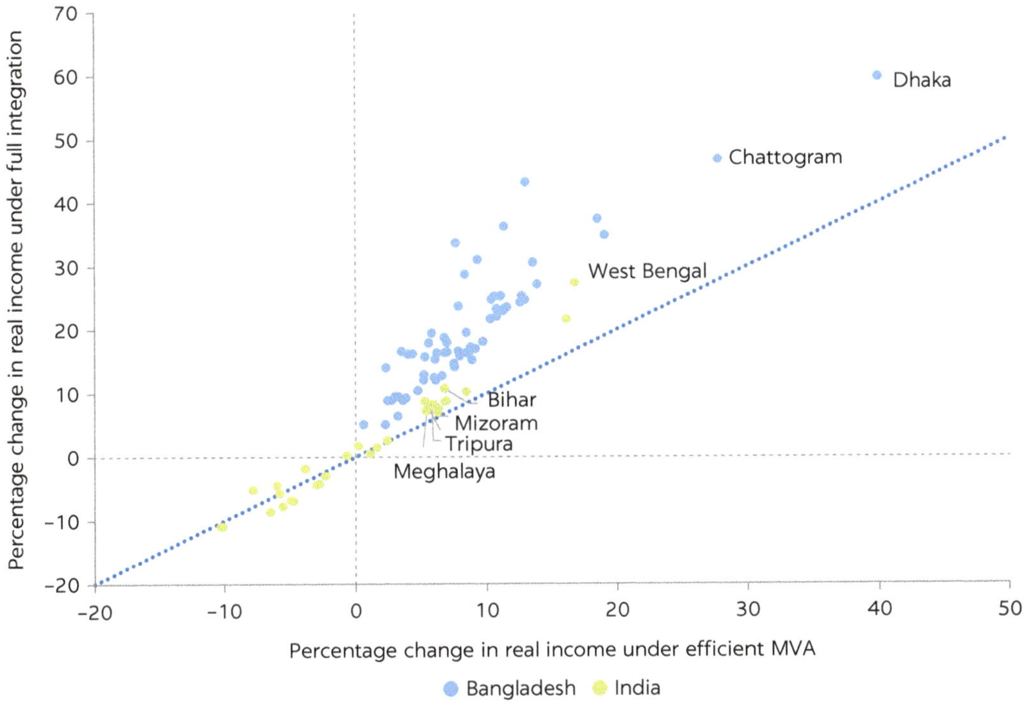

Source: World Bank analysis.

or transloading. As India is already party to the TIR, Bangladesh could join the same convention, making it possible to implement a proven international transit regime.

Second, mechanisms are needed that allow the transit countries (Bangladesh and India) to recoup the costs associated with the use of their infrastructure and services by vehicles registered abroad, based on universal principles on freedom of transit. With suitable transit arrangements, some of the road traffic currently moving through the Siliguri corridor in particular could transit across Bangladesh, yielding significant savings in shipping times.

Rationalizing and digitizing documents

The need to obtain documents, submit them, and have them checked or processed by different jurisdictions can add to the costs of trade. The MVA lists 11 documents that must be carried on a vehicle operated under its regulation. These documents are in addition to the more than 22 documents and 55 signatures required for trade between Bangladesh and India (CUTS International and IRU 2017). The burden on drivers to keep many documents in the vehicle is particularly heavy in South Asia, where most drivers are semiliterate.

One way of addressing the large number of documents could be to exploit the possibilities offered by IT and cross-border data sharing. The BBIN countries could significantly reduce the number of documents drivers have to carry by defining and adopting data standards and agreeing to share data among competent authorities that regulate road transport services. Transport regulators in many parts of the world use IT systems to check and verify the status of vehicles and drivers, including their working hours.

Rationalizing the selection of routes

The MVA restriction on routes and border posts that can be used by trucks is not based on the preferences of shippers and carriers. As a result, the benefits of road transport integration will not be fully realized. Ideally, countries should remove the constraint on routes and leave that decision to shippers and carriers. A second-best alternative would be to base the selection of routes and border posts on a detailed analysis of shippers' and carriers' preferences, such as that presented in chapter 2.

SEAMLESS CONNECTIVITY REQUIRES BETTER TRANSPORT INFRASTRUCTURE AND SERVICES

Differences in standards, axle-load limits, and quality hamper road transport operations between Bangladesh and India. For the same class of trucks, axle-load limits are consistently lower in Bangladesh than in India (table O.2). This difference could reflect weaker pavements in Bangladesh or a regulatory legacy in which limits have not kept pace with trends in trucking technology. The Bhutan Road Safety and Transport Authority (RSTA) Act of 1999 does not specify weight limits, relying instead on the weight limits specified by the vehicle manufacturer. In 2019 Bhutan's legislature approved raising the limits to 28 tonnes for 10-wheel vehicles, the most common configuration in South Asia. Differences in axle-load limits and vehicle dimensions have been cited as one of the reasons for denying India transit rights across Bangladeshi territory; they also explain why Bhutan did not implement the MVA.

Integration agreements, particularly the MVA, will increase traffic in some of the major corridors through Bangladesh, exacerbating congestion, unless measures are put in place to increase the effective capacity of the corridors on both sides of the border. Congestion in Bangladesh is a serious problem along all major corridors (figure O.4). Herrera Dappe and others (2020) find an average speed of 19 kilometers an hour along main corridors—less than half what it would have been under uncongested conditions. Reasons for congestion include

TABLE O.2 **Gross vehicle weight limits in Bangladesh and India (tonnes)**

VEHICLE TYPE	BANGLADESH	BHUTAN	INDIA	NEPAL
2 axle (1 front, 1 rear)	—	—	18.5	—
3 axle (1 front, 2 rear)	22	28	28.5	19
4 axle (steering + 3 axles)	25	—	31.0	—
5 axle (2 prime mover + 3 trailer)	38	—	43.5	—
6 axle (3 prime mover + 3 trailer)	41	—	44.0	—
7 axle (3 prime mover + 4 axle)	44	—	—	—

Source: World Bank staff estimates, based on data from various sources.
Note: — Not available.

FIGURE O.4
Actual versus free-flow travel time in Bangladesh, by corridor

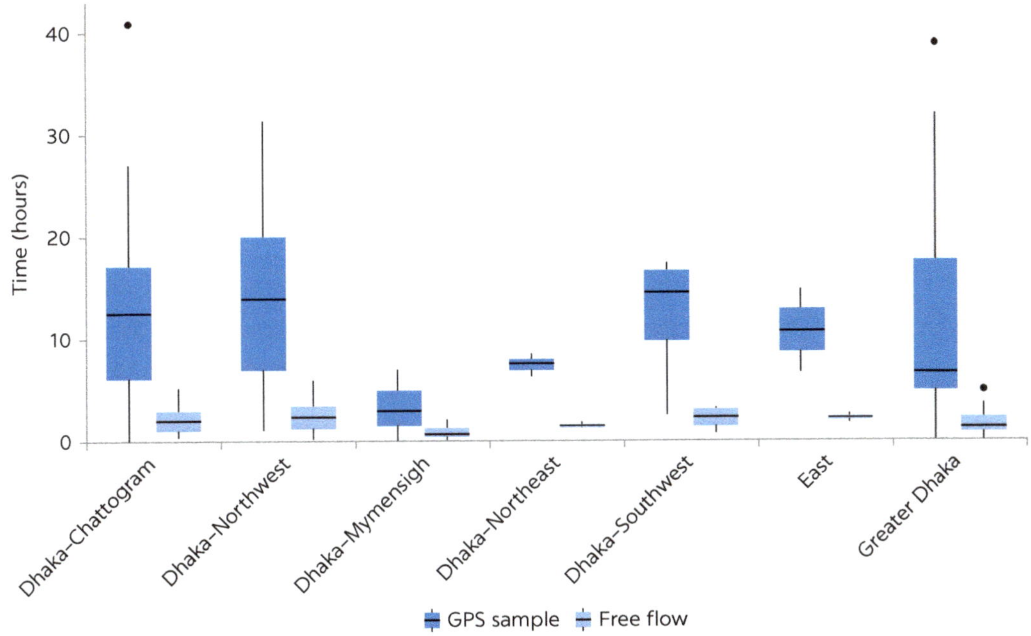

Source: Herrera Dappe and others 2020.
Note: The bottom of a box represents the first quartile, the middle bar the second quartile (median), and the top of the box the third quartile. The whiskers represent the highest and lowest values, excluding outliers. Dots are outliers.

the insufficient capacity of roads and bridges to handle current demand; the need to rely on inefficient ferries to cross rivers (because of the small number of bridges); the mismanaged system of weight checks at bridges; and policies, regulations, and procedures that create unnecessary trips. Road transport moves through various land ports on the Bangladesh–India border; most of them are connected through two-lane roads on both sides of the border, which are in poor condition.

Cargo movement between India and Bangladesh by rail is very limited, because of infrastructure challenges. Railways in the region use a combination of meter and broad-gauge lines, limiting cross-border movements. Bangladesh has had to construct both gauges in some parts of the network to interface with the Indian system, but there are still compatibility issues with the broad-gauge network of India. The Jamuna Bridge, which connects the western and eastern rail networks of Bangladesh, is the major barrier to rail transport because of structural problems that limit the loads that can be transported by rail.

Bangladesh's extensive river network presents challenges for navigation. The larger rivers are up to 50 meters deep; most of the lower Meghna River (the main route to Dhaka from the Bay of Bengal) is 10–25 meters deep. Bars have very shallow depths, however, especially at the confluences of the major rivers and their tributaries, at river bends, and in the wide delta area, limiting navigation. Poor navigation aid systems and very limited nighttime aids also limit safe navigation. Poor evacuation and handling infrastructure and the operational practices at river ports have long hampered the efficient handling of cargo. Improvements are under way in Bangladesh and India to improve several river terminals, including the Ashuganj River terminal in Bangladesh, which has road links and customs facilities for transit cargo to northeast India through the Akhaura (Bangladesh)–Agartala (Tripura, India) land border.

The Chattogram and Mongla ports in Bangladesh and Kolkata Port in India are among the most inefficient ports on the subcontinent (Herrera Dappe and Suárez-Alemán 2016). Chattogram Port handles about 90 percent of seagoing cargo in Bangladesh, with the remaining cargo handled by Mongla Port. Mongla's role is limited, because it faces challenges with respect to draft availability, handling infrastructure, and connectivity. Chattogram Port suffers from severe capacity constraints associated with inadequate infrastructure and processes. Because of the limited number of cranes to handle containers, the port relies on less efficient vessel-mounted cranes to handle large numbers of containers. Because of vehicle congestion inside the port, the absence of separate weighbridges for the entry and exit movement of vehicles, and the slow uplift of containers in the storage yard, the few port cranes work at only 8–12 cycles an hour instead of the optimal 22–28. These inefficiencies led to an average preberthing waiting time at Chattogram of 10 days, which is also highly variable as a result of frequent crane breakdowns. Chattogram and Kolkata (including Haldia Docks) are among the South Asian ports in which container vessels spend the longest time at berth, leading to the longest vessel turnaround times in the region.

The success of regional transport agreements relies partly on competitive markets for transport services in the signatory countries. Such markets do not exist in eastern South Asia. Trucking service markets in Bangladesh are not competitive. Thousands of operators, many of them using very small fleets or single units, provide trucking services, which should nurture competition. However, drivers unions, owners associations, and brokers related to them set prices and control access to cargo, interfering with the market mechanism and preventing full competition. According to one study, more than 85 percent of shippers interviewed believe there is no competition in logistics service markets in Bangladesh (Herrera Dappe and others 2020).

The role that associations, agents, and drivers play in controlling access to loads hinders the entry of international operators. International operators are not able to penetrate the market unless they work with local players who belong to unions and associations. Having to work with local players means that international operators do not have control over the quality of their services or the prices they charge.

Drivers unions and owners associations are large enough and well organized enough that they exert significant influence over policy reforms and market operations. For example, whenever the regulatory authority tries to set axle-load restrictions with severe penalties for overloading, the drivers union and associations call strikes to get the restrictions rescinded.

Several policies would improve regional connectivity

This section discusses key policy actions the countries should take to improve regional connectivity.

Standardizing infrastructure design

The interconnectivity of infrastructure and the interoperability of services is a defining attribute of networks; it is especially important in transport systems. Interconnectivity and interoperability across borders, based on transport infrastructure that is built to the same standards and specifications, provides the basis for allowing vehicles loaded to the same limits to cross borders without hindrance.

For the MVA corridors to allow seamless operations, they need to be built to the same minimum design standards, so that they can handle similar axle-load limits and vehicle configurations. Different load limits or vehicle dimensions may require goods to be transloaded or loads to be split, resulting in delays and high costs. Lack of standardization presents challenges for operators, who may not know in advance the limits on particular road sections in each country. The problem is compounded by the fact that weight limits at bridges are not notified in advance (before vehicles arrive), even along major regional corridors. Harmonization of axle-load and maximum vehicle / combination mass limits is essential for an integrated and efficient road transport industry in South Asia. It is particularly important for increasing the low level of intraregional trade. There is an urgent need to ensure that standardized regulations govern vehicle load limits and dimensions in the BBIN countries.

Increasing the level of service along regional corridors

For carrier and shippers to shift their cargo movements to optimal routes and modes once the MVA and all other transport integration agreements are implemented, the level of service of regional corridors needs to be improved. Policy makers need to think very carefully about where to invest, what to invest in, and what policies to implement to increase the level of service of corridors.

Policies and investments in transport have wider economic impacts. They are not spatially neutral, as the concentration of people and economic activities gives rise to agglomeration benefits. A regional transport master plan that identifies the mix of investments and policies that yield the greatest net benefits should be developed, considering all transport modes, both infrastructure and services, and the wider economic impacts of transport interventions. The master plan should be anchored in a transport model.

Expanding the effective capacity of core transport and logistics infrastructure will lead to a higher level of service along regional corridors. Key components of the transport and logistics system are highly congested, and projected growth will further strain the system. Connectivity needs to be improved by maintaining and expanding existing links and building new ones. For example, one of the potential road routes through Bangladesh that ensures the shortest travel time in Bangladesh connects Kolkata and Guwahati through the Hili and Mahendraganj/Dhanu-Kamalpur land ports and crosses the Jamuna River in Rangpur division, where there is currently no bridge. A new bridge over the Jamuna River and approach roads in Rangpur division would allow traffic to use such route. Improvement of land port facilities and development of off-border customs clearance facilities in Bangladesh and India would remove bottlenecks at the border.

The solution is not just to invest more, however, but to invest better, by focusing on the service gap instead of the infrastructure gap. Improving service requires much more than just capital expenditures. Improving the operation of the Chattogram, Mongla, and Kolkata ports, for example, would expand their effective capacity. Lack of proper maintenance of the transport infrastructure reduces the capacity of the network and leads to higher capital investment needs. Ensuring adequate funding for maintenance and proper execution will therefore be a step toward better investments.

Ensuring competition in transport service markets

Governments in eastern South Asia should ensure that transport service markets are competitive. Competitive markets would ensure that reductions in transport costs lead to reductions in the prices of transport service. They would also provide incentives for service providers to improve the quality of their services and invest in technology and equipment.

Ensuring competitive markets requires independent national competition authorities with the power to enforce competition laws in any market. Bangladesh's Competition Act aims to prevent collusion in the market and price-fixing by industry players through various mechanisms, such as bid-rigging, control over the supply of goods or services, and abuse of dominant position. However, the Bangladesh Competition Commission stipulated in the act is not yet fully functional.

Greening road transport

Transport integration will deepen the reliance on road transport for the movement of freight across eastern South Asia, because road corridors dominate rail and inland water corridors in terms of door-to-door time and cost. The route and mode choice analysis in this report shows that there will be a switch to shorter road routes, a shift of cargo from rail and inland water transport to road transport, and an increase in the modal share of coastal shipping. The impact on emissions from transport depends on the characteristics of the vehicles and fuels, congestion, and idling time. A thorough analysis is needed to assess it.

The route and mode choice analysis also indicates that improvements in the level of service of existing rail and river routes leading to even 50 percent reductions in time and cost along those routes or deteriorations in the reliability and safety of cargo on the road corridors through Bangladesh would not sustain the current shares of greener modes of transport, such as inland water or rail. There is therefore a need to reduce the environmental footprint of trucks in the region, as trucks will remain central to the movement of freight.

LOCAL BENEFITS CAN BE ENHANCED

Opening the borders to the movement of trucks and improving transport infrastructure along regional corridors would increase real wages more in some regions than in others. Indeed, in some regions economic activity might even decrease, as workers move to more competitive regions. The analysis presented in chapter 3 shows that although all districts in Bangladesh would see increases in real wages once the MVA is implemented, the gains would be uneven. The southwest of Bangladesh, traditionally a lagging region, would see some of the lowest increases in real wages and experience some of the largest outflows of workers (map O.8).

MAP O.8

Predicted percentage changes in number of workers in Bangladesh and India following adoption of the Motor Vehicles Agreement

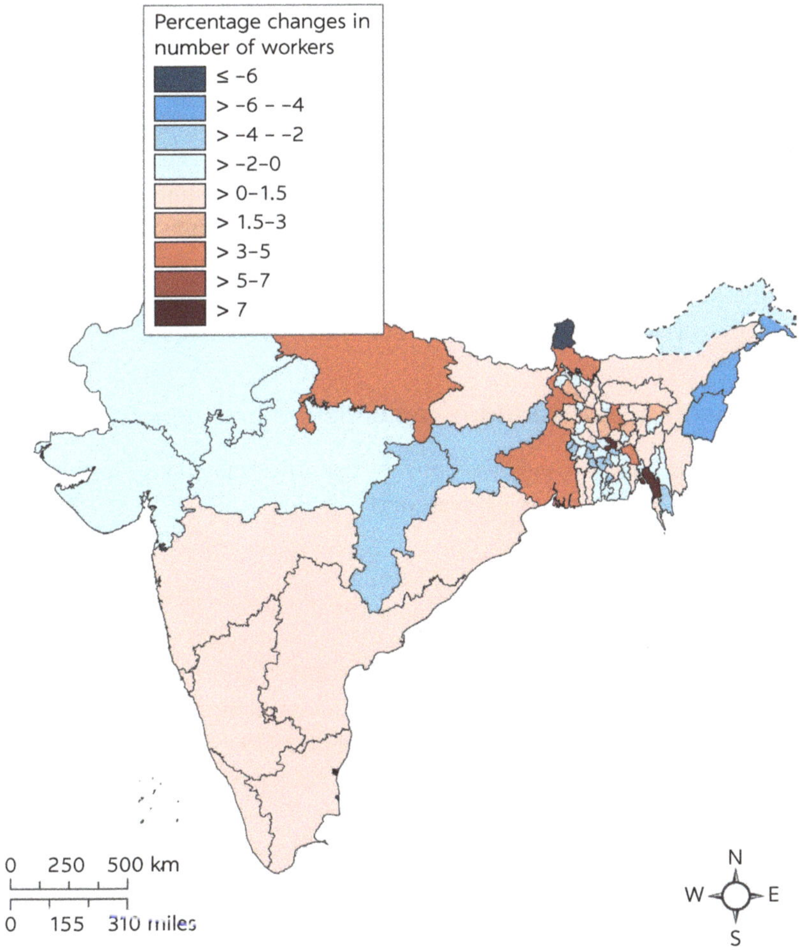

Source: World Bank analysis.

Regional corridors alone might not bring the level of economic activity needed to develop a lagging region. The regional corridor that would see the largest increase in the volume of trucks and cargo goes through the southwest of Bangladesh, connecting Kolkata through the Petrapole-Benapole border post, but those districts experience small increases in real wages and losses of economic activity. Unleashing income gains in rural areas requires that farmers and agricultural enterprises have access to the corridors and to transport and logistics services to reach local, regional, and global markets. A large body of empirical evidence shows that rural roads and rural markets yield significant localized benefits. They enable rural communities to increase production and sales and move up agricultural value chains.

Hurdles at all stages of agriculture value chains prevent the economic potential of rural communities in southwest Bangladesh and the broader eastern South Asia from being realized. Focus groups with women and men engaged in the cut flowers, mango, and fish-farming value chains in southwest Bangladesh reveal that they share many challenges, including a lack of pest management know-how; the high price of inputs; uncertainty regarding the price of outputs; a lack of infrastructure facilities, such as cold-chain capacity; and poor transport and road infrastructure.

In addition, women face gender-related challenges. They are much more likely to participate in the production stage of agriculture value chains than other stages; they are virtually absent from the transportation and commercialization stages. They face barriers to participation in agriculture value chains, at the macro (societal), meso (value chain/community), and micro (household/individual) levels. At the macro level, the main limiting factor is the strongly embedded social norm of *purdah*,[2] which prohibits women from leaving the boundaries of their homestead unaccompanied by their husband or a male relative. At the meso level, women's work is informal and goes unacknowledged. Their roles in value chains lack visibility, as they are seen as supporters and helpers rather than key players. Women also lack venues and opportunities to market their products. At the micro level, their lack of control over income from their participation in agricultural value chains limits their participation.

Complementary interventions can enhance local benefits

This section discusses key policy actions the countries should take to enhance benefits of regional integration in rural areas.

Connecting local markets

Regional trade and transport initiatives typically connect major economic centers and trade gateways in the countries they link. The initiatives are often designed around corridors that offer superior infrastructure, harmonized policies, and procedures to facilitate trade and transport and supportive institutional mechanisms to coordinate among the many stakeholders. Corridors are high-capacity systems that are most efficient when they facilitate the unimpeded movement of large volumes of traffic. In order to benefit the communities and centers in regions through which the corridors pass, it is important to create on- and off-ramps for rural communities and intermediate centers to access each corridor. As doing so could compromise the efficiency of a corridor, there is a need for careful design of local access solutions.

A proven solution for local access to corridors is through secondary roads and rural markets, as discussed in chapter 4. Rural communities connect to corridors through a cascade of market centers and secondary and tertiary networks of roads that form interconnected clusters. Local infrastructure can help consolidate traffic volumes, so that producers can benefit from the economies of scale that corridors offer without degrading the efficiency of the corridors with too many access points and impediments to traffic flow.

To help rural economies, it is important to carefully select and design bundles of markets and roads to complement corridor improvements. Bundles should be those that can spur local development, via agricultural marketing and increased income from farming, enhance opportunities to sell produce, and reduce losses from poor handling while produce is transported to larger markets. Consolidation can allow local produce to reach markets in distant centers, including export markets.

Three broad steps can help identify the package of roads and markets that could best leverage investments in regional corridors:

1. Identify a cluster of rural markets that are co-dependent as either origins of shipments or assembly markets, where shipments from small facilities are consolidated.

2. Classify the links that make up the connecting transports system based on the volume of traffic they carry.
3. Integrate the results of the first two steps to arrive at a package of markets and roads that maximizes returns for rural producers within a budget constraint for infrastructure.

The algorithm seeks to maximize returns from investments in a bundle of rural markets and roads needed to integrate a cluster of rural producers.

Improving local connectivity to corridors can reduce poverty by helping lagging regions benefit from domestic and regional trade. As South Asian countries invest in large-scale corridors for regional integration, it is important that they pay special attention to local connectivity, which is particularly important as the region is still predominantly rural and based on agriculture.

Improving women's participation in export-oriented agricultural value chains

Several measures can be taken to improve women's participation in export-oriented agricultural value chains. They need to be grounded in the realities of women's lives and the fact that gender norms change slowly.

The most effective strategies are ones that are applied to value chain products and processes in nodes in which women are already participating. Removing blockages to adding value at these nodes and increasing women's control of income over benefits can have direct impacts on returns to female value chain participants and be used to incrementally facilitate behavior and norms change. In designing these strategies, care should be exercised to ensure that there are no unintended consequences for women in terms of increases in violence against them.

At the macro level, governments can conduct mass and multimedia campaigns describing the importance of empowering women economically by increasing their access to productive employment and showing that doing so increases their prestige and the purchasing power of the household. Governments can also pass legislation that encourages the formation of women-led cooperative organizations. Governments also need to prioritize women when developing economic policies.

At the meso level, countries can provide technical assistance to help women form cooperatives and small and microenterprises. Technical support can be provided to mobilize the group; identify and formulate viable businesses; establish linkages downstream and upstream of the value chain; and explore venues to access finance, equipment, and technical training. At the community level, projects could create advocacy groups that seek to mobilize male opinion leaders—religious leaders, teachers, government officials, politicians—to advocate for changes in women's status.

At the household level, training and sensitization of men—and women—needs to work toward moving away from the local cultural norm of *purdah*. Value chain projects could provide training to small-scale farming families on adopting a "farming as a family business" approach that fosters more cooperative efforts between men and women in planning and managing family farm enterprises to maximize household profits. The farming-as-a-family business approach can also facilitate the delivery of agricultural extension services, capacity development, technology transfer, and access to productive inputs to women producers.

SUMMARY AND CONCLUDING REMARKS

Both geopolitical and economic considerations affect regional integration initiatives. By presenting innovative analysis that fills knowledge gaps in the realm of regional transport integration, this report seeks to strengthen the economic considerations that go into the design and implementation of regional integration policies in eastern South Asia. It provides detailed analyses of Bangladesh and India, but most of the findings and recommendations are relevant for the entire BBIN region, and the innovative analytical approach it explores can be used throughout the subregion.

The transport integration agreements in eastern South Asia represent a significant step toward the creation of a cross-border integrated transport market in the subregion, with the MVA the cornerstone of that integration. Unleashing the full potential of integration requires strengthening the agreements by adopting good practices from elsewhere; addressing gaps and inconsistencies in infrastructure and market failures in transport services; and adopting complementary policies that remove binding constraints caused by market imperfections, institutional failures, and socioreligious norms.

Looking ahead, a few questions stand out that require deeper analysis. One is the impact of the integration agreements, particularly the MVA, on competition in regional and domestic transport service markets. Although the MVA does not allow for cabotage or triangular permits, allowing the delivery of exports and the picking up of imports in a foreign country could have implications for the intensity of competition in regional markets, which could also affect domestic transport service markets if service providers shift their focus. A robust analysis of this area would require detailed data from service providers in affected countries to model their behavior and simulate the implementation of the agreement. A corollary is the likely impact on transport prices, based on the comparative advantage of each country's fleet.

A second issue is the environmental impact, particularly on emissions, of the route and mode shifts triggered by the agreements. Chapter 2 provides the foundation for the analysis of the impact on emissions from freight transport. Analysis of this issue needs to consider the characteristics of the vehicles and fuels used in the countries as well as congestion and idling time along the relevant corridors.

A third issue is the extent of binding constraints on labor, land, capital, and product markets that need to be removed through complementary policies in each country to amplify the gains and manage the risks of regional transport integration. This report looks at only a few binding constraints and potential complementary reforms. Country- and sector-specific analyses need to be undertaken to identify the binding constraints and potential reforms considering the countries' readiness for and feasibility of complementary reforms.

NOTES

1. Indian river-sea cargo vessels are of less than 6,000 gross tonnage.
2. *Purdah* means "curtain," implying female seclusion.

REFERENCES

ADB (Asian Development Bank), DFID (Department for International Development), JICA (Japan International Cooperation Agency), and World Bank. 2018. *The Web of Transport Corridors in South Asia*. Washington, DC: World Bank.

Alder, S., M. Roberts, and M. Tewari. 2018. "The Effects of Transport Infrastructure on India's Urban and Rural Development." Working Paper. https://smartnet.niua.org/sites/default/files/resources/alderrobertstewari_india_0.pdf.

Asturias, J., M. García-Santana, and R. R. Magdaleno. 2018. "Competition and the Welfare Gains from Transportation Infrastructure: Evidence from the Golden Quadrilateral of India." Working Paper 1816, Banco de España, Madrid.

CUTS International and IRU (International Road Transport Union). 2017. *Benefits of the TIR Convention for the Implementation of the BBIN Motor Vehicles Agreement*. Dhaka.

Bird, J., Y. Li, H. Z. Rahman, M. Rama, and A. J. Venables. 2018. *Toward Great Dhaka: A New Urban Development Paradigm Eastward*. Directions in Development. Washington, DC: World Bank.

Breinlich, H. 2006. "The Spatial Income Structure in the European Union—What Role for Economic Geography?" *Journal of Economic Geography* 6 (5): 593–617.

De, P., S. Raihan, and S. Kathuria. 2012. "Unlocking Bangladesh-India Trade: Emerging Potential and the Way Forward." Policy Research Working Paper 6155, World Bank, Washington, DC.

Donaldson, D., and R. Hornbeck. 2016. "Railroads and American Economic Growth: A 'Market Access' Approach." *Quarterly Journal of Economics* 131 (2): 799–858.

Hanson, G. H., 2005 "Market Potential, Increasing Returns, and Geographic Concentration." *Journal of International Economics* 67 (1): 1–24.

Head, K., and T. Mayer. 2006. "Regional Wage and Employment Responses to Market Potential in the EU." *Regional Science and Urban Economics* 36 (5): 573–95.

Herrera Dappe, M., C. Kunaka, M. Lebrand, and N. Weisskpot. 2020. *Moving Forward: Connectivity and Logistics to Sustain Bangladesh's Success*. International Development in Focus. Washington, DC: World Bank.

Herrera Dappe, M., and A. Suárez-Alemán. 2016. *Competitiveness of South Asia's Container Ports: A Comprehensive Assessment of Performance, Drivers, and Costs*. Directions in Development. Washington, DC: World Bank.

Hsieh, C., and P. J. Klenow. 2009. "Misallocation and Manufacturing TFP in China and India." *Quarterly Journal of Economics* 124 (4): 1403–48.

Kathuria, S., ed. 2018. *A Glass Half Full: The Promise of Regional Trade in South Asia*. South Asia Development Forum. Washington, DC: World Bank.

Kunaka, C., and R. Carruthers. 2014. *Trade and Transport Corridor Management Toolkit*. Washington, DC: World Bank.

Kunaka, C., V. Tanase, P. Latrille, and P. Krausz. 2013. *Quantitative Analysis of Road Transport Agreements (QuARTA)*. Washington, DC: World Bank.

Mayer, T. 2008. "Market Potential and Development." CEPR Discussion Paper 6798 . Center for Economic and Policy Research.

Redding, S. 2010. "The Empirics of New Economic Geography." *Journal of Regional Science* 50 (1): 297–311.

Redding, S., and A. Venables. 2004. "Economic Geography and International Inequality." *Journal of International Economics* 62 (1): 53–82.

Reserve Bank of India. 2019. "Handbook of Statistics on Indian States." New Delhi. https://m.rbi.org.in/Scripts/AnnualPublications.aspx?head=Handbook%20of%20Statistics%20on%20Indian%20States.

Roberts, M. 2016. "Identifying the Economic Potential of Indian Districts." Policy Research Working Paper 7623, World Bank, Washington, DC.

Srinivasan, T. G. 2020. "The Promise of Northeast India." In *Playing to Strengths: A Policy Framework for Mainstreaming Northeast India,* ed. S. Kathuria and P. Mathur. International Development in Focus. Washington, DC: World Bank.

1 Identifying the Gaps

AN ASSESSMENT OF THE MOTOR VEHICLES AGREEMENT

CHARLES KUNAKA

Road transport is the dominant mode of domestic and intraregional transport in South Asia; road freight transport accounts for more than 80 percent of all regional trade shipments. The cost and quality of road transport services is therefore critical to the trade competitiveness of countries in the region.

The sector suffers from major weaknesses and inefficiencies (Rahman and Rahman 2016; Herrera Dappe and others 2020). Weaknesses include the high costs and long delays of crossing borders, the age and lack of reliability of fleets, the poor quality of services, weak skills, and the high degree of atomization.

Despite its importance, little attention has been paid to the cross-border integration of road transport services in South Asia. Many of the trade and transport facilitation initiatives across the region emphasize improvements in connectivity through investments in infrastructure. It is often taken for granted that associated services will respond to infrastructure improvement and operators will increase the supply of services.

There is little evidence that the quality of road transport services is improving in tandem with investments in road infrastructure, however. International indexes such as the World Bank's Logistics Performance Index and Doing Business point to continuing weaknesses in logistics and trade facilitation. Performance lags most other regions across nearly all dimensions, especially quality, reliability, and time. Many weaknesses have roots in the policy and regulatory environment, which does not incentivize reform or innovation in services.

This chapter focuses on the regulatory aspects of cross-border road freight transport services in South Asia, as the exchange of traffic rights between countries is a fundamental step in reducing costs and improving the efficiency of transport and logistics services. It analyzes one recent initiative to establish a more integrated road transport system across the countries of northeast South Asia: the Motor Vehicles Agreement for the Regulation of Passenger, Personal, and Cargo Vehicular Traffic between Bangladesh, Bhutan, India, and Nepal (MVA), signed in 2015. It explores the extent to which the MVA supports the cross-border operation of road transport services and identifies the gaps that need to be addressed if the agreement is to deliver on its stated objectives of integrating trade and transport.

INTERNATIONAL APPROACHES TO THE REGULATION OF ROAD TRANSPORT SERVICES

Evidence from South Asia and Africa suggests that regional trade and transport corridors with limited competition in road transport services face higher prices than corridors with more competition (Teravaninthorn and Raballand 2009; Chemonics International 2011). It is therefore important for countries and regional organizations to invest in regulatory reform in the logistics services sector, including trucking, warehousing, and freight forwarding. Investing in infrastructure or trade facilitation initiatives will not lead to significant reductions in trade costs unless they are accompanied by meaningful services reform, especially in road transport services (Borchert, Gootiiz, and Mattoo 2010).

The MVA follows global practice in the regulation of international road transport services. As infrastructure has improved across most of the developing world, regulatory and procedural constraints in logistics services have become more pronounced. International agreements on road transport tend to provide only the basic framework; regional and bilateral agreements between states articulate more precise provisions.

Bilateral agreements are the main means by which international road transport services are regulated; hundreds of such agreements have been signed (Kunaka and others 2013). Recent analytical work suggests that some of these agreements can have a negative effect on trade and add to trade cost. Anecdotal evidence suggests that bilateral agreements can supersede more open agreements enacted at the regional or international level. Examples of agreements that can increase costs are agreements that have provisions on quotas or *tour de rôle*. Such agreements can limit the supply of services or sustain high prices. Prominent examples include agreements in West Africa, a region that Teravaninthorn and Raballand (2009) find to have the highest transport costs in Africa. In East Asia, the relaxation of quota provisions in the agreement between the Lao People's Democratic Republic and Thailand resulted in a 20 percent decline in transport prices, as Thai operators were able to offer more and more efficient services.

Most multilateral international legal instruments on transport and trade facilitation are elaborated under the auspices of global organizations or their specialized agencies (the United Nations, the World Customs Organization, the International Maritime Organization, and so forth). They therefore generally contain framework provisions that are acceptable to all members of the organization, irrespective of their level of development or geographic location. It is then up to the countries themselves to define more detailed implementing provisions, which they usually do through regional, subregional, or bilateral treaties and national legislation. Regional and subregional treaties are common where countries are integrated in formal entities, but regional integration does not exclude bilateral cooperation between members.

Some of the major international legal instruments on road transport include the following:

- the Convention on International Transport of Goods under Cover of TIR (Transports Internationaux Routiers) Carnets (TIR Convention), on customs transit
- the Accord Européen Relatif au Transport International des Marchandises Dangereuses par Route, on the transport of dangerous goods by road

- the Vienna Convention on road traffic
- the Agreement on the International Carriage of Perishable Foodstuffs and on the Special Equipment to Be Used for Such Carriage (ATP), on the transport of perishable foodstuffs
- the European Agreement Concerning the Work of Crews of Vehicles Engaged in International Road Transport (AETR), on driving and rest time rules and the application of related on-board checking equipment (tachographs).

Other multilateral trade agreements that are relevant to transport operations include the following:

- the Convention on the Contract for the International Carriage of Goods by Road (CMR), on road infrastructure development, road traffic safety, vehicle technical requirements, facilitation of border crossing, and the transport of dangerous and perishable goods
- the General Agreement on Tariffs and Trade (GATT)
- the General Agreement on Trade in Services (GATS).

Also relevant are pieces of European Union (EU) legislation that have mandatory application to transport operators registered in third countries operating in EU territory on the basis of bilateral agreements. Such arrangements exist between Europe and Asia and between Europe and Africa. Several international instruments that are influential have been adopted under the auspices of the United Nations Economic Commission for Europe (UNECE).

Regions other than Europe have also pursued agreements between groups of countries (table 1.1). Prominent examples other than the MVA include following:

- the Cross Border Transport Agreement (CBTA) agreement, signed by the Lao People's Democratic Republic, Thailand, and Vietnam for the facilitation of the cross-border transport of goods and people
- the original tripartite agreement on road transport signed by Kenya, Tanzania, and Uganda, which has since been opened to all member countries of the East African Community
- the Agreement on International Land Transport (Latin American Integration Association [ALADI]), signed by Argentina, Bolivia, Brazil, Chile, Paraguay, Peru, and Uruguay for the facilitation of the cross-border transport of goods and people.

Regional agreements tend to reflect the operating environment and offer more pragmatic provisions for participating countries than do multilateral agreements. Some of them can be self-executing, in that they do not need to be adapted through national legislation but become legally enforceable as soon as the agreement has been ratified by a participating country.

In some cases, provisions on transport are embedded in agreements on trade. Regulation of road transport services in India and Nepal, for example, is part of the India–Nepal Treaty of Transit. Other international trade agreements include transport road provisions as part of deeper integration schemes. Some of the provisions in the United States–Mexico–Canada Agreement (USMCA), for example, were in the North American Free Trade Agreement (NAFTA). Standalone transport agreements are thus not the only type of arrangements countries can pursue.

TABLE 1.1 **Examples of regional agreements or templates on road transport**

REGION	AGREEMENT AND MODEL TITLE	NUMBER OF PARTICIPATING COUNTRIES
Africa	Memorandum of Understanding on Road Transportation in the Common Customs Area pursuant to the Customs Union Agreement between the Governments of Botswana, Lesotho, South Africa, and Swaziland	4
	SATCC (Southern African Transport and Communication Commission) Model Bilateral Agreement on the Regulation of Cross-Border Freight Road Transport	15
	Tripartite Agreement on Road Transport (Uganda, Kenya, Tanzania)	3[a]
Black Sea Region	Memorandum of Understanding on the Facilitation of Road Transport of Goods in the Black Sea Economic Cooperation Region; Agreement on Multilateral Transit Permits	7
Europe (including Caucasus)	Recommended Model Bilateral Agreement on Road Transport between European Conference of Ministers of Transport (ECMT) member countries	45[b]
	South-East European Cooperation Initiative (SECI) Memorandum of Understanding on the Facilitation of International Road Transport of Goods	10
South America	Agreement on International Land Transport (Latin American Integration Association [ALADI])	7
South Asia	Motor Vehicles Agreement for the Regulation of Passenger, Personal and Cargo Vehicular Traffic between Bangladesh, Bhutan, India, and Nepal (MVA)	4[c]
South-East Asia	Agreement between and among the governments of the Lao People's Democratic Republic, the Kingdom of Thailand, and the Socialist Republic of Vietnam for Facilitation of Cross-Border Transport of Goods and People (the Cross-Border Transport Agreement [CBTA])	3

Source: Based on Kunaka and others 2013.

a. The provisions of the agreement have since been incorporated in a wider agreement for all countries that are members of the East African Community.

b. The model has been used by several pairs of countries. The exact number and the extent to which it has been followed is difficult to determine.

c. Four countries signed the Motor Vehicles Agreement (Bangladesh, Bhutan, India, and Nepal). Bhutan pulled out after its parliament failed to ratify it.

Where transport is included in general agreements on trade, the agreements may not include explicit provisions on some aspects. In the case of NAFTA, for instance, Fox and Londoño-Kent (2014) found that despite the liberal regime and substantial investments in infrastructure, technology, and equipment, significant barriers to efficient truck transportation between the United States and Mexico remained. As a result, vehicles transiting from the United States to Mexico would spend three to five days at the border, and crossing the border involved several pieces of equipment for drayage and three to four drivers. Standalone agreements have the advantage that they can cover many of the technical dimensions as well as reflect the political economy context that can affect the efficiency of operations.

Where regional agreements are not signed, it is common for groups of countries to adopt template agreements that can be signed by pairs of countries. The intention is that as more and more pairs sign similar agreements, progress toward regional convergence in practices will occur. Examples of template agreements include the model bilateral agreement adopted under the auspices of the Southern African Transport and Communication Commission (SATCC), which was part of the Southern African Development Community and the European Conference of Ministers of Transport (ECMT). These template agreements offer sets of provisions that can be accepted by most countries; they do not need to be best practice. The ECMT is indirectly supported by a progressive multilateral permit and quota system that allows free access to bilateral, transit, and third-country transport market segments for transport operators in the territory of other ECMT participating states. Evidence abounds that the ECMT system has been successful in developing an efficient European road transport environment that is contested, though with some persisting restrictions (Kunaka and Carruthers 2014).

It is also common for countries to be party to agreements and instruments at different levels—global, regional, bilateral—and to reflect their provisions in domestic law. This process often works well, provided there are no contradictions across the instruments. Agreements that involve a large number of parties are often of a general nature—to reflect the varying interests and circumstances of the participants. It is common to include more specific provisions at the bilateral or domestic level. Bilateral road transport agreements are a preferred approach to regulating cross-border road transport services. There can therefore be a continuum of provisions, from the broad to the very explicit, enshrined in domestic legislation.

Modern regional agreements on road transport emphasize the importance of focusing on the quality, not the quantity, of services (see, for example, Kunaka and others 2013), because quantity restrictions tend to limit supply, raise prices, and encourage suboptimal operations. A common recommendation from research on road transport is to establish the actual effect of the regulatory barriers between countries and the effects permit and quota systems have on the supply and costs of transport services between countries. Teravaninthorn and Raballand (2009) recommended reviewing bilateral agreements as a means of reducing transport costs in Africa. In Southern Africa, freight forwarders have long argued that bilateral agreements, although seemingly sound, are rigid and include inadequate management procedures, which render them unsuited to the provision of efficient transport services (Nick Poree Associates 2010). Emphasizing the regulation of quality encourages the entry into the market of operators that meet minimum standards, which encourages innovation and helps create safer and more contested markets.

Regulatory efforts generally focus on the three main elements that have to cross international borders in order to achieve efficient operations: the vehicle, its driver, and the goods being carried (box 1.1). Delays faced by any one of the three result in additional costs. Many regional and interstate agreements include provisions relating to the three. The MVA covers all three, but not to a consistent depth, as analyzed below.

BOX 1.1

The three main elements of international transport agreements: The vehicle, the driver, and the load

International instruments should include efficient procedures to allow the vehicle, its load, and its driver to cross international borders as easily as possible.

The vehicle: Provisions need to cover the permit the vehicle needs to have and how it is issued; any fees that need to be paid to cover costs of infrastructure and other services that are used in the host country; insurance; vehicle weights and dimensions to suit the existing infrastructure; and how vehicles are registered and their worthiness to be on the roads determined.

In some instances, documents need to be carried on the vehicle attesting to its compliance with the above requirements. Increasingly, however, verification can be done electronically. For instance, it is possible to

continued

Box 1.1, *continued*

allow countries access to one another's vehicle registration databases or digital systems on the vehicle to verify roadworthiness.

The driver: Drivers need visas or permits that allow them to operate their vehicles across the border. Some agreements set limits as to how deep into a country a foreign driver may operate. In such instances, operators may establish depots and facilities to allow drivers to offload their vehicles and turn around. The agreement may specify the nationality of the driver that can take the truck this maximum distance.

The most important considerations for drivers are driver's licenses and visas. Most agreements adopt mutual recognition of valid driver's licenses or international driving permits. Certifications from the immigration authorities are required to verify the identity of individuals entering or leaving the country. One way of facilitating visa issuance is for the national authorities responsible for international road transport to act as intermediaries.

The load: The purpose of allowing cross-border operations is to reduce the costs and delays of trading goods. As such, it is important that there be appropriate customs and border management protocols to allow goods to cross expeditiously and be cleared at their final destination. A well-designed transit regime is often called for domestic movement after crossing the border or international transit in which goods need to cross the territory of a third country. Unless the transit regime is clear and efficient, it can be a source of delay and cost.

One area that is often difficult to address is vehicle weights and dimensions. Both factors impose heavy costs on operators or the agencies responsible for the maintenance of road infrastructure. Some agreements include standards on weights and dimensions to which international corridors should be built, in order to allow seamless operations. Even then, however, control over vehicle overload is important. Controls need to be effective without being overly duplicative.

REGULATION OF ROAD TRANSPORT SERVICES IN SOUTH ASIA

Unlike other regions, South Asia has gaps in its regime for regulating cross-border road transport services. Only a few countries, notably India, have agreements with their neighbors on road transport services (table 1.2). Most countries do not have explicit agreements, with transport services often regulated through agreements on trade, such as the transit treaty between India and Nepal.

Given the absence of bilateral agreements on road transport between some South Asian countries, the MVA fills a critical void. Multilateral agreements are generally a more efficient way to establish a common operating environment across several countries, especially countries that are geographically contiguous. Such agreements provide for seamless transport services across borders, obviating the need to transload at international boundaries. They also include related regulations covering the passage of drivers, the passage of goods, insurance, and taxes and levies, which can speed cross-border transit.

The MVA is the result of an initiative to draft an all–South Asia agreement under the auspices of the South Asian Association of Regional Cooperation (SAARC). Reaching region-wide agreements on road and rail transport proved difficult, as countries could not converge on a set of common provisions. When no region-wide agreement could be reached, four countries—Bangladesh, Bhutan, India, and Nepal (BBIN)—decided to proceed with an agreement covering northeast South Asia.

TABLE 1.2 **Dates of bilateral regulatory frameworks for road transport in South Asia**

COUNTRY	BHUTAN	INDIA	NEPAL
Bangladesh	No agreement	1999, 2001	No agreement
Bhutan		2016	No agreement
India			2006

Source: World Bank.

The MVA was signed in Bhutan on June 15, 2015. It has since been ratified by Bangladesh, India, and Nepal. In 2017 the legislature of Bhutan declined to ratify the agreement, citing gaps and conflicts between the agreement and the national council in such areas as immigration, routes and infrastructure, ability to compete, and environmental impacts, among other concerns. Technically, it is possible for Bhutan to ratify the agreement at any time.

The MVA contains many elements found in similar agreements in other regions. Its 17 articles cover the following, among other topics:

- definition of terms
- types of permits and how they can be issued
- documents that should be carried on the vehicle
- visa regime for vehicle drivers and crews
- restrictions and exclusions (types of vehicles or traffic that may be excluded from coverage by the agreement)
- fees and charges that may be levied
- road signs and signals
- force majeure
- procedures for vehicle searches
- insurance
- facilitation of business
- dispute settlement and administrative processes, including consultation processes.

The MVA seems to address many of the essential items that are part of regulating road transport services. To ensure that there are no gaps, the agreement provides that the authorities revert to national laws if the agreement does not provide coverage.

METHODOLOGY FOR ASSESSING THE MOTOR VEHICLES AGREEMENT

The World Trade Organization (WTO 2006) developed a pioneering approach to the assessment of bilateral air services agreements. The approach for the Quantitative Air Services Agreement Review (QUASAR) offered fresh insights into the content and coverage of the agreements for pairs of countries across the globe. It sought to offer a detailed and, as far as possible, comprehensive analysis of market access features of bilateral air services agreements. QUASAR combined a methodology and a database of information drawn from a variety of sources.

The QUASAR is part of a family of quantitative techniques that has since been adopted for the comparison of the constitutions of countries (Law and Versteeg 2012). Kunaka and others (2013) built on the approach, developing a quantitative approach to the assessment and comparison of bilateral road transport agreements. Their approach takes into consideration the fact that in road transport, factors outside any agreements have a significant impact on the content and coverage of an agreement and that technical provisions, or the lack hereof, may have significant impacts.

A quantitative approach provides a structured way of identifying the coverage and potential weakness of any one agreement and revealing how it compares with others with a similar purpose. The methodology is based on scores for various elements that reflect their expected impact on the market openness of an agreement. The template for the analysis is based on Kunaka and others (2013). It is designed around 11 features that are essential for measuring the openness of an agreement:

1. *Limitations of the scope of the agreement.* The carriage of certain types of cargo, such as hazardous goods, may be forbidden. There may also be geographic limitations on the scope of the agreement. For example, trucks of one contracting party may be allowed to penetrate the territory of the other contracting party only to a certain point, where transloading of cargo can take place. It is also possible that certain regions of the territory of one contracting party are excluded from the scope of the agreement. (All agreements, bilateral and multilateral, are obviously restricted in their geographic scope to the territory of the contracting parties. Such a restriction is not considered a geographic limitation of scope.)

2. *Transport permit/authorization requirements and complexities/restrictions of transport permit management.* Any permit requirement may lead to quantitative restrictions of the number of trips feasible within a given period of time. Determination of the number of bilaterally exchanged permits and the techniques of permit delivery/bureaucracy can make life difficult for transport operators. Various conditions of permit use may also be burdensome and restrictive.

3. *List of types of traffic exempted from permit requirements.* A list of bilaterally agreed upon permit-free transport operations clearly indicates whether the contracting parties intend to facilitate operations of a noncommercial nature. A list of permit-free operations is particularly valuable if a general permit/quota obligation otherwise applies under the scope of the bilateral agreement.

4. *List of types of traffic exempted from quota requirements.* Where a permit system and restrictive quotas apply, it important to list any type of traffic—normally of noncommercial nature but subject to the permit system—that is exempt from the quota limitations.

5. *Cabotage traffic limitations.* If allowed, cabotage transport (transport between two internal points in the territory of one contracting party by operators registered in the territory of the other contracting party) may help reduce the number of empty vehicle runs.

6. *Transit quota limitations.* Attention should be paid to quantitative restrictions of transit traffic. An open-ended transit traffic regime should be recognized by giving it a high mark. This issue should be analyzed in the light of

Article 5 of the GATT on freedom of transit, which tolerates no quantitative restrictions of this type of traffic.

7. *Triangular/third-country traffic limitations.* Mutual enactment of triangular freight transport operations is an effective way to increase the efficiency of operations. It helps increase the share of laden runs, facilitating trade transactions through reduced transport costs.

8. *Prescribed routes and border-crossing points.* Operators can optimize their freight runs when given the freedom to choose the most convenient route on the basis of traffic, transport technology, and trade requirements, factoring in possible physical infrastructure limitations. Restrictions on route choice may diminish the flexibility and quality of operations and run against the provisions of GATT Article 5.

9. *Taxation-related limitations.* Any taxes, charges, and fees on international road freight transport operations should be reasonable and proportionate, duly considering relevant provisions of GATT Article 5. Ideally, mutual tax and duty exemptions apply on transport operation, vehicles, and spare parts used for such activities. Transit taxes cannot be levied.

10. *Facilitation measures (driver, vehicle, cargo).* Practical facilitation measures include the acceptance of international weight and vehicle technical inspection certificates, the rapid issuance of visas to professional drivers, smooth border-crossing operations, and the strict application of the nondiscrimination principle. All are important for efficient and reliable international road freight transport operations.

11. *Transparency requirements in place.* The exchange of information on changes in national legislation, border-crossing requirements, and many other circumstances of international road freight transport is indispensable in today's rapidly evolving commercial environment. Ideally, decisions of a joint committee that may be established to implement the agreement should be accessible to all actors. Bilateral agreements should include methods for resolving disputes between contracting parties, including the possibility of appeal against measures in case of infringements.

These features have different effects on the openness of the regulatory environment; they therefore need to be weighted differently (table 1.3). Kunaka and others (2013) reviewed more than 70 agreements across all regions of the world and defined the scoring methodology that was used for the review of the MVA. The weights attached to each criteria reflect its assessed impact on the cross-border operation of road transport services.

The quantitative analysis yields a score of 52 out of 100 for the MVA. The agreement shows strengths in several areas, including comprehensive treatment of relevant topics, clearly stated permit requirements, and definition of traffic that is exempt from the permit requirement. And although transit is not clearly specified, the MVA appears to allow for transit operations.

The agreement also has several weaknesses and ambiguities that could hamper the design of efficient operations:

- It does not specifically address transit operations.
- It fails to define allowed vehicle weights and dimensions.
- It does not provide for triangular permits and cabotage (which are common in similar agreements).

TABLE 1.3 **Assessment of the Motor Vehicles Agreement against the ideal agreement on cross-border freight traffic**

FEATURE	FEATURES OF IDEAL MODEL AND ASSOCIATED WEIGHTING	FEATURES AND SCORE OF MOTOR VEHICLE AGREEMENT
Limitations of scope	• All territories of the parties fall under the scope of the agreement. • There is no distance (or time) limitation to penetrate any of the territories of the contracting parties. • There is no exclusivity of means of transport registered for one contracting party. • There is no exclusivity of carriers for contracting parties. • No operations are totally prohibited. • Permits are issued for at least one year. • No special authorizations are needed, except for overweight and oversize (abnormal) cargos. Maximum points: 5	• There are no limitations on territory in each state. • There is no limit on distance, but the agreement does not affect existing bilateral agreements. The agreement between India and Nepal limits Indian trucks to no more than 24 hours within Nepal. Score: 3
Transport permit requirements, permit management	• Bilateral traffic is not subject to quotas (open-ended). • Permits are exchanged before year-end for the following year. • Permits are not tradable. • Additional quotas are available for modern vehicles and/or combined transport. • There is no queuing (*tour de rôle*) for freight sharing. • There is no double approval in individual permit procedures. Maximum points: 15	• The agreement does not provide for quotas, but countries consult on number of vehicles to be issued permits. • Permits have to be countersigned by other part within 30 days. • The number of permits will be shared equally by states connected by a particular route. • Permits are valid for a period of one year and are not tradable. • There is no provision for *tour de rôle.* Score: 7
Traffic exempted from permits	• The types of traffic that are exempt from permit obligation are listed. • The agreement caters to all types of traffic, with no exemptions Maximum points: 10	• The agreement includes no major exemptions, except for "nonregular" traffic (occasional operations), which does not require full insurance. Score: 8
Traffic exempted from quotas	• The types of traffic exempt from quota obligation are listed. • All types of traffic listed in the questionnaire are exempt from quota limits. Maximum points: 8	• There are no specific exemptions from quotas except "nonregular" traffic. Score: 4
Cabotage traffic limitations	• Cabotage is allowed without any restriction (open-ended). Maximum points: 5	• Cabotage is not allowed. Score: 1
Transit quota limitations	• Transit operations are allowed in an open-ended manner. Maximum points: 15	• Transit quotas are not specifically provided for, but the agreement implies that transit operations are allowed. Score: 10
Triangular/ third-country traffic limitations	• Triangular traffic is allowed in an open-ended manner. Maximum points: 9	• Triangular traffic is not mentioned, but the agreement provides for carriage of third-country cargo. Score: 4
Prescribed routes and border crossing points	• No routes are prescribed for any operation. • Clear support is provided for the development of roadside services. Maximum points: 8	• The agreement provides for operations only on specified routes and through designated border-crossing points. In December 2019, Bangladesh, India, and Nepal agreed on a set of designated routes for MVA operations between them. Score: 3

continued

TABLE 1.3, *continued*

FEATURE	FEATURES OF IDEAL MODEL AND ASSOCIATED WEIGHTING	FEATURES AND SCORE OF MOTOR VEHICLE AGREEMENT
Taxation-related limitations	• Tax exemption is in place for ownership taxes, registration taxes, taxes for running of the vehicle, and special taxes on transport services. • Fuel in built-in tankers, lubricants, and spare parts is exempt from all import duties. • The initial and terminal legs of combined transport are exempt from tolls and duties. Maximum points: 8	• Vehicles are exempt from additional taxes except tolls and other service charges that must be paid at the border. Score: 4
Facilitation measures	• Reference to vehicle weight certificate is included (per UN convention). • Reference to vehicle technical inspection certificate is included (per UN convention). • Use of vehicle combination with units registered in different countries with one permit is allowed. • Provisions on mutual recognition of driving licenses are included. • Carrier has right to establish offices and/or appoint representatives and/or agencies in the territory of the other contracting parties. • Nondiscriminatory treatment (of goods, vehicles, and drivers) is clearly stated as an obligation. • Provisions are in place on (a) preferential facilitation measures for drivers (simplified immigration formalities, such as passport/visa, driving licenses, and so forth); vehicles (registration, road worthiness, weights and dimensions, insurance); and goods (customs, quality-phytosanitary-veterinary checks) and (b) special expeditious treatment for transport of special cargoes (hazardous goods, livestock and perishable goods, temporary admission of certain goods and means of transport). Maximum points: 10	• The agreement does not specify technical specifications of vehicles, including weights and dimensions; it lists 10 documents that must be carried on each passenger vehicle and 9 on each goods vehicle. Score: 4
Transparency	• A joint committee is in place • Joint committee decisions are made public. • Clear infringement procedure is in place. • Right of appeal is mentioned • Exchange of information is an obligation. • Registration of the agreement with the UN Secretary General is prescribed. • The pieces of national legislation are easy to access • Dispute settlement arrangements are in place. • Procedures of amendment are in place. Maximum points: 7	• The agreement does not provide for registration with United Nations. • The agreement includes a dispute-settlement mechanism, mainly through negotiation between states. • All issues not covered in the agreement will be addressed through the national laws of each country. Score: 4

Source: Author's assessment based on Kunaka and others 2013.

- It limits operations to only prescribed routes, in a region with fairly complex patterns of movement.
- It allows participating states to resort to national law in cases of gaps or conflict between regional and domestic requirements—a possible source of uncertainty for operators, as it opens the possibility of countries using their domestic requirements to prevent regionally integrated services.

The MVA's score of 52 is almost identical to the average for the selected agreements of 53. The most open of the other regional agreements is the CBTA, in South East Asia (table 1.4). Trade among members of the Association of South East Asia Nations (ASEAN) accounts for an average 23 percent of total trade of the partner economies (ASEAN Secretariat 2018). Growth in ASEAN has been driven by regional value chains, which very much depend on road transport and sea shipping. Important gaps in road infrastructure connectivity remain. The cost of infrastructure improvements within ASEAN is estimated at more than $110 billion a year—at least twice as much as ASEAN member states have historically spent on infrastructure (World Bank 2019). In transport, the priority links form an ASEAN highway network. The CBTA therefore has to be seen from the point of view of facilitating intraregional trade connectivity.

Demand for regional transport in South Asia remains low, and intraregional trade is modest. The score of the MVA reflects the limited demand for greater capacity and efficiency. The MVA—and most other regional agreements—also illustrates the fact that transport agreements are not always negotiated for transport objectives. In some cases, the purpose of an agreement is more to indicate political cooperation than necessarily to facilitate economic integration.

The high score of the trilateral CBTA mainly reflects its no-permit regime, which automatically prohibits quotas for any type of operation except cabotage, bans route restrictions, provides at least partial tax exemption, and includes a number of agreed upon facilitation and transparency measures. A comparison by Kunaka and others (2013) of the scores of the multilateral and bilateral agreements for the same geographic relations/regions finds that the openness of these schemes is relatively close in the same region. However, multilateral road

TABLE 1.4 **Scoring of intraregional and multilateral agreements and models**

REGION	AGREEMENT, MEMORANDUM OF AGREEMENT, OR MODEL	SCORE
Southeast Asia	Agreement between and among the Governments of the Lao People's Democratic Republic, the Kingdom of Thailand, and the Socialist Republic of Vietnam for Facilitation of Cross-Border Transport of Goods and People (Cross Border Transport Agreement [CBTA])	75
Europe	South-East European Cooperation Initiative (SECI) Memorandum of Understanding on the Facilitation of International Road Transport of Goods	59
Europe	Recommended Model Bilateral Agreement on Road Transport between European Conference of Ministers of Transport (ECMT) Member Countries	57
South America	Agreement on International Land Transport (Latin American Integration Association [ALADI])	56
South Asia	Motor Vehicles Agreement for the Regulation of Passenger, Personal and Cargo Vehicular Traffic Between Bangladesh, Bhutan, India, and Nepal (MVA)	52
Africa	Memorandum of Understanding on Road Transportation in the Common Customs Area pursuant to the Customs Union Agreement between the Governments of Botswana, Lesotho, South Africa, and Swaziland (Memorandum of Understanding of the Southern Africa Customs Union [SACU])	46
	Tripartite Agreement on Road Transport Uganda-Kenya-Tanzania	40
Black Sea Region	Memorandum of Understanding on Facilitation of Road Transport of Goods in the Black Sea Economic Cooperation (BSEC) Region together with the BSEC Agreement on Multilateral Transit Permits	40

Source: Adapted from Kunaka and others 2013.

transport agreements are generally less open than bilateral agreements. This finding is very different from the WTO's (2006) finding on air transport, where multilateral agreements have higher scores than bilateral agreements. It suggests that countries are less willing to open up to a wide set of neighbors at the same time, preferring to do so on the basis of reciprocity with selected partners. In air transport, the more parties to an agreement, the more open it is. Many considerations other than just transport efficiency thus influence the conclusion of regional agreements on road transport services.

STRENGTHENING THE MOTOR VEHICLES AGREEMENT

The MVA addresses many of the issues that have contributed to operational problems in other regions of the world. Three of these issues are fees and charges for services received in a foreign territory, insurance, and visas for crews.

Like other agreements, the MVA provides for nondiscriminatory treatment of commercial charges on highways. Where fees are payable, the agreement provides that they shall be collected at the point of entry. The agreement explicitly provides that no additional fees shall be payable on the way, especially fees levied by municipal authorities. It also provides for the temporary admission of vehicles free of customs duty. These measures are progressive, consistent with some of the more open agreements. However, the agreement does not address the transit regime of guarantees on the goods. This lapse may not be an issue where the member countries have ratified the necessary international agreements or are party to relevant instruments, such as the Transports Internationaux Routiers (TIR). However, of the four BBIN states, only India is party to the TIR.

A general problem in trading across borders is liability in the event that a vehicle causes injury or death, or cargo is lost or damaged. The MVA covers this issue by requiring that operators have comprehensive insurance for every vehicle conducting cross-border operations. Only "nonregular" (occasional) operations are exempt from comprehensive insurance. For efficient movement of trucks along a trade corridor, it is important to have an insurance program that covers both the transport units and their cargo while transiting the corridor. Ultimately, it may become necessary for states to adopt a region-wide insurance scheme, without which it can be difficult to compensate for injuries or damage in a foreign territory. Examples of regional schemes that could serve as templates include the brown card scheme that is used for regional transport services in West Africa (de Matons 2014).

The MVA acknowledges that there are areas it does not cover. It provides two ways that some of these areas can be dealt with: protocols to the agreement, and reversion to the domestic laws of the participating countries. Several protocols are being drafted and negotiated by the parties to the MVA, such as those on designated corridors and some aspects of transit. However, there are numerous other issues that would still need to be addressed to complement the agreement and make it much more effective. They include the role of state-owned enterprises in some countries; the role of associations of operators, drivers, or agents and their associated political economy influences; the setting of benchmark prices by some regulatory authorities and the impact that can have on market contestation; and regulation of ancillary logistics services, such as warehousing. All of these issues are important but beyond the scope of this chapter.

The following recommendations are therefore limited to a few matters that would normally have been included in an agreement such as the MVA.

Standardizing infrastructure design

The interconnectivity of infrastructure and services is a defining attribute of networks; it is especially important in transport systems. Interconnectivity across borders, based on transport infrastructure that is built to the same standards and specifications, provides the basis for allowing vehicles loaded to the same limits to cross borders without hindrance. Different load limits may require goods to be transloaded or loads split, resulting in delays and high costs. Harmonization of axle load and maximum vehicle/combination mass limits is essential to integrated and efficient road transport industry in South Asia. It is particularly important for increasing the low level of intraregional trade. Vehicle load limits should ideally be the same in all BBIN countries.

Differences in axle-load limits and vehicle dimensions (table 1.5) have been cited as one of the reasons why the MVA has not been implemented in Bangladesh and Bhutan. There is an urgent need to ensure that standardized regulations govern vehicle-load limits and dimensions in the BBIN countries.

Infrastructure standardization is important for the seamless cross-border operation of road transport services. The main corridors and routes used for international road transport services need to have the same minimum design standards, so that they can handle the same axle-load limits. The main goal of standardization of axle limits along corridors is to eliminate or weaken arguments that can be used to deny access to markets or transport routes. Care should be taken to avoid significant discrepancies between theory and practice. In some cases, the regulatory framework is liberal, modern, and comprehensive; but because of low or no enforcement, bad practices dominate, and market functioning continues to be unhealthy, impeding competition. Transport and logistics services include all services related to the movement, handling, and processing of goods.

The countries of northeast South Asia have in place a basic interconnected road network. However, road transport operations face several hurdles that need to be addressed to operationalize the MVA.

One discrepancy is vehicle weights and dimensions. For the same class of trucks, axle-load limits are consistently lower in Bangladesh than in India (see table 1.5). This difference could reflect weaker pavements in Bangladesh or

TABLE 1.5 **Gross vehicle weight limits in Bangladesh and India (tonnes)**

VEHICLE TYPE	BANGLADESH	BHUTAN	INDIA	NEPAL
2 axle (1 front, 1 rear)	—	—	18.5	—
3 axle (1 front, 2 rear)	22	28	28.5	19
4 axle (steering + 3 axles)	25	—	31	—
5 axle (2 prime mover + 3 trailer)	38	—	43.5	—
6 axle (3 prime mover + 3 trailer)	41	—	44	—
7 axle (3 prime mover + 4 axle)	44	—	—	—

Source: World Bank staff estimates, based on data from various sources.
Note: — Not available.

a regulatory legacy in which limits have not kept pace with trends in trucking technology. The Bhutan Road Safety and Transport Authority (RSTA) Act of 1999 does not specify weight limits, relying instead on the weight limits specified by the vehicle manufacturer. In 2019 the legislature approved raising the limits to 28 tonnes for 10-wheel vehicles, the most common configuration in South Asia.

Differences in axle-load limits are cited as one reason for denying India transit rights across Bangladeshi territory. Lack of standardization presents challenges for operators, who may not know in advance what the limits are in each country, let alone along specific routes. The problem is compounded by the fact that weight limits at bridges are not notified in advance (before vehicles arrive), even along major regional corridors.

Most trucks in Bhutan are two-axle vehicles that carry payloads of only 10 tonnes. Bangladesh and India have the largest fleet sizes. As coastal countries, they have a comparative advantage in the carriage of international trade traffic, partly because of the trade imbalance. As imports greatly exceed exports, most trucks return from Bhutan empty, usually to ports to pick up goods. Such a pattern favors coastal country fleets, which, in the absence of cabotage, are better able to pick up goods and reduce empty runs.

Harmonizing driver's licensing and visa regimes

It is important for countries to negotiate complementary reforms—on road signage, driver training, insurance, and related dimensions, for example. The MVA requires vehicle crews to carry passports and be issued multiple-entry visas valid for at least one year. However, the agreement does not state where the visas should be issued. In some regions, agreements explicitly state that visas may be obtained at the border, which saves crews the burden of having to travel to the capital for consular services. Bhutan's National Council identified the issuance of multiple-entry visas that are valid for at least a year as one of the reasons for not ratifying the agreement (Legislative Committee of the National Council of Bhutan 2016), because Bhutan legislation allows for visitors traveling on ordinary passports to stay for a maximum of 30 days. According to the MVA, in the case of inconsistencies, national legislation shall apply.

Establishing an efficient regional transit regime

A well-functioning transit regime is a prerequisite for efficient cross-border road transport operations. The MVA does not provide much detail on transit, other than acknowledging that the agreement covers transit movements. The absence of integrated and modern transit regimes has long been an impediment to transit traffic across South Asia. Ongoing and planned improvements in intra- and interregional connectivity are adding to the urgency of developing such regimes. Policy makers can borrow from several international practices and exploit the new capabilities offered by information technology (IT) in data sharing by customs administrations. In fact, there are examples of the use of IT to better manage transit between some of the MVA countries, a case in point being the use of electronic cargo tracking between India and Nepal. Still, there is need for a region wide system to support the MVA.

Because of the shape of borders in the region, Bangladesh could serve as a transit country for trade between northeast India and the rest of India as well as for Bhutan and Nepal. The cross-border movement of vehicles—for transit or the delivery of goods—is not currently possible. Goods therefore have to be offloaded from trucks at the border and transferred to vehicles from the other country, and locomotives need to be changed for rail transport. The MVA provides a framework for facilitating the transit of Indian vehicles from the rest of India to the northeast states across Bangladesh—a move that would halve travel distance to about 500 kilometers.

A functional through-transit system for the countries of South Asia and between South Asia and the ASEAN has the potential to transform the trade-facilitation environment in the region, especially for its landlocked countries. The problem is a very specific one that requires a practical transit solution on a few identified road corridors with significant traffic potential.

Two considerations are critical. First, a functional transit procedure through Bangladesh is needed that allows the seamless movement of goods between West Bengal and the northeast states of India, with no significant waiting time at the border or en route because of inspections or transloading. Second, adequate mechanisms are needed that allow Bangladesh to recoup the costs associated with the use of its infrastructure and services by foreign registered vehicles, based on universal principles on freedom of transit. With suitable transit arrangements, some of the road traffic currently moving through the Siliguri Corridor in particular could transit across Bangladesh, yielding significant savings in shipping times.

Rationalizing and sharing documents electronically

The costs associated with obtaining, submitting, and having documents checked or processed by different jurisdictions adds significantly to the costs of trade in the region. The Organisation for Economic Co-operation and Development (OECD) estimates that such costs account for as much as 3 percent of the total costs of trade (WTO 2015). To expedite the clearance of goods through its borders, the South Asia region should move toward a legally binding trade facilitation agreement consistent with the WTO Trade Facilitation Agreement (TFA).

The MVA lists 11 documents that must be carried on a vehicle operated under its regulation:

- valid registration certificate
- certificate of fitness
- insurance policy
- permit
- certificate indicating vehicle's emission level and that pollution is under control
- driver's licenses
- passports of all crew
- passenger list (for passenger vehicles)
- way bill (for goods vehicles)
- commercial invoices and packing lists
- lists of personal goods of the crew.

These documents are in addition to the several documents and signatures that are required for trade between Bangladesh and India (CUTS International and IRU 2017). In some regions of the world, many of the documents required under the MVA are conditions for the issuance of a permit and do not need to be carried in the vehicle. Increasingly, IT is being exploited to transmit trade information, obviating the need to carry physical copies of documents. The MVA places a significant burden on drivers to keep several documents on the vehicle. This burden is particularly heavy in South Asia, where most drivers are semiliterate.

One way of addressing the large number of documents could be to implement the provisions of the WTO TFA and exploit the possibilities offered by IT and cross-border data sharing. By defining and adopting data standards and agreeing to share data among competent authorities that regulate road transport services, the BBIN countries could significantly reduce the number of documents drivers have to carry. Transport regulators in many parts of the world use IT systems to check and verify the status of vehicles and drivers, including their working hours. The lack of regulation of driver working hours is an important gap in the MVA—and one that could compromise safety. The European Union uses digital tachography and other technologies to track driver working hours and habits. The BBIN countries already have the basic infrastructure in place to track drivers and vehicles, including the electronic cargo-tracking systems used by customs.

Providing for multimodal logistics

Although road transport is the dominant mode of transport in the BBIN countries, India and Bangladesh also have extensive networks of interconnected railways and inland waterways. They carry very small and declining shares of traffic, however. Some of the measures of the MVA have the potential to support the development of a multimodal transport and logistics system across the region, allowing road transport to provide first- and last-mile connectivity to rail and inland water terminals, some located across borders. However, operationalizing proper multimodal logistics requires that the transit regime that is designed be flexible in terms of transport modes and that the vehicle standards proposed above take account of the loading requirements of the other modes of transport. There are already several junctions and nodes in the BBIN region where the three main modes of surface transport interface and could exchange regional traffic.

SUMMARY AND CONCLUDING REMARKS

Appropriate and effective regulatory regimes are essential to cross-border road transport operations. Operators have to have a clear understanding of the requirements they need to meet to offer services in a foreign territory, as the cost of infringements can be very high. The MVA is an important element for the establishment of an integrated road transport market in South Asia.

The content and scope of road transport agreements are usually useful indicators of the issues the participating countries consider important. Countries can also use such agreements to telegraph other objectives, some of which may be political or social in nature. The issues multilateral—and bilateral—road transport agreements exclude can offer important signals.

The analysis in this chapter is based on a quantitative assessment of the extent to which the MVA deals with provisions that are known to be important for the efficient regulation of cross-border transport operations. The approach provides a more objective analysis than would be possible through purely qualitative approaches. It has the added advantage of enabling comparison between the MVA and similar agreements in other regions of the world.

The foregoing analysis shows that the MVA scores in the middle of a sample of similar agreements. It covers well over half of the features that are important in the regulation of international road transport services. Some of its key features include provisions on the issuance and administration of permits, clarity on the types of traffic that it regulates, and the way in which taxes are treated in foreign territories. The agreement also provides for the designation of routes on which regional services can operate. All these provisions are critical for organizing cross-border operations.

The agreement is missing or weak on some important elements. Chief among them are standards for the design of infrastructure on which services are permitted, rules on the training and issuance of driver's licenses, and general principles for transit movements. These technical elements can prevent full realization of the benefits of the liberalization of services that the agreement entails, at least in principle. Negotiation of features such as these normally take time, as would their implementation. Implementation of new standards for infrastructure, for instance, can involve large capital outlays and are feasible only over long periods of time. Still, it is important that steps be taken to fill the gaps in coverage of the MVA. Without such action, the lack of agreement on the more technical standards can still prevent efficient cross-border road transport operations in the region.

The MVA is a significant step toward creating a cross-border integrated road transport market in South Asia. Integration should result in more contested markets, lower prices, and higher quality. However, there is need for the negotiation of additional provisions to address gaps in regulation that may continue to hamper seamless cross border operations.

REFERENCES

ASEAN Secretariat. 2018. *ASEAN Statistical Highlights 2018: ASEAN Singapore 2018*. Jakarta.

Borchert, I., B. Gootiiz, and A. Mattoo. 2010. "Trade Policy Restrictiveness in Transportation." Presentation at the OECD Expert Meeting on Transport Services, World Bank, Washington, DC, November.

Chemonics International. 2011. *Study on Impact of Transportation Monopoly: Report on the Roads Goods Transport Industry of Nepal*. Kathmandu: US Agency for International Development (USAID).

CUTS International, and IRU (International Road Transport Union). 2017. *Benefits of the TIR Convention for the Implementation of the BBIN Motor Vehicles Agreement*. Dhaka.

Fox, A., and P. Londoño-Kent. 2014. "U.S.–Canada and U.S.–Mexico Border Crossing for Trucks: 20 Years after NAFTA." Paper presented at the conference "NAFTA at 20: Effects on the North American Market," Federal Reserve Bank of Dallas, Houston, June 5–6.

Herrera Dappe, M., C. Kunaka, M. Lebrand, and N. Weisskopf. 2020. *Moving Forward: Connectivity and Logistics to Sustain Bangladesh's Success*. Washington, DC: World Bank.

Kunaka, C., and R. Carruthers. 2014. *Trade and Transport Corridor Management Toolkit*. Washington, DC: World Bank.

Kunaka, C., V. Tanase, P. Latrille, and P. Krausz. 2013. *Quantitative Analysis of Road Transport Agreements (QuARTA)*. Washington, DC: World Bank.

Law, D., and M. Versteeg. 2012. "The Declining Influence of the United States Constitution." *New York University Law Review* 87: 1–86.

Legislative Committee of the National Council of Bhutan. 2016. *Review Report on Motor Vehicles Agreement for the Regulation of Passenger and Cargo Vehicular Traffic between Bangladesh, Bhutan, India and Nepal.* Thimphu.

de Matons, J. G. 2014. *A Review of International Legal Instruments: Facilitation of Transport and Trade in Africa,* 2nd ed. Washington, DC: World Bank.

Nick Poree Associates. 2010. *Facilitation of Road Transport Market Liberalisation in the SADC Region.* Final Report. Gaborone, Botswana: Southern African Development Community (SADC).

Rahman, K. M., and T. Rahman. 2016. *Cost Benefit Analysis of Cooperation in Motor Vehicle Agreement in Bangladesh, Bhutan, India and Nepal Region: Bangladesh Priorities.* Dhaka: Copenhagen Consensus Center.

Teravaninthorn, S., and G. Raballand. 2009. *Transport Prices and Costs in Africa: A Review of the Main International Corridors.* Washington, DC: World Bank.

World Bank. 2019. *Report on the Initial Priority Infrastructure Pipeline Project List.* Jakarta.

WTO (World Trade Organization). 2006. "Quantitative Air Services Agreements Review (QUASAR)." WTO S/C/W/270/Add.1-3. Geneva: WTO.

WTO (World Trade Organization). 2015. "Implementing the Trade Facilitation Agreement." In *Aid for Trade at a Glance 2015: Reducing Trade Costs for Inclusive, Sustainable Growth.* Geneva.

2 Analysis of Route and Mode Transport Choice in Eastern South Asia Following Integration Agreements

GERARD DE JONG, MANISH SHARMA, MARCO KOUWENHOVEN, GIJS VAN ECK, YASHAR ARAGHI, RACHIT MITTAL, MAYANK PRATAP, MATÍAS HERRERA DAPPE, AND MEGERSA ABATE

Trade plays a central role in the economic development of countries, because accessing regional and global markets provides a broader market base for domestic natural resources and manufactured goods. Trade also benefits consumers, by offering them more affordable goods and services. Trade can be particularly beneficial for developing countries, which can use their lower-cost labor to establish labor-intensive, export-focused manufacturing. The ready-made garment and textile sector in Bangladesh is one such example, contributing about 84 percent of all goods exports from Bangladesh.

Geographically contiguous countries can benefit from intraregional trade. Intraregional trade accounts for 50 percent of total trade in East Asia and Pacific and 22 percent in Sub-Saharan Africa. In contrast, it accounts for just 5 percent of total trade in South Asia (Kathuria 2018). The inadequacy of physical infrastructure and logistics services and thick borders have been the key reasons preventing the scaling up of regional trade in South Asia.

Northeast India faces severe connectivity challenges, as trade routes through Bangladesh are virtually nonexistent. Before the partition of India, in 1947, trade and commerce between northeast India and the rest of India and the outside world passed through the territory of what is now Bangladesh. Rail and river transit across the erstwhile East Pakistan continued until 1965, when all transit routes were suspended, as a result of the war between India and Pakistan. Although the governments of India and Bangladesh restored river transit in 1972, until recently no substantial progress was made on road and rail transit/transshipment (Rahmatullah 2009). As a result, cargo to and from northeast India transported by road/rail must circumvent Bangladesh, increasing transit time and cost in the region. Transporting cargo through Bangladesh would reduce the lead distance between Kolkata and Agartala by about 1,100 kilometers.

Export-import (EXIM) cargo from northeast India and Bangladesh moves through seaports in the two countries. Indian use of the Chattogram Port in Bangladesh would dramatically reduce lead distances. Bangladeshi use of the Indian seaports at Kolkata and Haldia would yield economic benefits, through a reduction in cost.

Bangladesh's inland waterway transport (IWT) network provides an alternative to the road and rail network for connecting northeast India with the rest of India. But the network is used to transport only a small volume of transit cargo, mainly because of a lack of adequate physical infrastructure, including the fairway and terminals. Use of the IWT network for cargo transiting to and from northeast India and cargo moving between India and Bangladesh could benefit India and Bangladesh.

Several recent bilateral and multilateral agreements aim to facilitate cross-border trade in South Asia by integrating transport and logistics services:

1. The Motor Vehicles Agreement (MVA) between Bangladesh, Bhutan, India, and Nepal (known as the BBIN countries), signed in 2015, seeks to facilitate the unrestricted cross-border movement of cargo, passenger, and personal vehicles between the BBIN countries.[1] Under the agreement, trucks carrying EXIM or transit cargo can move inside the territories of other countries without the need for transshipment to local trucks at the border land ports. Currently, cargo movement to and from northeast India occurs through the Siliguri corridor (known as the "chicken's neck"). Trucks have to go around Bangladesh, increasing the distance and transit time and cost. The agreement is expected to open new and shorter routes through Bangladesh.

2. The Protocol on Inland Water Transit and Trade (PIWTT), signed by India and Bangladesh in 2009 and subsequently amended to add new routes and ports, seeks to facilitate cargo movement through Bangladesh's vast inland waterway network. It outlines new measures to facilitate inland water trade, develop infrastructure, and better integrate transport and logistics facilities in the two countries.

3. The Agreement on Coastal Shipping (ACS), signed by India and Bangladesh in 2015, seeks to facilitate the coastal movement of cargo through river-sea vessels directly from ports in India to ports in Bangladesh. Limited direct shipping between seaports in both countries is taking place primarily because of restrictions on vessel size. Both governments are planning to allow use of larger vessels in a revision of the agreement planned for 2020.

4. The Agreement for the use of Chattogram and Mongla ports (ACMP), signed by Bangladesh and India in 2018, seeks to allow the movement of goods between northeast India and the rest of India through Chattogram and Mongla ports. The agreement stipulates specific routes to connect both ports with northeast India.

The integration agreements have the potential to create new regional corridors, by opening domestic routes to regional traffic and changing the way freight moves across eastern South Asia. Effective implementation of the agreements requires the development of transport and logistics infrastructure and services, laws and regulations, and standard operating procedures to ensure hurdle-free and cost-efficient cross-border movement.

The potential traffic shift to new routes and modes from the current preferred routes and modes needs to be studied in order to facilitate proactive infrastructure capacity planning and the identification of desired service levels to enable the shift. Two key questions need answers:

- What factors or attributes of logistics service govern the route and mode choice of cargo owners and transporters in India and Bangladesh?
- What are the expected benefits in level of service from new routes and modes over existing corridors that can enable the shift of cargo?

This chapter aims to answer these questions through implementation of stated preference (SP) experiments in northeast India and Bangladesh, with a focus on the MVA, PIWTT, and ACS.

EXISTING CORRIDORS, ROUTES, AND MODE CHOICE

Implementation of the integration agreements between India and Bangladesh would potentially affect three types of cargo movement: domestic cargo movement between northeast India and the rest of India, EXIM cargo movement to and from northeast India, and bilateral trade between India and Bangladesh. This section describes the current routes and modes in each of these cases.

Movement of domestic and export-import cargo

Domestic and EXIM cargo movements take place through similar route and mode combinations. Northeast India is dependent on road and rail connectivity for the transport of goods to and from the rest of India. Road and rail networks pass through the Siliguri corridor. Two main routes connect northeast India with the rest of the country. The route passing through Kolkata connects the eastern and southern regions as well as the Kolkata and Haldia ports, the EXIM gateways for northeast India. The road and rail routes passing through Muzaffarpur and Patna in Bihar connect northern and western India with northeast India. Because of its good connectivity, Guwahati, in Assam, acts as a hub for trade between northeast India and the rest of India and between northeast Indian states (map 2.1).

Assam is the key cargo-generating and consumption center in northeast India. Northeast India spans seven states, which collectively contribute 2.8 percent to India's GDP and about 1.5 percent of the GDP contributed by manufacturing activities. The distribution within the region is highly skewed, with Assam contributing about 61 percent of the region's GDP, followed by Tripura, which provides 9 percent and Meghalaya (7 percent) (Central Statistics Office). Assam also contributes 75 percent of the region's manufacturing output (Indiastat). About 3.7 percent of India's population lives in northeast India, of which 69 percent live in Assam, according to the 2011 Census of India.

The key industries that produce goods for trade are natural resources–based industries, such as tea, cement, steel, and oil and gas refinery. Other industries with a sizable presence are fast-moving consumer goods (FMCG) and processed foods. The region also receives food grains, fruits and vegetables, consumer durables, fly ash, and FMCG products from the rest of India. Table 2.1 shows the movement of key commodities across existing route and mode combinations.

MAP 2.1

Industrial clusters and the connectivity network in northeast India

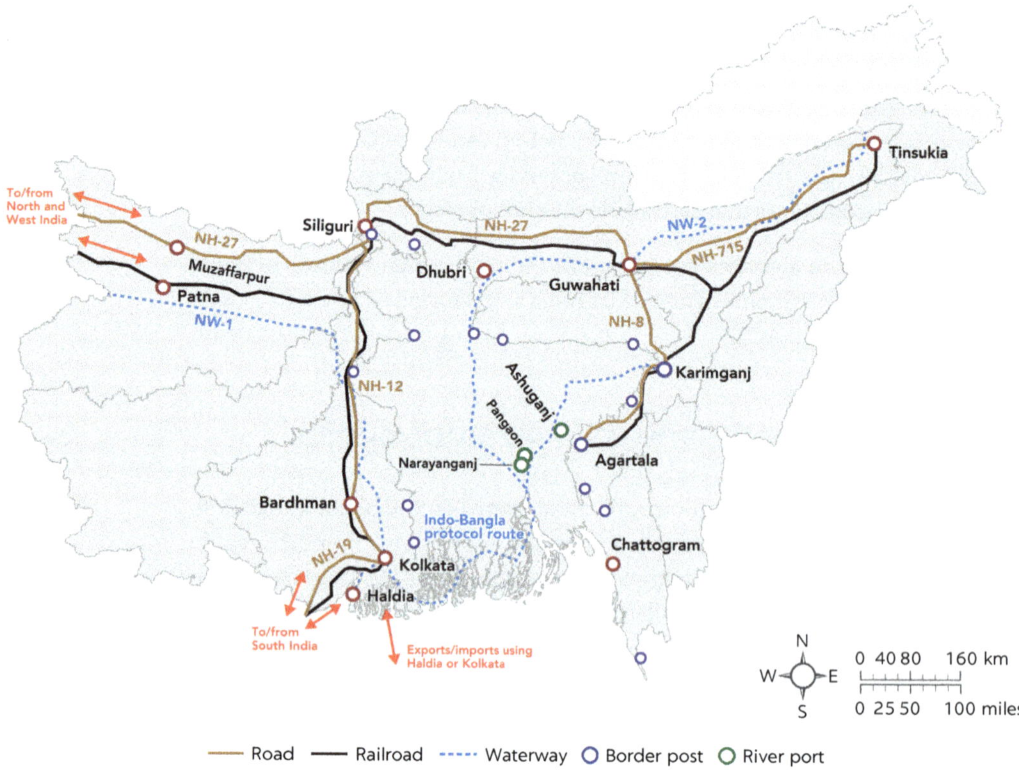

Source: World Bank

TABLE 2.1 **Domestic and export-import movement of commodities in northeast India**

COMMODITY	ROUTE	TRANSPORT MODE
Cement: Fly ash	Patna–Guwahati Kolkata–Guwahati	Rail
Cement: Finished products	Within northeast India	Road, with limited rail share
Crude oil	Patna–Guwahati	Pipeline
Petroleum, oil, and lubricant products	Within northeast India	Road, with limited rail share
Steel: Raw material	Kolkata–Guwahati	Road, with limited rail share
Steel: Products	Within northeast India	Road
Food grain	Patna–Guwahati Kolkata–Agartala	Rail, with very intermittent inland waterway movement to Agartala
Tea	Guwahati–Kolkata	Road and rail
Fast-moving consumer goods	Patna–Guwahati Kolkata–Guwahati	Road
Household goods	Patna–Guwahati Kolkata–Guwahati	Road and rail

Source: World Bank.

Cement industry. The cement plants in Assam and Meghalaya region depend on the eastern states of Bihar and West Bengal for their fly ash. Limestone from Meghalaya is supplied to cement plants in the eastern states. The movement of cement is limited largely within northeast India, with very limited supply to western states. Fly ash is transported by rail; limestone is transported mainly by road. Cement is distributed within the region largely by road. In some cases where cement is moved to eastern states, plants with rail siding use the rail network.

Petroleum and natural gas industry. The industry is concentrated in Assam, with a small presence in Tripura and Mizoram. Refineries are located in Digboi, Bongaigaon, Guwahati, and Numaligarh in the state of Assam. The major consumption centers for these refineries are the northeastern states, with any surplus supplied to the state of Sikkim or exported to countries in the region. Crude oil for the refineries is procured from the Barauni refinery in Bihar through pipelines. Finished products are distributed within the region by road; supply to other regions is through road and to a lesser extent rail.

Steel industry. Steel plants are located in Meghalaya. They source their raw materials from West Bengal and Odisha. Finished products are distributed mainly within northeast India. Raw materials such as iron ore pellets and sponge iron are moved largely by truck, with a marginal share by rail. Steel products are distributed within northeast India by road. Trucks transport steel products to the eastern states, as lower volumes of supply make rail transport costlier. The rail network is used in the rainy season, when trucks are often unavailable.

Food grain industry. The main sources of food grain supply to northeast India are the surplus production states of Punjab, Haryana, Uttar Pradesh, and Bihar. Food grains are sent directly to the zonal distribution center at Guwahati by rail. They are then distributed to other states in the region by road. The Food Corporation of India has also used the inland waterway route to the Ashuganj river port in Bangladesh and onward by road through the Akhaura border for the supply of food grains to the Agartala region. However, this movement has been very intermittent.

Tea industry. Assam and Arunachal Pradesh are the major tea producers in the region, with most commercial tea production contributed by Assam. Processed tea from Assam is distributed to the rest of India. Both rail (containers) and road networks are used to transport tea.

FMCG industry. The FMCG industry in the region is very small, to cover local demand. The deficit is met by supply from the rest of India. Goods are moved to Guwahati and then distributed to various states, mainly by truck.

Household goods. Household goods, including consumer durables, are supplied from the rest of India, mainly Delhi, Maharashtra, Gujarat, Karnataka, Rajasthan, and West Bengal. They are transported by road and rail. Guwahati acts as the distribution hub in the region.

Multiple challenges cause frequent delays in the transport of cargo to and from Guwahati by road. It takes about 8–10 days for cargo to reach Guwahati from Kolkata over a road distance of about 1,000 kilometers. The key reasons for the long transit time are low average speed because of hilly terrain in the region and heavy congestion.

The roads are not suitable for transporting heavy cargo, such as project equipment, as the strength and design of the road cannot handle the weight and size of the cargo. Even in such cases, use of the inland waterway network is limited, because of low least available depth and inadequate terminal handling facilities, among other factors.

Transport along the rail network is faster, with the trip from Guwahati to Kolkata taking two to three days. However, the smaller industry size, lack of rail sidings in the region, and lack of rakes limit the use of rail as the preferred transport mode.[2] During the rainy season, road transport is hampered by landslides, making rail the preferred mode for some industries.

Movement of bilateral cargo

Total annual goods trade between Bangladesh and India amounted to $9 billion in 2018 (International Trade Center). The main commodities traded between India and Bangladesh are exports of cotton and fabric, automobiles, machinery and equipment, food grains, chemicals, fruits and vegetables, and steel and metal products from India and exports of fabric and yarn, and apparel from Bangladesh. Bilateral cargo movement between India and Bangladesh occurs largely through the cross-border road network, as Bangladesh is landlocked on three sides by India. IWT is the second-most favored mode of transport, which caters predominantly to bulk products such as fly ash. The shares of rail and sea are very limited in bilateral trade.

Road transport moves through various land customs stations and land ports on the India–Bangladesh border. The land customs stations handling most of the bilateral cargo are Petrapole-Benapole, Ghijadanga-Bhomra, Changrabandha-Burimari, Mahadipur-Sonamasjid, Hili, Agartala-Akhaura, and Golakganj-Sonahat. Petrapole-Benapole handles most industrial cargo; the commodities handled at other ports are mostly construction materials and agricultural products.

Inland water transport (IWT) has the second-largest share of bilateral trade between India and Bangladesh. Bilateral cargo is transported along inland waterways through the Indo–Bangla protocol routes. The major movement of cargo is between Kolkata/Haldia and the river ports in the Dhaka region (Dhaka, Narayanganj, and the Pangaon container terminal). According to data from the Inland Waterway Authority of India (IWAI), the total cargo carried through IWT was about 3.2 million tonnes in fiscal 2019, of which about 96 percent was fly ash exported to cement companies in Bangladesh.

Bilateral cargo is also transported by sea. Sea-based trade is highly skewed toward containerized exports from India, contributing more than 95 percent of trade volumes. There is very limited direct cargo movement between India and Bangladesh through seaports. Major freight movement is on the transshipment route through the ports of Colombo or Singapore, which increases transport time and cost.

Cargo movement between India and Bangladesh by rail is very limited, because of infrastructure challenges. The commodities transported by rail are construction material (stone) and coal. Bangladesh's rail network consists mainly of meter gauge, which creates compatibility issues with the broad-gauge network of India. The load-carrying capacity of the Jamuna Bridge, which connects the western and eastern rail networks of Bangladesh, is the major barrier to rail transport.

Potential route and mode choices

The potential route and mode choices expected to materialize following implementation of the integration agreements between India and Bangladesh include

TABLE 2.2 **Potential route and mode choices following implementation of integration agreements**

MOVEMENT TYPE	EXISTING ROUTES AND MODES	POTENTIAL NEW ROUTES AND MODE CHOICES
Domestic cargo between northeast India and the rest of country	• Road through Siliguri corridor • Rail through Siliguri corridor	Road: • Guwahati to Kolkata via Bangladesh • Agartala to Kolkata via Bangladesh • Agartala to North India via northwest Bangladesh (Rajshahi/Rangpur region) Inland water: • Indo-Bangla protocol routes Multimodal: • Agartala to Kolkata by road (up to Ashuganj river port) and IWT protocol route
Export-import (EXIM) cargo to and from northeast India	EXIM through Haldia Port • Road through Siliguri corridor • Rail through Siliguri corridor	EXIM through Haldia Port Road: • Guwahati to Haldia via Bangladesh • Agartala to Haldia via Bangladesh Inland water: • Guwahati to Haldia via NW-2 and protocol route Multimodal: • Agartala to Haldia by road (up to Ashuganj river port) and IWT protocol route
		EXIM through Chattogram Port Road: • Guwahati/Agartala to Chattogram via Sabroom • Guwahati to Chattogram via Sylhet Rail: • Guwahati/Agartala to Chattogram via Sabroom Inland water: • Guwahati to Chattogram via NW-2 and Meghna River Multimodal: • Agartala to Chattogram by road (up to Ashuganj river port) and Inland water transport route to Chattogram • Guwahati to Chattogram by road (up to Karimganj) and Inland water transport route to Chattogram
Bilateral trade between India and Bangladesh	Road: • Movement through land customs stations/ports Sea: • Transshipment to Chattogram via Colombo/ Singapore Inland water: • Protocol routes between India and Bangladesh	Rail: • Movement through the Kolkata-Ranaghat Gede-Bangabandhu-Dhaka rail Sea: • Coastal movement between Indian ports and Chattogram Port

Source: World Bank.

single-mode as well as multimodal options transiting through Bangladesh. Twenty-four route and mode choices across the three movement types have been identified (table 2.2). Seven are currently used; the remaining 17 are new route and mode choices expected to materialize following implementation of the agreements (map 2.2).

MAP 2.2

Potential new route and mode choices following implementation of integration agreements

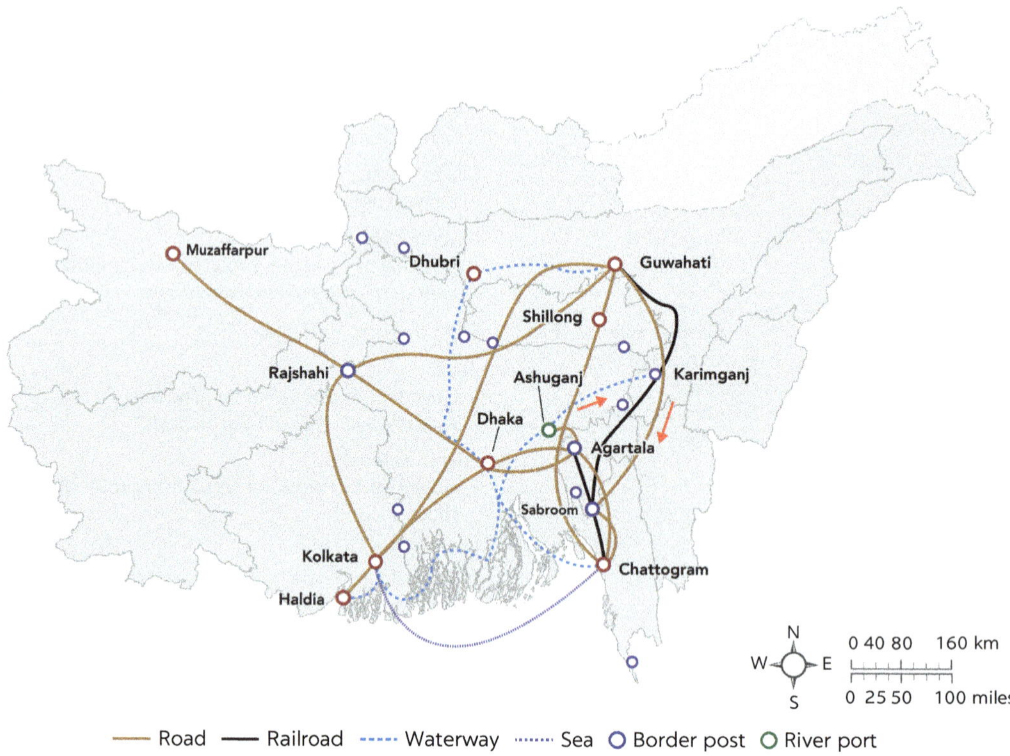

Source: World Bank.

METHODOLOGICAL APPROACH AND DATA

Stated-preference (SP) experiments were conducted to assess the preferences of users across route and mode choices. In such experiments, respondents are shown hypothetical alternatives that are described in terms of scores on multiple attributes of the alternatives and asked to choose between, rank, or rate the alternatives. In revealed-preference (RP) surveys, respondents are asked to record their actual choices in real choice problems. In the case of freight mode choice, for instance, an RP survey would ask shippers to provide the actual mode they use for shipments. A mode choice SP survey would present hypothetical mode choice alternatives to the shipper (road, rail, inland waterways, sea), each with specific assumptions on level-of-service attributes (for example, transport time, costs, reliability).

An advantage of an SP survey is that it allows preferences to be elicited for a situation that does not yet exist, such as a situation with considerably fewer border restrictions between India and Bangladesh and better-integrated transport infrastructure for freight transport. It is important to aim for realism in SP experiments, by using the current situation as a point of reference. For this reason, the SP survey conducted for this study was set up in the context of current shipments of the interviewed firms, modifying the attribute levels of these observed shipments. This kind of SP is called a customized SP, or pivot design.

A pilot survey of about 20 percent of the target population was conducted to gain a clear idea of the model coefficients or priors to be defined for the main SP experiment. Annex 2A describes the pilot survey. Box 2.1 presents the setup and implementation methodology of the SP experiments. Annex 2A describes the recruitment and survey method.

The stated-preference sampling

The design framework ensured that the mode and route choices of all relevant stakeholders were captured.[3] Shippers and 3PLs were interviewed, with a focus on mode choice. Road carriers were interviewed about the route choice for road transport. Table 2.3 presents the target sample distribution, which was selected based on the cargo volumes for different movement types, and the actual sample.

The three movement types were divided based on four dimensions: commodity types, geographic location, existing routes, and existing modes. Annex 2A shows the sample distribution across all dimensions.

BOX 2.1

Stated-preference experiments

The survey consisted of three SP experiments, including one unlabeled (abstract) experiment and two labeled experiments (see Louviere, Hensher, and Swait 2000 for a general introduction to SP experiments and de Jong 2008 and Tavasszy and de Jong 2014 for examples of SP experiments in freight transport). In the unlabeled experiments, alternatives were presented as generic names (Route 1, Route 2). These unlabeled route choices ensured unbiased responses and yielded a deeper understanding of the attributes that determine which route a respondent wants to use.

SP1 was an unlabeled or abstract experiment administered to both shippers/third-party logistics service providers (3PLs) and carriers (road haulage). SP2 and SP3 were labeled experiments. SP2 was conducted for carriers and SP3 for shippers/3PL players. In these experiments, the names of the routes or modes were shown. SP2 assessed the route choices of the respondents; SP3 assessed the overall choice influencing route, mode, and port choice of respondents. Each respondent participated in two experiments: shippers and 3PL players in SP1 and SP3, and road carriers in SP1 and SP2.

SP1 consisted of 10 choice screens, one of which was a dominant question (to check whether the respondent was paying attention and making rational choices). SP2 and SP3 contained 12 choice screens for each experiment. Each respondent was thus asked to make 22 choices.

After the efficient design (Rose and others 2008) was created, the number of blocks (design tables) for each experiment was determined based on analysis of a pilot survey. Four blocks for the design table were designed for each experiment using NGENE software (Choicemetrics 2018). For each respondent and each SP, a random draw determined which block of choice cards was presented. In the final sample of respondents, for each SP experiment, each block occurred the same number of times. Choice screens within each experiment were presented in random order. For SP2 and SP3, a random draw determined the order in which alternatives were shown to respondents. For each respondent, the order in which the alternatives were shown remained constant; the order varied only between respondents.

The number of alternatives was limited to a maximum of four, to ensure that respondents were not overburdened with choices. Too many alternatives often result in partial nonresponse and use of simplifying heuristics (such as always choosing the left-hand side alternative). SP1 and SP2 consisted of binary alternatives, as the objective was to capture choices between Route A versus Route B in SP1 and the route through the Siliguri corridor versus the route through Bangladesh in SP2. Four alternatives were used for SP3 experiments, which considered a combination of route and mode choices.

TABLE 2.3 **Sample distribution**

MOVEMENT TYPE	SHIPPERS/THIRD-PARTY LOGISTICS SERVICE PROVIDERS		CARRIERS (ROAD HAULAGE)	
	TARGET	ACTUAL	TARGET	ACTUAL
Domestic cargo	150	183	75	130
Export-import cargo	25	30	25	25
Bilateral trade	75	93	50	52

Source: World Bank.

Commodities. Commodities were selected in a way that ensured that a significant share of movement was captured. In the case of domestic and EXIM movement, the selected commodities covered about 80 percent of movement to northeast India and about 72 percent of movement from northeast India. The commodities selected for the bilateral movement represented about 73 percent of imports to and 54 percent of exports from India.

Geographic location. Respondents were divided into three categories based on their location: northeast India, the rest of India (mainly East India), and Bangladesh. These categories ensured that both shippers and carriers were selected from all three regions.

Existing routes. The existing routes for domestic cargo movement were divided into four corridors for the distribution of the respondents: Corridor A: Guwahati–Patna; Corridor B: Guwahati–Kolkata; Corridor C: Agartala–Patna; and Corridor D: Agartala–Kolkata.

- Guwahati represents origins and destinations located in Assam, Meghalaya, Manipur, Nagaland, and Arunachal Pradesh.
- Agartala represents origins and destinations located in Tripura, Mizoram.
- Kolkata represents origins and destinations located in West Bengal (including the Port of Haldia), Jharkhand, and states in southern India.
- Patna represents origins and destinations located in northern and western India.

The selected existing corridors for EXIM cargo movement were Guwahati–Kolkata (Corridor B) and Agartala–Kolkata (Corridor D). The major seaport used for EXIM of commodities used by industries and logistics services providers in northeast India is Haldia, in Kolkata. These categories were selected to survey the route and mode choices of these players.

For bilateral trade, the existing corridors selected were the road using the Petrapole-Benapole customs station, the road using other land customs stations, and the sea. Petrapole-Benapole was selected because it has the largest share of trade via road.

Existing mode. Road and rail are currently the dominant modes of transport used by industries and logistics service providers in northeast India for domestic and EXIM cargo movement. For bilateral trade, roads are the main mode of transport, with sea the second-most preferred mode for freight movement between India and Bangladesh.

Determinants of mode and route choice

The experiment assesses the choices of the routes and modes based on different attribute levels. The attributes for the experiments were selected based on the attributes recommended by the literature on SP experiments of freight transport, and the attributes that influence decisions about the mode and route choice in the region were studied.

Most of the SP surveys carried out in the freight transport sector consider transport costs and transport time. An additional reason for including these attributes is that most transport infrastructure projects and policies (for example, road pricing or trade/transport agreements) can be simulated by changing these variables in the model. Including these attribute variables greatly increases the relevance of policy in the model. The most often used attribute after transport time and cost is the probability of delay, an important determinant of hypothetical route and mode choice in freight.

Pilot surveys with the firms located or operating in the study area corridors allow factors other than transport time and costs influencing route and mode choices to be identified and ranked. The responses revealed that the selection of route and mode depends on multiple attributes, including the following:

- *Transport time.* Transport time is a key factor for most industries. It affects inventory carrying cost for shippers and the utilization of assets by carriers.
- *Transport cost.* Transport cost has a major impact on the route and mode choices by shippers and carriers.
- *Probability of delay.* The probability of delay is the most critical attribute for export-oriented industries, such as tea.
- *Frequency of operation / availability of transport.* Frequency affects the selection of some transport modes. To incorporate this attribute in the SP experiments, respondents were asked to assume that trains run at least once a day.
- *Presence of end-to-end service providers and cargo aggregators.* To use rail transport, industries are required to book a rake of 2,500 tonnes; for IWT, typical barge sizes are 800–1,000 tonnes. Shippers with smaller volumes of bulk cargo depend on cargo aggregators for rail and IWT services. This factor was incorporated into the SP experiment by asking respondents to indicate a typical shipment size and to make choices about that size of shipment, which were considered in the econometric model.
- *Number of handlings or transshipments.* Interviews with the tea industry revealed that the number of handlings is one of the key parameters for selection of route and mode. Handling increases the risk of damage and the ingress of foreign particles, resulting in rejection of the shipment, especially in the case of exports.
- *Administrative issues related to customs and other operations for the cross-border movement of cargo.* The efficiency of administrative and customs processes at the border were identified as key attributes for movement through Bangladesh. It influences door-to-door transport time and cost. Respondents were asked to assume that border issues would be resolved following implementation of the agreements and policies.
- *Impact on quality of goods.* The petrochemical and chemical shipments must meet specific quality requirements. The preference for route and mode for these types of industries may depend on the level of control the industry can exercise. For example, a chemical company can have more control over quality if its products are transported by rail than it can if they are transported by tanker barge. Because this attribute is relevant for only some sectors, it was not included in the SP experiments.

- *Probability of damage or theft.* This attribute is not often used in the literature but was confirmed as important. It was therefore included as an attribute.

Based on the review of the literature and preliminary surveys, the following attributes for the SP experiments were selected:

- door-to-door transport time (five levels)
- total transport costs (five levels)
- number of transshipments (three levels)
- probability of a delay of more than 24 hours (three levels)
- probability of cargo damage and theft (three levels)
- border waiting time (three levels).

The values of time and cost of the chosen mode and route and the unchosen modes and routes are based on data and expert knowledge on the relative time and cost of the alternatives.

Econometric models for mode and route choice

Both mode and route are discrete variables (they can take only a limited number of values). They are also of a purely qualitative nature (a possible outcome would be "road transport" for mode choice or "Siliguri corridor" for route choice). As a result, standard regression models—which are designed to explain continuous, quantitative variables—cannot be used. Instead, a special category of models called discrete choice models should be used (Ben-Akiva and Lerman 1985; Train 2003). Tavasszy and de Jong (2014) discuss the application of these methods in freight transport modeling.

Different discrete choice models for carriers and shippers were estimated, because it is assumed that road transport carriers do not decide on mode choice but influence route choice for road transport and that mode choice (sometimes including the choice of port and route) is based on decisions by shippers. The shipper and carrier models were estimated for the three transport types: domestic transport in India, EXIM transport in India, and bilateral transport between Bangladesh and India.

The shipper models interact time and cost with firm size, containerized goods, and the value of the goods per tonne. For the carrier models, the same is true, except nonbulk goods (food and nonfood) are used instead of containerized goods. The interactions between the attributes offered in the SP and characteristics of firms and shipments are included to account for observed heterogeneity. For instance, a large firm's response to changes in cost could be different from that of a small firm. Interactions that were not significant were dropped. Both shipper and carrier models included the logarithm of cost to capture nonlinearities. Nonlinear time specifications were tested in the shipper models, but they were not statistically significant and therefore were dropped.

Shippers choose between multiple modes and in some cases multiple routes. To test whether there is more substitution between certain modes and routes, different multinomial nested logit model structures were tested for the three transport types. A nesting structure is preferred in the shipper models for domestic and bilateral trade, where the results show more substitution between routes than between modes. For carriers, nonnested multinomial logit models were used. All models were estimated by the maximum likelihood method using the SP data.[4]

RESULTS OF MODE AND ROUTE CHOICE MODEL ESTIMATION

The estimated coefficients for the mode and route choice models have plausible signs and magnitudes. For domestic carriers, routes through Bangladesh have a negative constant (–0.62), which reduces the chance that carriers will select routes through Bangladesh (table 2.4). As expected, longer time and higher cost make a route less attractive, as do more frequent delays, more frequent theft and damage, and longer waiting time at the border. The coefficients for the interactions with time and cost should be regarded as influences that are added to the overall influence of time or cost. The cost coefficient for large firms in the carriers-bilateral segment is –5.50 + 3.69 = –1.81, which implies that they are less sensitive than the average-size firm. Nonbulk nonfood commodities in the carriers-bilateral segment are less sensitive to time than bulk commodities (the reference category), which can be explained by the fact that bulk products may be required in a production process for further processing.

In the shipper models (table 2.5), longer time, higher cost, more frequent delays, more frequent theft and damage, longer waiting time at the border, and more transshipments for a certain mode lower the probability of choosing that mode.

TABLE 2.4 **Determinants of route choice by carriers**

	TRANSPORT TYPE		
	DOMESTIC	EXPORT-IMPORT	BILATERAL
Bangladesh dummy	−0.62*** (−2.8)	1.19*** (2.7)	0.16 (1.4)
Time (in hours)	−0.023*** (−5.0)	−0.040*** (−7.3)	−0.028*** (−5.2)
Time for nonbulk nonfood	0.0071** (2.0)		
Time for large firms		0.0060*** (4.6)	0.019*** (3.8)
Time for goods with low value per tonne	0.0060 (1.3)		
Time for goods with high value per tonne	−0.042*** (−5.5)		
Time for goods with unknown value per tonne	−0.052*** (−8.4)		
Cost (in Rs)	−24.80*** (−12.5)	−12.29*** (−6.0)	−5.50*** (−8.7)
Cost for nonbulk food		−1.06 (−0.6)	
Cost for large firms			3.69*** (6.8)
Cost for containerized goods	3.66** (2.3)		3.03*** (5.5)
Cost for goods with low value per tonne	10.68*** (6.2)		

table continues on next page

TABLE 2.4, *continued*

	TRANSPORT TYPE		
	DOMESTIC	EXPORT-IMPORT	BILATERAL
Percentage of delay (reliability)	−0.019*** (−4.5)		−0.024*** (−4.9)
Percentage of damage and theft	−0.044*** (−5.5)	−0.024*** (−2.0)	−0.058*** (−5.3)
Waiting time at the border (hours)	−0.037** (−2.6)	−0.081*** (−2.7)	−0.038*** (−5.2)
Scale coefficient SP experiment 2	1.00[a]	1.00[a]	1.00[a]
Scale coefficient SP experiment 1	0.47*** (10.7)	0.96*** (5.5)	1.16*** (5.1)
Observations	2,604	525	840
Final loglikelihood	−678.1	−141.2	−445.9
Degrees of freedom	13	8	10
$Rho^2(0)$	0.62	0.61	0.23
$Rho^2(c)$	0.50	0.53	0.23

Source: World Bank.
Notes: Figures in parentheses are *t*-statistics.
a. Coefficient was fixed at 1.
Significance level: * = 10 percent, ** = 5 percent, *** = 1 percent.

TABLE 2.5 **Determinants of mode, route, and port choice by shippers**

	TRANSPORT TYPE		
	DOMESTIC	EXPORT-IMPORT	BILATERAL
Bangladesh dummy	0.98*** (8.9)	−0.26 (−0.8)	0.59 (1.6)
Rail dummy	−0.25 (−1.4)	−0.75** (−2.4)	0.20 (0.5)
Inland waterways dummy	−1.01*** (−4.9)	−0.033 (−0.1)	0.38 (1.0)
Time (hours)	−0.017*** (−7.6)	−0.021*** (−7.8)	−0.0047*** (−8.4)
Time for large firms		0.0092*** (3.8)	0.0019*** (3.6)
Time for containerized goods	0.0089*** (4.6)		
Time for goods with low value per tonne		0.011*** (4.0)	
Time for goods with unknown value per tonne			−0.0047*** (−3.9)
Cost (in Rs)	−2.56*** (−6.4)	−7.95*** (−10.1)	−1.31*** (−18.3)
Cost for large firms		2.50*** (2.9)	
Cost for containerized goods	0.52 (1.4)	−4.08*** (−3.1)	

table continues on next page

TABLE 2.5, *continued*

	TRANSPORT TYPE		
	DOMESTIC	EXPORT-IMPORT	BILATERAL
Cost for goods with high value per tonne	−0.91*** (−4.2)		
Cost for goods with unknown value per tonne	−4.81*** (−9.9)		
Percentage of delay (reliability)	−0.0050*** (−3.6)	−0.020*** (−4.7)	−0.0052*** (−5.0)
Percentage of damage and theft	−0.024*** (−6.8)	−0.037*** (−4.5)	−0.020*** (−6.2)
Waiting time at the border (hours)	−0.0071** (−2.3)	−0.014 (−1.5)	
Number of transshipments			−0.039 (−1.5)
Scale coefficient of SP experiment 3	1.00[a]	1.00[a]	1.00[a]
Scale coefficient of SP experiment 1	2.08*** (10.3)	1.74*** (7.5)	5.97*** (5.8)
Nesting coefficient for routes of same mode	0.72*** (11.1)		
Nesting coefficient for road and nonroad nests			0.78*** (6.1)
Observations	3,938	760	1,980
Final loglikelihood	−2,876.4	−338.1	−1,598.9
Degrees of freedom	14	13	12
$Rho^2(0)$	0.32	0.56	0.25
$Rho^2(c)$	0.26	0.51	0.22

Source: World Bank.
Note: Figures in parentheses are t-statistic.
a. Coefficient was fixed at 1.
Significance level: * = 10 percent, ** = 5 percent, *** = 1 percent.

The willingness of shippers and carriers to pay for improvements in service levels indicates the importance of each attribute. The estimated coefficients of the route and mode choice models are used to estimate the monetary value of travel and time waiting at the border, reliability, transshipment, and theft and damage for shippers and carriers.[5]

Time is not as important as cost for carriers transporting goods between northeast India and the rest of India or EXIM from/to northeast India, but it is more important than cost for carriers transporting bilateral trade between Bangladesh and India. The estimated value of time (in Indian rupees per hour per shipment) for road carriers transporting goods between northeast India and the rest of India or EXIM from/to northeast India is lower than the median transport cost per hour; it is higher than the median transport cost per hour for carriers transporting bilateral trade between Bangladesh and India (table 2.6). Time is also not as important for carriers, as is usually found in SP analyses in the Western world (where it comes close to the mean transport costs per hour, according to de Jong and others 2014).

For domestic and EXIM freight, the value of time is higher for shippers than carriers; for bilateral trade, the carriers' value of time is higher than that of shippers (see table 2.6). In the Western world, the value of time for carriers is usually higher than that of shippers (de Jong and others 2014). The fact that the analysis finds a reversal of this pattern for freight moving across India may have to do with the much longer land-based travel times in India, which makes it more difficult for shippers to ignore the interest cost on the value of goods in transit.[6]

TABLE 2.6 **Willingness to pay by carriers and shippers (Indian rupees per shipment)**

TYPE OF TRADE/CARRIER	TRANSPORT MODE			
	ROAD	RAIL	RIVER	SEA
Value of time (per hour)				
Domestic, carriers	88	n.a.	n.a.	n.a.
Domestic, shippers	240	323	248	n.a.
Export-import, carriers	143	n.a.	n.a.	n.a.
EXIM, shippers	372	313	377	n.a.
Bilateral, carriers	495	n.a.	n.a.	n.a.
Bilateral, shippers	211	291	370	393
Value of reliability (per 1 percentage point increase in probability of delay)				
Domestic, carriers	83	n.a.	n.a.	n.a.
Domestic, shippers	132	177	136	n.a.
Export-import, carriers	n.a.	n.a.	n.a.	n.a.
Export-import, shippers	193	163	195	n.a.
Bilateral, carriers	618	n.a.	n.a.	n.a.
Bilateral, shippers	290	401	509	541
Value of theft/damage (per 1 percentage point increase in probability of theft/damage)				
Domestic, carriers	189	n.a.	n.a.	n.a.
Domestic, shippers	633	850	653	n.a.
Export-import, carriers	92	n.a.	n.a.	n.a.
Export-import, shippers	1,425	1,200	1,442	n.a.
Bilateral, carriers	1,528	n.a.	n.a.	n.a.
Bilateral, shippers	1,112	1,537	1,951	2,074
Value of transshipments (per transshipment)				
Domestic, carriers	n.a.	n.a.	n.a.	n.a.
Domestic, shippers	n.a.	n.a.	n.a.	n.a.
Export-import, carriers	n.a.	n.a.	n.a.	n.a.
Export-import, shippers	n.a.	n.a.	n.a.	n.a.
Bilateral, carriers	n.a.	n.a.	n.a.	n.a.
Bilateral, shippers	2,153	2,976	3,777	4,016
Value of border waiting time (per hour)				
Domestic, carriers	159	n.a.	n.a.	n.a.
Domestic, shippers	186	250	192	n.a.
Export-import, carriers	309	n.a.	n.a.	n.a.
Export-import, shippers	552	464	558	n.a.
Bilateral, carriers	1,002	n.a.	n.a.	n.a.
Bilateral, shippers	n.a.	n.a.	n.a.	n.a.

Source: World Bank.
Note: n.a. = Not applicable.

The values for reliability average about Rs 300 per shipment, with a large variance (see table 2.6). A value of Rs 300 means that a 1 percentage point reduction in the probability of delays of more than 24 hours (for example, from 10 percent to 9 percent) is valued at Rs 300. The result implies that on average, a 1 percent change in the frequency of delay is worth about the same as 1 hour of transport time. Carriers and shippers involved in bilateral trade between Bangladesh and India place the highest value on reliability; carriers and shippers involved in domestic freight movements between northeast India and the rest of India place the lowest value on it.

The value placed on avoiding theft and damage varies widely across movement types, probably reflecting differences in the values of the goods shipped. The mean value of about Rs 1,100 means that a 1 percentage point reduction in the probability of damage or theft (for example, from 10 percent to 9 percent) is valued at Rs 1,100 per shipment. This figure is three to four times the average value of time per hour. High values are found for bilateral trade and EXIM (shippers) to and from northeast India for all modes. These values also depend on the shipment size. Per tonne, road values will therefore be highest.

Transshipment is more onerous for modes with larger shipment sizes. Reducing the number of transshipments by one is worth about 10 hours of travel time. Shippers engaged in bilateral trade are willing to pay about Rs 2,100 to reduce the number of transshipments in road transport by one, about Rs 3,000 in the case of rail, and about Rs 4,000 in the case of river and sea transport.

A reduction of an hour of waiting time at the border is worth more for carriers and shippers involved in bilateral movements than for carriers and shippers involved in domestic movements between northeast India and the rest of India and trade between northeast India and the rest of the world. Bilateral movements have to cross the border; other movements have alternatives, which can explain the difference in willingness to pay. The average value for an hour of waiting time at the border is about the same as the average value of an hour in general. A reduction of an hour of waiting time at the border is worth less than the transport costs per hour for domestic movements between northeast India and the rest of India, but it could be worth as much, or even more than, the transport costs per hour of bilateral trade and trade between northeast India and the rest of the world.

For the most part, decision-makers are inelastic with respect to changes in price and time. For road transport, the price elasticity of the number of tonnes are −0.51 for domestic, −0.13 for EXIM, and −0.25 for bilateral freight. For rail transport, the price elasticity of the number of tonnes is −1.00 for domestic, −2.44 for EXIM, and −1.14 for bilateral freight. These estimates are within the range typically found in the literature, except for the elasticities for EXIM freight, which are higher (in absolute value), indicating strong price sensitivity in northeast India. The time elasticities for both modes are a bit lower (in absolute values) than the price elasticities.

The success of the integration agreements in triggering changes to more efficient routes and modes across eastern South Asia requires improving infrastructure and service delivery in an integrated manner. Elasticity estimates vary greatly across commodity groups and origin–destination pairs. They also depend strongly on the availability of port and rail infrastructure. This heterogeneity suggests that reductions in border delays or travel time (through implementation of cross-border integration agreements) or pure pricing instruments (such as road pricing for trucks) will have limited mode/route substitution impacts unless they are complemented with policies that improve infrastructure for rail, river transport, and coastal shipping. The high willingness-to-pay estimates for travel and wait time savings; reliability; and lower chances of theft, damage, and border delays call for tackling both hard and soft infrastructure deficiencies to ensure that trade and transport facilitation bottlenecks at borders do not erode improvements in road, rail, and river connectivity.

SIMULATION RESULTS FOR THE ANALYSIS OF MODE AND ROUTE CHOICE

This section examines the potential for the modal and route shifts that the integration agreements and a set of complementary policies may induce.

Simulation method

Mode and route choice models were used to predict the potential mode and route shift of a series of policy measures that facilitate cross-border trade between India and Bangladesh in a number of corridors. The simulations use the database of all carriers and shippers that participated in the SP survey, weighted by their reported annual transported volume. The following corridors are considered:

- domestic transport: Guwahati–Kolkata, Agartala–Patna, Agartala–Kolkata
- EXIM transport: Guwahati–Kolkata, Agartala–Kolkata
- bilateral transport: India–Bangladesh, Bangladesh–India.

Most of these corridors offer road, rail, inland waterway, and sea transport alternatives. In each corridor (and separately for domestic, EXIM, and bilateral transport), the choice is modeled in two steps:

- *Route choice modeling.* For road transport, the distribution over routes in each corridor is predicted by simulating the route choice of all carriers with the estimated carrier (route choice) models. The estimated carrier models apply to road transport and are therefore not applicable to model the choice between rail, inland waterways, and sea routes. These route choices are therefore simulated by a deterministic model that assigns the entire volume to the fastest route.
- *Mode choice modeling.* Based on the predicted route shares, weighted-average level-of-service attributes are calculated for each available mode in each corridor. Thereafter, the mode choice is predicted by simulating the mode choice of all shippers with the estimated shipper (mode choice) models.

The estimated mode and route choice models are first applied to model the mode and route choice of all respondents in the SP data (separately for domestic, EXIM, and bilateral transport) in the base year (2019). The mode-specific constants for road, rail, inland waterways, and sea are then recalibrated for each corridor to match the current mode shares in that corridor (annex 2B presents the costs and time elasticities after calibration). Thereafter, the recalibrated model is applied for two scenarios for the same year (2025). In the first scenario (the reference case for 2025), no policy measures are adopted. Assumptions are made about the overall growth in transport by commodity type between 2019 and 2025,[7] keeping the mode and route shares unchanged. In the second scenario, policy measures are adopted. When they are implemented, the attractiveness of most alternatives improves, and new travel alternatives (routes) through Bangladesh become available.

Simulated policy measures

The policy measure scenario assumes that the MVA is implemented without restrictions on the border posts and corridors trucks can use, as well as the PIWTT and ACS, and some infrastructure intervention recommendations are implemented to improve the level of service in some corridors (table 2.7). Expansion of the effective capacity of roads to key land ports and along regional corridors will reduce travel time and costs. It can be increased through a mix of infrastructure investments, policies to increase containerization, cargo aggregation, and reductions in the share of empty running trucks and overall congestion on the roads. One of the potential road routes through Bangladesh that ensures the lowest travel time in Bangladesh connects Kolkata and Guwahati through the Hili and Mahendraganj/Dhanua-Kamalpur land ports and crosses the Jamuna River in Rangpur division, where there is currently no bridge. It is assumed that a new bridge over the Jamuna River and approach roads in Rangpur division will be built and existing bridges will be rehabilitated.

Policy measures that reduce border times and the number of transshipments are key to ensuring that the implementation of the integration agreements will lead to a shift of freight traffic to optimal routes and modes. Construction of dedicated lanes at land ports and berths at Chattogram Port for transit cargo, improvement of land port facilities, increase in the effective capacity of evacuation infrastructure at Chattogram Port, deployment of modern information technology infrastructure at relevant land ports and seaports, development of

TABLE 2.7 **Measures to facilitate shift to new mode and route alternatives**

MEASURE	IMPACT ON LEVEL-OF-SERVICE ATTRIBUTES
Expansion of effective capacity of roads to key land ports and along regional corridors	Reduces travel time and cost
Construction of a new bridge over the Jamuna River in Rangpur division and approach roads and the rehabilitation of existing bridges	Reduces travel time and cost
Construction of dedicated lanes at land ports and berths at Chattogram Port for transit cargo	Reduces border waiting time Reduces probability of delay, theft, and damage
Increase in the effective capacity of evacuation infrastructure at Chattogram Port	Reduces probability of delay, theft, and damage Reduces travel time
Improvement of land port facilities	Reduces border waiting time
Deployment of modern information technology infrastructure at relevant land ports and seaports	Reduces border waiting time and probability of delay
Development of off-border customs clearance facilities in Bangladesh and India	Reduces border waiting time Reduces number of transshipments
Improved collaboration between customs authorities of Bangladesh and India through adoption of standard operating procedures for cross-country transport	Reduces border waiting time
Standardization of policies and regulations, such as vehicle and road design standards, following implementation of the integration agreements	Reduces border waiting time Reduces number of transshipments

off-border custom clearance facilities in Bangladesh and India, improved collaboration between customs authorities of Bangladesh and India through adoption of standard operating procedures for cross-country transport, and standardization of policies and regulations, such as vehicle and road design standards, will reduce border waiting times, number of transhipments, travel time and probability of delay, theft and damage of cargo.

In the model simulation, each transport alternative (mode and route) is described by the following level-of-service attributes: travel time (hours); travel costs (Rs/tonne); probability of delay more than 24 hours (percent); chance of theft or damage (percent); number of transshipments; and border waiting time (hours). Annex 2C presents the level-of-service attributes for the mode and route alternatives available after the implementation of the integration agreements.

Some of these alternatives lead to large reductions in distance and consequently transport cost and time. A truck traveling from Guwahati to Kolkata via the Siliguri corridor takes on average 164 hours and pays Rs 3,129 per tonne. In the scenario in which the policy measures are implemented, the truck can use the route through the Petrapole-Benapole land port, which will take on average 126 hours plus 8 hours waiting time at the border and cost Rs 2,479 per tonne, reducing the time by 18 percent and the cost by 21 percent. The differences are even more pronounced for a truck traveling from Agartala to Kolkata. Via the Siliguri corridor, it takes 250 hours and costs Rs 4,940 per tonne; through Petrapole-Benapole, it will take 80 hours plus 8 hours waiting time at the border and cost Rs 1,597 per tonne—a 65 percent reduction in time and a 68 percent reduction in cost. It takes a truck traveling between Agartala and Patna 237 hours and costs Rs 4,614 per tonne through the Siliguri corridor. Using the route through Hili would take 122 hours plus 8 hours at the border and cost Rs 3,177 per tonne—a 45 percent reduction in time and a 31 percent reduction in cost.

For the probability of delay and theft or damage, it is difficult to determine the effect of the policies. For current routes, the average of the base-year values and European reference values is used. For new routes that become available after policy implementation, the average values of current routes are taken. The assumption is made that there is no systematic difference between routes in India and Bangladesh in terms of delays, theft, or damage. Should any of these assumptions not be realized, the predicted mode and route shift would be different. It is assumed that by 2025, all policies will have been implemented, though not necessarily at the same time.

Predicted mode and route shares

For the domestic movement of cargo through Kolkata to northeast India, after implementation of the agreements, the choice of route and mode will be highly skewed toward road transport via the Petrapole-Benapole border (map 2.3 and table 2.8). The Hili border will be the preferred route for movement to Agartala through Patna. Rail transport through the Siliguri corridor will be used for movement to Guwahati through Kolkata and to Agartala through Patna.

There will be a decline in the share of rail transport, however, from 18 percent to 10 percent for Guwahati–Kolkata and from 39 percent to 25 percent for Kolkata–Guwahati, as a result of the attractive new road alternative. An even larger reduction in the rail share is predicted for Agartala–Kolkata (from 17 percent to 6 percent), Kolkata–Agartala (from 27 percent to 2 percent),

MAP 2.3

Predicted freight traffic between northeast India and rest of India in 2025 if agreements are implemented

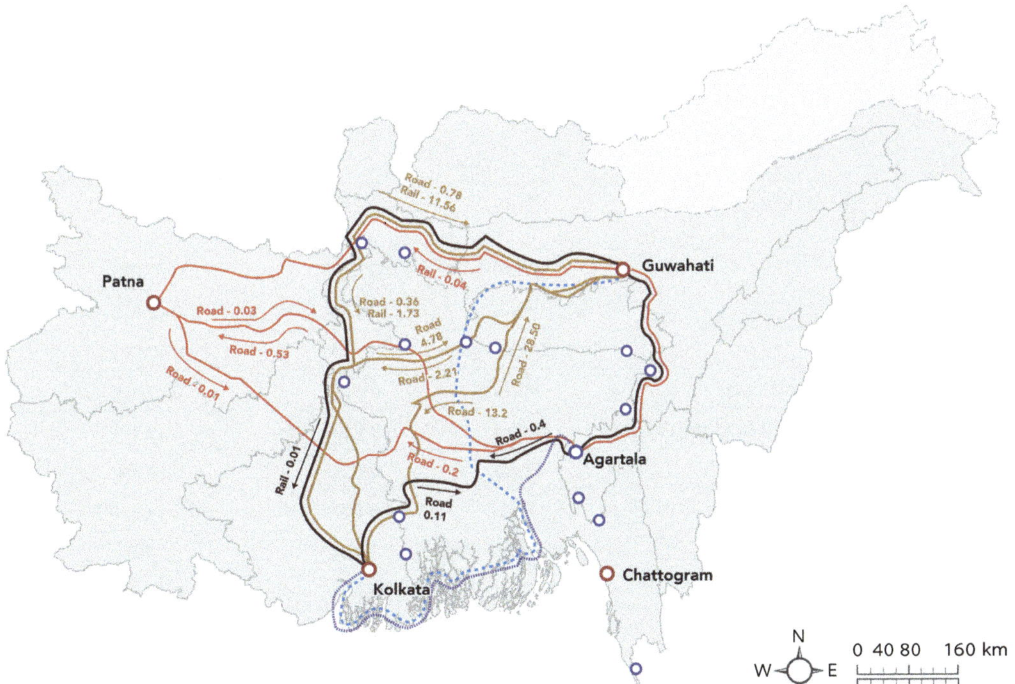

Guwahati-Kolkata (and vice versa)
—— Road and rail route
----- PIWTT route

Kolkata-Agartala (and vice versa)
—— Railroad and rail route
······· PIWTT route

Patna-Agartala (and vice versa)
—— Railroad and rail route

(Unit: million tonnes)
O Border post

Source: World Bank.

TABLE 2.8 **Predicted freight traffic between northeast India and rest of India in 2025 if agreements are implemented, by route and mode**

ORIGIN-DESTINATION	ROUTE	MODE	ROUTE SHARE	ANNUAL TRAFFIC IN 2025 (MILLION TONNES)
Guwahati-Kolkata	Via Gobrakura-Ghasuapara and Petrapole-Benapole land ports	Road	75 (0)	13.2 (0)
	Via Dhanua-Mahendraganj and Hili land ports	Road	13 (0)	2.2 (0)
	Via Siliguri corridor	Road	2 (82)	0.4 (9.3)
	Via inland waterways	Inland waterways	0 (0)	0 (0)
	Via Siliguri corridor	Rail	10 (18)	1.7 (2.0)
Kolkata-Guwahati	Via Petrapole-Benapole and Gobrakura-Ghasuapara land ports	Road	62 (0)	28.5 (0)
	Via Siliguri corridor	Road	2 (61)	0.8 (15.7)
	Via Siliguri corridor	Rail	25 (39)	11.6 (10.1)
	Via Inland waterways	Inland waterways	0 (0)	0 (0)
	Via Hili and Dhanua-Mahendraganj land ports	Road	10 (0)	4.8 (0)

table continues on next page

TABLE 2.8, *continued*

ORIGIN-DESTINATION	ROUTE	MODE	ROUTE SHARE	ANNUAL TRAFFIC IN 2025 (MILLION TONNES)
Agartala–Kolkata	Via Agartala-Akhaura and Petrapole-Benapole land ports	Road	98 (0)	0.4 (0)
	Via Siliguri corridor	Road	0 (72)	0 (0.18)
	Via Siliguri corridor	Rail	2 (28)	0.01 (0.07)
	Via inland waterways	Inland waterways	0 (0)	0 (0)
Kolkata–Agartala	Via Petrapole-Benapole and Akhaura-Agartala land port	Road	98 (0)	0.11 (0)
	Via Siliguri corridor	Road	0 (66)	0 (0.05)
	Via Siliguri corridor	Rail	2 (27)	0 (0.02)
	Via inland waterways	Inland waterways	0 (7)	0 (0.01)
Agartala–Patna	Via Agartala-Akhaura and Hili land ports	Road	69 (0)	0.53 (0)
	Via Agartala-Akhaura and Darshana land ports	Road	25 (0)	0.19 (0)
	Via Siliguri corridor	Road	0 (83)	0 (0.34)
	Via Siliguri corridor	Rail	6 (17)	0.04 (0.07)
	Inland waterways	Inland waterways	0 (0)	0 (0)
Patna–Agartala	Via Hili and Akhaura/Agartala land ports	Road	65 (0)	0.03 (0)
	Via Darshana and Agartala/Akhaura land ports	Road	23 (0)	0.01 (0)
	Via Siliguri corridor	Road	0 (71)	0 (0.02)
	Via Siliguri corridor	Rail	11 (29)	0 (0.01)
	Via inland waterways	IWT	0 (0)	0 (0)

Source: World Bank.
Note: Figures in parentheses are base-year figures.

Patna–Agartala (from 29 percent to 11 percent) and Agartala–Patna (from 28 percent to 2 percent). For Guwahati–Kolkata and Kolkata–Guwahati, interventions that lead to a 25 percent reduction in rail costs and times would be sufficient to maintain the original base-year market shares (of about 18 and 39 percent, respectively) in 2025 with implementation of the agreements. For the other domestic corridors, even with 25 percent time and cost reductions, the rail shares would still be below those of the base year; additional cost and time reductions would be necessary to maintain the base-year share.

The share of inland waterways, which had a 7 percent market share on the Kolkata–Agartala corridor in the base year (which amounted to only 10,000 tonnes) drops to zero. To regain this market share of 7 percent for IWT, even a 50 percent reduction in time and cost would not be sufficient (such reductions lead to a market share for IWT of just 3 percent after implementation of the agreements). This finding implies that substantial reductions are needed in reliability, theft or damage of cargo, and border delays along IWT routes to remain competitive alternatives.

Almost all trade between northeast India and the rest of the world is transported to and from seaports by road, both with and without the policy measures (map 2.4 and table 2.9). However, after the agreements are implemented, shippers in northeast India clearly prefer the Chattogram Port over the Kolkata and Haldia ports, leading to an almost complete shift of flows from Kolkata/Haldia to Chattogram. This result seems to be intuitive, as the Chattogram Port is closer,

MAP 2.4

Predicted freight traffic of exports from and imports to northeast India in 2025 if agreements are implemented

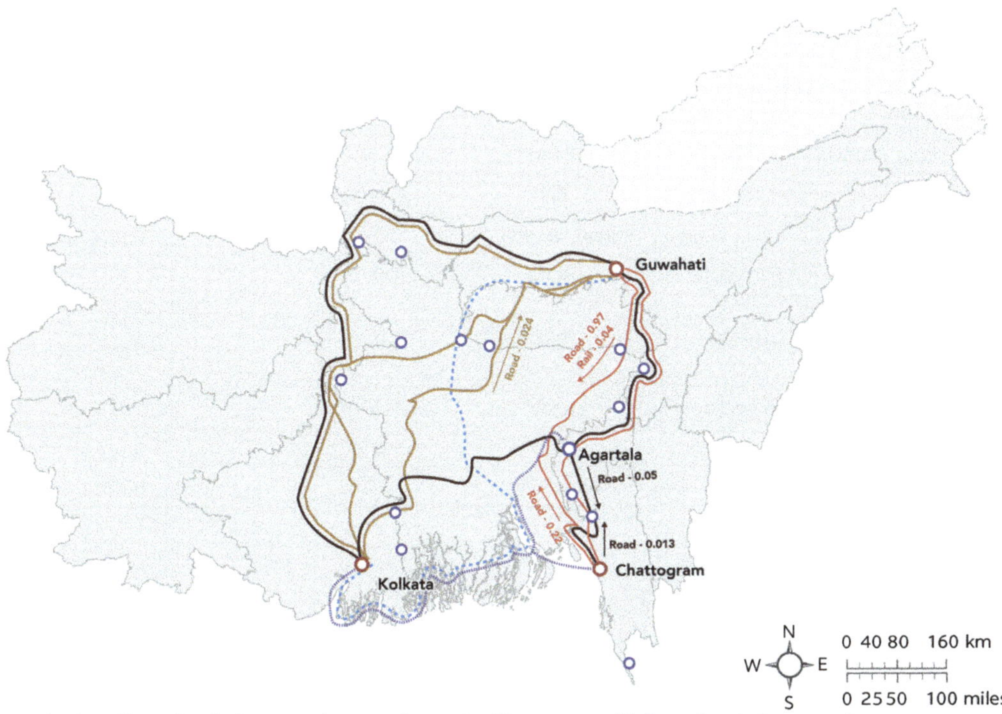

Guwahati–Kolkata (and vice versa)

—— Road and rail route

----- PIWTT route

Guwahati–Chattogram (and vice versa)

—— Road and rail route

Agartala–Chattogram/Kolkata (and vice versa)

—— Road and rail route

········ PIWTT route

(Unit: million tonnes)

O Border post

Source: World Bank.

TABLE 2.9 **Predicted freight traffic of exports from and imports to northeast India in 2025 if agreements are implemented, by route and mode**

ORIGIN-DESTINATION	ROUTE	MODE	ROUTE SHARE (PERCENT)	ANNUAL TRAFFIC IN 2025 (MILLION TONNES)
Guwahati–abroad	Via Sylhet to Chattogram	Road	93 (0)	0.97 (0)
	Via Sylhet to Chattogram	Rail	4 (0)	0.04 (0)
	Via Siliguri corridor to Kolkata	Road	0 (95)	0 (0.71)
	Via other routes to Kolkata or Chattogram	Road	3 (0)	0.03 (0)
	Via Siliguri corridor to Kolkata	Rail	0 (5)	0 (0.04)
	Via inland waterways to Kolkata	Inland waterways	0 (0)	0 (0)
Abroad–Guwahati	From Chattogram via Sylhet	Road	95 (0)	0.22 (0)
	From Chattogram via Sylhet	Rail	0 (0)	0 (0)
	From Kolkata via Siliguri corridor	Road	0 (98)	0 (0.13)
	From Kolkata or Chattogram via other routes	Road	3 (0)	0.007 (0)
	From Kolkata via Siliguri corridor	Rail	0 (0)	0 (0)
	From Kolkata via inland waterways	Inland waterways	2 (2)	0.004 (0.003)

table continues on next page

TABLE 2.9, *continued*

ORIGIN-DESTINATION	ROUTE	MODE	ROUTE SHARE (PERCENT)	ANNUAL TRAFFIC IN 2025 (MILLION TONNES)
Agartala–abroad	Via the Sabroom-Ramgarh land port to Chattogram	Road	99 (0)	0.05 (0)
	Via the Sabroom-Ramgarh land port to Chattogram	Rail	1 (0)	0.001 (0)
	Via the Siliguri corridor to Kolkata	Road	0 (95)	0 (0.04)
	Via the Siliguri corridor to Kolkata	Rail	0 (5)	0 (0.002)
	Via inland waterways	Inland waterways	0 (0)	0 (0)
Abroad–Agartala	From Chattogram via the Ramgarh-Sabroom land port	Road	100 (0)	0.01 (0)
	From Chattogram via the Sabroom-Ramgarh land port	Rail	0 (0)	0 (0)
	From Kolkata via the Siliguri corridor	Road	0 (100)	0 (0.01)
	From Kolkata via the Siliguri corridor	Rail	0 (0)	0 (0)
	Via inland waterways	Inland waterways	0 (0)	0 (0)

Source: World Bank.
Note: Figures in parentheses are base-year figures.

reducing the transport time and costs for EXIM (other attribute values of the alternatives are similar in this scenario). The Sylhet (Dawki-Tamabil) and Sabroom-Ramgarh land ports are the key land ports expected to facilitate the movement of EXIM to and from Guwahati and Agartala, respectively.

For EXIM to and from Guwahati, IWT retains its small share and rail loses its market share when the agreements are implemented. Rail also loses market share in the movement of exports from Agartala. Interventions leading to a 25 percent reduction in rail costs and times for Guwahati will maintain the base-year market share of 5 percent for rail (the rail share becomes 9 percent). For the rail link connecting Agartala, additional time and cost reductions would be needed.

Once the integration agreements are in place, coastal shipping will become more prominent in bilateral trade between Bangladesh and India (map 2.5 and table 2.10). Currently, the road route through Petrapole-Benapole plays a key role in the two countries' bilateral trade, with a share of 76–97 percent, depending on the direction. IWT is the second-most-used mode for exports from India (18 percent), but not for exports from Bangladesh. When the agreements are in place, the route through the Petrapole-Benapole land port (road transport) will remain the key route facilitating bilateral freight movement, with a mode share of 86–95 percent, depending on the direction. However, the share of costal shipping will raise to 5–11 percent, depending on the direction.

Rail and inland waterways will see declines in their market shares for bilateral transport after implementation of the agreements. Interventions leading to a 50 percent reduction in rail costs and times would reduce the market share of rail to 1 percent instead of zero. Similarly, interventions leading to a 50 percent reduction in IWT costs and time would reduce the market share of IWT from India to Bangladesh from 18 to 11 percent instead of 3 percent.

The results show that shippers and carriers react strongly to the time and cost advantages offered by the new alternatives through Bangladesh, especially for road transport. If, of course, reliability declined (because of unpredictable delays caused by congestion, for example); damage and theft increased; or waiting

MAP 2.5
Predicted bilateral freight traffic in 2025 if agreements are implemented

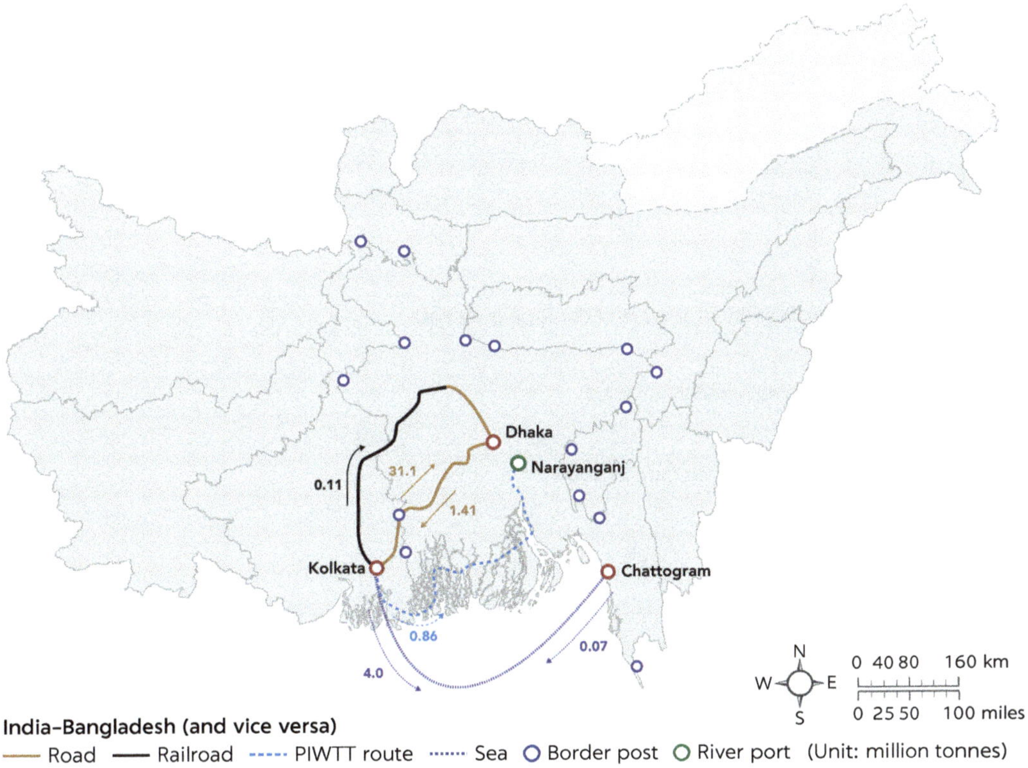

Source: World Bank.

TABLE 2.10 **Predicted bilateral freight traffic in 2025 if agreements are implemented, by route and mode**

ORIGIN–DESTINATION	ROUTES	MODE	ROUTE SHARE (PERCENT)	ANNUAL TRAFFIC IN 2025 (MILLION TONNES)
India–Bangladesh	Via Petrapole-Benapole	Road	86 (76)	31.1 (13.4)
	Via coastal movement from Haldia to Chattogram Port	Coastal shipping	11 (4)	4.0 (0.75)
	Via Gede (partly by road)	Rail	0 (2)	0.11 (0.34)
	Via inland waterways	Inland waterways	3 (18)	0.86 (3.16)
Bangladesh–India	Via Benapole-Petrapole	Road	95 (97)	1.41(0.78)
	Via coastal movement from Chattogram to Haldia Port	Coastal shipping	5 (3)	0.07 (0.02)
	Via Gede (partly by road)	Rail	0 (0)	0 (0)
	Via inland waterways	Inland waterways	0 (0)	0 (0)

Source: World Bank.
Note: Figures in parentheses are base-year figures.

times at the border were longer than expected, the shift to road transport routes through Bangladesh would be more modest.

Such situations can be simulated using the model presented in this chapter, by testing different assumptions about these factors by mode and route. For instance, if the roads in Bangladesh have twice as many delays, theft and damage, and border waiting times as assumed earlier, the Siliguri road corridor would

TABLE 2.11 **Predicted domestic freight traffic from Guwahati to Kolkata in 2025 if agreements are implemented, under alternative level-of-service attributes**

LEVEL-OF-SERVICE VARIANTS	SHARE OF PETRAPOLE-BENAPOLE ROUTE (PERCENT)	SHARE OF HILI ROUTE (PERCENT)
Probability of delays of more than 24 hours (percent)		
0	76	13
9 (as assumed in table 2.8)	75	13
18	75	13
40	73	12
Probability of theft and damage (percent)		
0	76	13
4 (as assumed in table 2.8)	75	13
10	74	12
Border waiting time in hours		
0	77	13
8 (as assumed in table 2.8)	75	13
20	74	12

Source: World Bank.

have a 4 percent share on the Guwahati–Kolkata route after implementation of the agreements rather than the 2 percent shown in table 2.8.

The importance of reliability, damage and theft, and waiting times at the border can also be assessed using the model presented in this chapter to help policy makers prioritize interventions. Using the routes through the Petrapole-Benapole and Hili land ports for domestic freight traffic from Guwahati to Kolkata, the analysis shows that changes in each of the level-of-service attributes have a similar and small effect on the shares of both routes. For instance, reducing the probability of delays or the probability of theft from the levels assumed in table 2.8 to zero have a similar effect on the shares of the Petrapole-Benapole and Hili routes (table 2.11).

SUMMARY AND CONCLUDING REMARKS

Recent agreements in the region—particularly the MVA, the PIWTT, and the ACS—aim to open new corridors to facilitate the movement of freight and trade in India and Bangladesh. The results of SP experiments and an econometric model indicate a very high preference for shifting to the new routes and mode choices for freight moving between northeast India and the rest of India and between northeast India and the rest of the world. For bilateral movement between India and Bangladesh, the road route would still be preferred, although there would be a significant shift toward coastal areas.

The predicted shifts in routes and modes of freight transport are based on the assumptions that complementary policies and interventions are implemented together with the agreements to significantly improve the level-of-service attributes for potential choices. Improvement in the level-of-service attributes assumed in the experiments need to be realized to achieve the predicted route and mode shift.

Ideally, countries should not prescribe the routes and modes to be used for freight transport, leaving that decision to shippers and carriers unless there are important safety, security, or environmental reasons to limit the volume of traffic along certain areas. If countries do prescribe the routes and border posts to be used—which is the case under the MVA—the selection should be based on shippers' and carriers' preferences. If it is not, the integration agreements could have limited or no effect on transport costs, patterns, and volumes. The BBIN countries should consider removing the restrictions on specific routes.

The shorter routes through Bangladesh and the elimination of transshipment at border points would reduce travel times and costs. However, the upgrading and development of connectivity infrastructure, handling infrastructure at land ports, and automation of cross-border processes need to occur to ensure that the time savings are not offset. It will be important to ensure that no additional costs, such as facilitation payments or accident costs, are incurred on the new routes through Bangladesh. Reducing manual interventions and checks through automation and IT-based solutions may be required.

Unpredictable border crossing times and congestion along the new routes could potentially increase the probability of delays. Process definition and standardization at the borders and upgrading of infrastructure to eliminate congestion will be needed to reduce the probability of delays. Proper sealing of trucks and security surveillance along the corridors will be required to reduce the chances of theft and damage.

Harmonization and standardization of regulations and integration of customs processes will be needed to ensure seamless integration. Implementation of the MVA will mean that mandatory transshipment at land ports will no longer be necessary. It will be important to ensure that no additional transshipments are required because of differences in axle-load limits or gauges between the two countries. Infrastructure constraints and customs process delays at the borders would increase congestion, increasing border waiting time. Integrating cross-border IT infrastructure, facilitating off-border customs clearances, and upgrading land port connectivity will be required to eliminate infrastructure constraints and process delays.

The strength of the analysis presented in this chapter is that it is based on interviews with actual shippers and carriers in the relevant corridors on their behavior when it comes to deciding which modes and routes to take. These behavioral data were used in discrete choice models that account for differences in the characteristics of the shipments and the firms (observed heterogeneity) as well as different substitution patterns between modes (nested logit), where shifts between rail, IWT, and sea transport are more likely than between any of these modes and road transport. This approach is not common at all in freight transport analysis, where most models are based on aggregate data.

A disadvantage of the methodology is that the data collected are stated preferences of decision-makers in an experimental context, because the context of the implementation of the agreements does not yet exist. Actual behavior of shippers and carriers when the agreements are implemented could differ from the behavior stated in the SP survey (hypothetical bias). To minimize such effects, the experiments were conducted in the contexts of actual shipments and the models were calibrated to observed market shares.

ANNEX 2.A: SURVEY

Pilot survey

A pilot survey of about 20 percent of the target population (85 respondents) was conducted to gain a clear idea of the model coefficients or priors to be defined for the main SP experiment. Initially, the value of the coefficients for the pilot surveys was based on the relevant literature. From the analysis of the choices made by respondents during the pilot survey, the prior values were refined. The refined prior values were then used for the statistical design and the most relevant levels of attributes for SP experiments. The questionnaires and Android application were also adapted based on the requirements discovered in the pilot stage.

The analysis of pilot-stage data yielded results with the expected signs on the coefficients. In the logit models for the SP1 shippers group, the coefficients for time, cost, delay, and theft had the expected signs and were significant (at the 5 percent level). Only the number-of-transshipments attribute was not significant, although for shippers' EXIM and bilateral segments, it had the expected sign. Seventy-one interviews from the pilot stage could be used for econometric modeling and shift estimations.

Recruitment and survey method

In the sample plan, a master list of industries and logistics service providers by commodities and geographies was prepared. The recruitment and survey of respondents was done in two steps:

- *Step 1: Telephone interviews of the screening questionnaire.* Representatives of industry and logistics service providers were contacted by phone to determine whether their cargo movement type was relevant to the study and whether they used at least one route or mode tested in the study. Only relevant respondents were considered. An appointment for a face-to-face interview was scheduled during the phone interview.
- *Step 2: Face-to-face interview through Computer Assisted Personal Interview (CAPI).* The SP experiments were modeled in an Android-based application. All SP experiments were conducted face to face on Android devices (tablets and smartphones) carried by enumerators. The data were autotransmitted to a central server from the devices upon completion of the experiment.

CAPI methodology was adopted for this study, given the limited understanding of SP experiments among target respondents in northeast India and Bangladesh. Enumerators spent considerable time explaining the experiment methodology and hypothetical situations. They also guided respondents for correct data responses to the questionnaire, based on which the SP experiments were generated in the application. Only respondents who completed two SP experiments were considered for the data analysis.

Distribution of sample

Tables 2A.1–2A.4 show the distribution of the sample.

TABLE 2A.1 Distribution of respondents by commodity type

TYPE OF CARGO MOVEMENT	COMMODITY	NUMBER OF RESPONDENTS			
		SHIPPERS/PROVIDERS OF THIRD-PARTY LOGISTICS SERVICES		CARRIERS (ROAD HAULAGE)	
		TARGET	ACTUAL	TARGET	ACTUAL
Domestic and export-import	Minerals, marble, stone	20–40	32	10–20	15
	Household goods	20–40	21	10–20	39
	Fruits and vegetables	20–40	19	10–20	22
	Food products, fast-moving consumer goods	20–40	27	10–20	21
	Cement, clinker, fly ash	10–20	10	8–15	12
	Petroleum, oil, lubricants, chemicals, petrochemicals	10–20	10	8–15	13
	Iron, steel	10–20	17	5–10	5
	Tea	10–20	18	5–10	8
	Food grains	1–5	4	1–5	9
	Other	20–40	55	10–20	11
	Total	175	213	100	155
Bilateral	Food grains	10–20	12	7–15	7
	Fruits, vegetables	10–20	11	7–15	7
	Apparels and textile raw materials	10–20	14	7–15	10
	Automobiles and spare parts	5–10	9	4–8	4
	Construction materials	5–10	8	4–8	6
	Fast-moving consumer goods	5–10	17	4–8	7
	Other	10–20	22	10–20	11
	Total	75	93	50	52

Source: World Bank.

TABLE 2A.2 Distribution of respondents by geographic location

TYPE OF CARGO MOVEMENT	LOCATION	NUMBER OF RESPONDENTS			
		SHIPPERS/PROVIDERS OF THIRD-PARTY LOGISTICS SERVICES		CARRIERS (ROAD HAULAGE)	
		TARGET	ACTUAL	TARGET	ACTUAL
Domestic and export-import	Northeast India	50–80	94	40–60	66
	Rest of India	95–125	119	40–60	89
	Total	175	213	100	155
Bilateral	India	30–40	54	20–30	36
	Bangladesh	30–40	39	20–30	16
	Total	75	93	50	52

Source: World Bank.

TABLE 2A.3 **Distribution of respondents by existing routes**

TYPE OF CARGO MOVEMENT	ROUTE	NUMBER OF RESPONDENTS			
		SHIPPERS/PROVIDERS OF THIRD-PARTY LOGISTICS SERVICES		CARRIERS (ROAD HAULAGE)	
		TARGET	ACTUAL	TARGET	ACTUAL
Domestic	Corridor A: Guwahati-Patna	0	0	0	0
	Corridor B: Guwahati-Kolkata	60–120	114	25–45	87
	Corridor C: Agartala-Patna	15–50	32	15–25	18
	Corridor D: Agartala-Kolkata	15–50	37	15–25	25
	Total	150	183	75	130
Export-import	Corridor B: Guwahati-Kolkata	10–15	20	10–15	15
	Corridor D: Agartala-Kolkata	10–15	10	10–15	10
	Total	25	30	25	25
Bilateral	Road using Petrapole-Benapole land customs station	20–40	44	20–30	35
	Road using other land customs station	20–40	49	20–30	17
	Total	75	93	50	52

Source: World Bank.

TABLE 2A.4 **Distribution of respondents by existing mode**

TYPE OF CARGO MOVEMENT	MODE OF TRANSPORT	NUMBER OF RESPONDENTS			
		SHIPPERS/PROVIDERS OF THIRD-PARTY LOGISTICS SERVICES		CARRIERS (ROAD HAULAGE)	
		TARGET	ACTUAL	TARGET	ACTUAL
Domestic and export-import	Road	125–150	144	100	155
	Rail	50–75	61, other (8)[a]		
	Total	175	213	100	155
Bilateral	Road	40–50	60		43
	Sea	20–35	22, other (11)[a]		3, other (6)[a]
	Total	75	93	50	52

Source: World Bank.
a. "Other" refers to inland waterway and/or rail modes.

ANNEX 2.B: CALIBRATED ELASTICITIES

TABLE 2B.1 **Calibrated cost and time elasticities by mode**

ELASTICITY	ROAD	RAIL	RIVER	SEA
Cost elasticities				
Domestic	-0.51	-1.00	-1.44	n.a.
EXIM	-0.13	-2.27	-2.27	n.a.
Bilateral	-0.23	-1.14	-0.86	-1.09
Time elasticities				
Domestic	-0.32	-0.49	-2.26	n.a.
EXIM	-0.04	-0.66	-0.61	n.a.
Bilateral	-0.23	-0.80	-1.11	-1.82

Source: World Bank.
Note: n.a. = Not applicable.

ANNEX 2.C: LEVEL-OF-SERVICE ATTRIBUTES

Tables 2C.1–2C.3 show the level-of-service attributes.

TABLE 2C.1 **Level-of-service attributes of domestic cargo, by route**

ROUTE	TRANSPORT TIME (HOURS)	TRANSPORT COST (RS/ TONNE)	NUMBER OF TRANSSHIPMENTS	BORDER WAITING TIME (HOURS)
Guwahati–Kolkata via Petrapole-Benapol (road)	126	2,479	1	8
Guwahati–Kolkata via Siliguri Corridor (road)	164	3,329	1	0
Guwahati–Kolkata via Siliguri Corridor (rail)	126	2,686	2	0
Guwahati–Kolkata via Hili (road)	134	2,742	1	8
Guwahati–Kolkata via PIWTT route (inland water transport)	504	2,903	2	12
Agartala–Kolkata via Siliguri Corridor (road)	250	4,940	1	0
Agartala–Kolkata via Siliguri Corridor (rail)	147	3,660	2	0
Agartala–Kolkata via Petrapole-Benapole (road)	80	1,597	1	8
Agartala–Kolkata via PIWTT route (inland water transport)	386	1,963	1	12
Agartala–Patna via Siliguri Corridor (road)	237	4,616	1	0
Agartala–Patna via Siliguri Corridor (rail)	144	3,544	2	0
Agartala–Patna via Hili (road)	122	3,177	1	8
Agartala–Patna via Gede-Darshana (road)	127	3,351	1	8

Source: World Bank.

TABLE 2C.2 **Level-of-service attributes of EXIM cargo, by route**

ROUTE	TRANSPORT TIME (HOURS)	TRANSPORT COST (RS/ TONNE)	NUMBER OF TRANSSHIPMENTS	BORDER WAITING TIME (HOURS)
Guwahati–Kolkata via Petrapole-Benapole (road)	126	2,479	1	8
Guwahati–Kolkata via Siliguri Corridor (road)	164	3,329	1	0
Guwahati–Kolkata via Siliguri Corridor (rail)	126	2,686	2	0
Guwahati–Kolkata via Hili (road)	134	2,742	1	8
Guwahati–Kolkata via PIWTT route (inland water transport)	504	2,903	2	12
Guwahati–Chattogram via Sabroom-Ramgarh (road)	154	2,576	1	4
Guwahati–Chattogram via Sabroom-Ramgarh (rail)	118	2,012	2	6
Guwahati–Chattogram via Dawki-Tamabil (road)	103	2,033	1	4
Guwahati–Chattogram via Dawki-Tamabil (rail)	112	1,650	2	6
Guwahati–Chattogram via PIWTT route (inland water transport)	375	1,959	2	6
Guwahati–Chattogram via Karimganj (Multimodal)	293	2,132	2	6
Agartala–Kolkata via Siliguri Corridor (road)	250	4,940	1	0
Agartala–Kolkata via Siliguri Corridor (rail)	147	3,660	2	0
Agartala–Kolkata via Petrapole-Benapole (road)	80	1,597	1	8
Agartala–Kolkata via PIWTT route (IWT)	386	1,963	2	12
Agartala–Chattogram via Sabroom-Ramgarh (road)	72	1,031	1	4
Agartala–Chattogram via Sabroom-Ramgarh (rail)	96	982	2	6
Agartala–Chattogram via Ashuganj (Multimodal)	226	1,032	2	6

Source: World Bank.

TABLE 2C.3 **Level-of-service attributes of bilateral cargo, by route**

ROUTE	TRANSPORT TIME (HOURS)	TRANSPORT COST (RS/TONNE)	NUMBER OF TRANSSHIPMENTS	BORDER WAITING TIME (HOURS)
Kolkata–Dhaka via Petrapole/Benapol (road)	138	1,095	0	4
Kolkata–Dhaka via Gede (road + rail)	201	1,513	2	6
Kolkata–Narayanganj via PIWTT route (inland water transport)	434	1,939	3	6
Kolkata–Dhaka via Chattogram and Colombo (sea)	610	9,837	2	—
Kolkata–Dhaka via Gede (rail)	202	1,513	2	6
Kolkata–Dhaka via Chattogram (sea)	293	2,139	2	—

Source: World Bank.

NOTES

1. Bhutan signed the agreement but subsequently pulled out after its parliament failed to ratify it.
2. A rake is a line of coupled freight wagons, passenger coaches, or railcars (excluding the locomotive) that typically move together.
3. The minimum number of interviews for estimating a separate standard submodel was 25.
4. Models were also estimated using RP data collected through the surveys, but the results did not lead to better models. The estimated RP models have positive cost coefficients (domestic), do not converge (EXIM), or have very extreme time and cost coefficients (bilateral). In the models in which the SP coefficients are fixed, very unrealistic RP-scale factors are estimated for EXIM and bilateral. The models estimated on both RP and SP data do not converge and therefore cannot be used. The RP data were therefore found to be unsuitable for model estimation and were not used in the rest of this project. One possible reason for the models not converging is the spatial aggregation of the applied level of service. All combinations of origins and destinations are mapped onto one of the few distinguished corridors.
5. Shippers' willingness to pay when using different modes are different, because a logarithmic formulation for costs is used. As a result, the willingness to pay becomes dependent on the level of the transport cost per mode in the model, which are different. The interaction variables for time and cost with the attributes of the shipments (such as the high value of the goods per tonne), and the correlations between modes and shipment attributes, also affect differences in the willingness to pay between modes.
6. This study did not ask shippers to restrict themselves to the goods-related consequences of time changes, as would have been done in a value-of-time survey, because the study is about mode and route choice, not about disentangling the components of the value of time. Whatever factors decision-makers include in mode and route choice therefore matters.
7. The projected EXIM and domestic cargo movements were calculated based on the historic growth rates of commodities in Assam and Tripura, national growth rates, and state GDP at constant 2011 prices. Bilateral cargo movement was calculated based on the average growth rate of trade between Bangladesh and India between 2016 and 2018 (about 12.6 percent a year) and the growth rate of apparel from Bangladesh (about 8.8 percent a year, according to the Export Promotion Bureau).

REFERENCES

Ben-Akiva, M. E., and S. R. Lerman. 1985. *Discrete Choice Analysis, Theory and Application to Travel Demand.* Cambridge, MA: MIT Press.

Choicemetrics. 2018. *Ngene 1.2 User Manual & Reference Guide.* Sydney.

De Jong, G. C. 2008. "Value of Freight Travel-Time Savings." In *Handbook of Transport Modelling,* ed. D. A. Hensher and K. J. Button. Amsterdam: Elsevier.

De Jong, G. C., M. Kouwenhoven, J. Bates, P. Koster, E. Verhoef, L. Tavasszy, and P. Warffemius. 2014. "New SP-Values of Time and Reliability for Freight Transport in the Netherlands." *Transportation Research Part E* 64: 71–87.

Kathuria, S., ed. 2018. *A Glass Half Full: The Promise of Regional Trade in South Asia.* South Asia Development Forum. Washington, DC: World Bank.

Louviere, J., D. Hensher, and J. Swait. 2000. *Stated Choice Methods: Analysis and Applications.* Cambridge: Cambridge University Press.

PwC and Significance. 2019. "Route and Mode Choice Analysis in Eastern South Asia." Final Report 3, for the World Bank Group.

Rahmatullah, M. 2009. "Regional Connectivity: Opportunities for Bangladesh to be a Transport Hub." *Journal of Bangladesh Institute of Planners* 2: 13–29

Rose, J., M. Bliemer, D. Hensher, and A. Collins. 2008. "Designing Efficient Stated Choice Experiments in the Presence of Reference Alternatives." *Transportation Research BL* 42 (4): 395–406.

Tavasszy, L. A., and G. C. de Jong., eds. 2014. *Modelling Freight Transport.* Elsevier Insights Series. London: Elsevier.

Train, K. 2003. *Discrete Choice Methods with Simulation.* Cambridge: Cambridge University Press.

3 Economic Gains and Losses from Integrating Road Transport between Bangladesh and India

MATÍAS HERRERA DAPPE, MATHILDE LEBRAND, AND DIANA VAN PATTEN

The Motor Vehicles Agreement will facilitate the seamless movement of passenger, personal, and cargo vehicles between Bangladesh and India. The opening of new regional corridors as well as the push for deeper regional integration is expected to bring economic gains for both countries. Reducing transport times for Indian trucks traveling to and from the northeast will better integrate that part of India with the rest of the country. Regional integration will give consumers and producers in both countries access to cheaper goods and intermediate inputs and increase the size of their export markets.

Deeper integration can lead some regions to gain more than others, however, and some regions may even lose out as a result. International evidence points to the increasing importance of regions with less costly access to foreign markets, such as border or port regions, which stand to reap the largest gains from trade liberalization and connectivity enhancements. In regions that are not competitive enough, workers and companies may move away toward better economic opportunities.

How regions adjust is shaped by the magnitude of improved market access; local comparative advantage (endowments of primary factors, technology, preferences); the mobility of people; and changes in technology that allow for scale and clustering. The quality of the domestic transport network affects which regions will remain isolated and which regions will benefit from more integration with foreign markets. Integration agreements can either increase or decrease a country's internal fragmentation. It is therefore important to understand the impact of integrating road transport services on the economic geography of Bangladesh and India.

This chapter examines the wider economic benefits of allowing Bangladeshi and Indian trucks to ply the roads of both countries and analyzes how doing so is likely to affect the economic geography of each country. It presents the results of a spatial general equilibrium model that was developed and calibrated for Bangladesh and India. It applies insights from research on the New Economic Geography to examine how regions within countries are likely to adjust to trade and transport shocks from new transit routes and improved regional integration.

The chapter is organized as follows. The first section discusses the wider economic benefits of regional corridors and the mechanisms through which benefits are realized. The second section presents the spatial general equilibrium model used to predict the impacts of integrating road transport services on prices of intermediate and final goods, wages, and economic activity. The third, fourth, and fifth sections discuss the potential wider economic benefits of different integration scenarios. The last section summarizes the findings and discusses what is needed for the predicted benefits of integration to fully materialize.

WIDER ECONOMIC BENEFITS OF REGIONAL CORRIDORS

Corridors affect what happens around them, not just in them. Integrating road transport services will trigger a reduction in generalized transport costs between northeastern India and the rest of India and between Bangladesh and India, which will lead to changes in the pattern of freight flows and an increase in the volume of freight. By opening regional corridors, the MVA can be transformational, unleashing a chain of multiple impacts beyond reductions in generalized transport costs, potentially affecting broader socioeconomic outcomes (ADB and others 2018). The economic impacts of regional corridors work through agglomeration effects, increased trade and migration, and changes in the local economic structure, among other areas. These long-term impacts ultimately yield wider economic benefits, such as the growth of income and consumption, new jobs, and poverty reduction (figure 3.1).

Corridors can have heterogeneous effects across population groups and geographical areas. Some regions could gain more than others, for example, because

FIGURE 3.1

Intermediate outcomes and wider economic benefits of a corridor intervention package

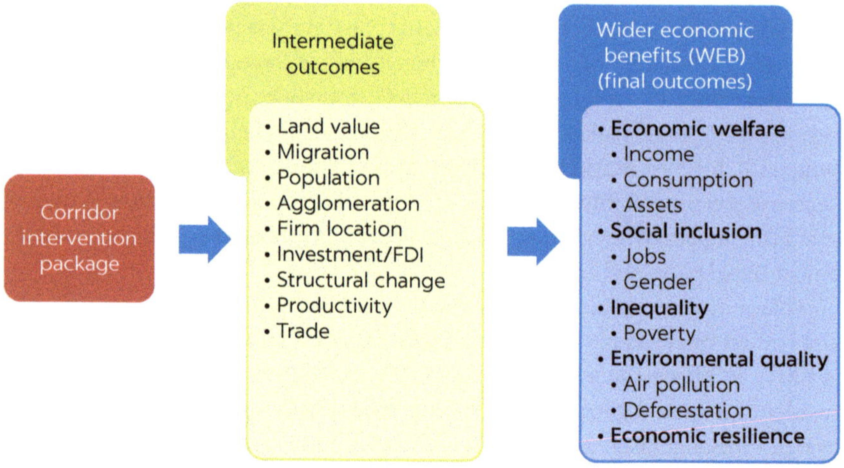

Source: ADB and others 2018.
Note: FDI = foreign direct investment.

of a higher concentration of skilled labor and agglomeration economies. Some regions could lose out, as economic activity relocates to other regions.

Spatially differentiated impacts of corridors are particularly important in South Asia, where economic growth has been associated with increasing spatial inequality, as metropolitan regions often expand much more rapidly than peripheral regions. Low-income areas in South Asia often coincide with border regions. Implementation of the MVA will have effects on economic activity along the regional corridors, including at or near the borders.

New regional corridors and deeper regional integration affect the prices of goods, wages, and land rents, which drive workers' decisions to migrate and firms' decisions about whether and where to produce. New regional corridors will reduce transport time and therefore transport costs, which decreases the price of imports for consumers and increases the prices local exporters receive. Production of traded goods increases in regions with lower transport costs and better access to foreign markets; if there are no significant frictions in the labor market, workers benefit from higher wages. Higher wages and lower import prices attract workers to regions that benefit from improvements in connectivity to other markets. These regions become more crowded, competition for land becomes fiercer, and land prices increase. The effect of a reduction in transport costs or improvement in market access depends on how all these forces affect markets across a country.

Research in quantitative spatial economics mimics the behavior of firms and workers in deciding what, how much, and where to produce. Their decisions are reconciled through general equilibrium models that can be calibrated based on the observed level of variables such as population density and economic activity in each location. Because of their meaningful connection with regional data, these models can be used to assess the effects of interventions that reduce transport costs or increase market access on the spatial distribution of economic activity.

ASSESSING THE WIDER ECONOMIC BENEFITS OF INTEGRATING ROAD TRANSPORT SERVICES WITH A SPATIAL GENERAL EQUILIBRIUM MODEL

The spatial general equilibrium model assesses the effects of integrating road transport services on the integration of regions with other domestic and foreign markets in India and Bangladesh. It looks at how the opening of new transit routes for Indian trucks and improved access to regional markets through land borders yields changes in economic activity, wages, and prices of intermediate and final goods. The model relies on work on Germany (Ahlfeldt and others 2015) and follows a growing literature on the spatial impacts of transport (see, for example, the work of Fajgelbaum and Redding 2014 on Argentina, Donaldson 2018 on India, Lall and Lebrand 2019 on the Belt and Road Initiative in Central Asia, Balboni 2019 on Vietnam, and Herrera Dappe and Lebrand 2020 on Bangladesh). The model (described in detail in the annex and by Herrera Dappe, Lebrand, and Van Patten 2021) has three main building blocks—geography, economic activity, and workers–which are connected by the goods prices, land rents, and wages that prevail in each location. Consistent with the idea of a general equilibrium, prices and wages adjust to balance supply and demand in each location.

Geography

The model allows for spatial granularity at the state level for India and at the district level for Bangladesh, considering the 38 states and union territories of India and the 64 districts of Bangladesh. Each region is characterized by its location, land area, livability, and firm productivity. Livability captures the quality of life in a district, which is determined by factors such as the quality of education and health services. It influences where people chose to live. The productivity of firms differs across locations, because of factors such as the infrastructure and technology available. A good transport network allows firms to access cheaper intermediate goods and be more competitive. The transport network connects all locations with one another, within and across countries. The model focuses on trade between Bangladesh and India through land border posts. It does not consider trade through maritime routes.

Economic activity

Firms choose the amount of output and inputs—labor, capital, and intermediate goods—used in production. Firms buy intermediate goods from other firms in the same or other locations, including foreign locations, when trade through land borders is considered.

Workers

Workers choose where in their country they live. All workers derive their income from employment and spend it on goods and services produced locally or imported from other regions in their country or from other countries. Workers' decisions on where to live and where to work depend on housing rents, wages, and livability across regions.

Calibration of the model

The information needed to calibrate the model comes from traditional data sources such as surveys and geocoded information on the transport network. Four types of data at the state and district level are used: transport costs, land size, labor force, and wages. The labor force includes the working-age population (people 15 and older). All wages are monthly and are expressed in dollars. Data on the labor force and wages in India come from the 2011 Periodic Labor Force Survey; data on Bangladesh come from the 2010 Labor Force Survey. The main parameters of the model are calibrated using country-specific data sources or commonly used values in the literature (see annex 3.A).

Transport costs are measured as a function of the travel time to reach other locations from the most populated district (upazila) in each Indian state (Bangladeshi district). Travel time, calculated using GIS network techniques, is the shortest time given all possible routes in the road network. Travel times in Bangladesh are based on actual speeds collected from more than 200 intercity road segments across the country and random speed assignment to the remaining segments based on the distribution of speeds in nearby segments. Travel times in India come from Krishna and Van Leemput (2018), based on GPS data from Blackbuk, an Indian logistics company that provides an online marketplace platform for freight shipments.

Scenarios

In the baseline, Indian trucks are not allowed to use Bangladeshi routes and must bypass Bangladesh through the Siliguri corridor to reach the northeast, and Bangladeshi trucks are not allowed in India. For cargo crossing the border between Bangladesh and India at Benapole-Petrapole, it takes on average 138 hours, including 28 hours spent transloading cargo to and from Bangladeshi and Indian trucks. Three scenarios were considered to assess the trade and welfare impacts of allowing Indian trucks to ply Bangladeshi roads and Bangladeshi trucks to ply Indian roads relative to the baseline.

Inefficient MVA. The first scenario considers the opening of new corridors through Bangladesh for Indian trucks transporting cargo to and from northeast India and Indian exports to and imports from Bangladesh (map 3.1).[1] It also allows Bangladeshi trucks to enter India to deliver exports and pick up imports using the same corridors.

MAP 3.1

Land ports and road corridors in Bangladesh

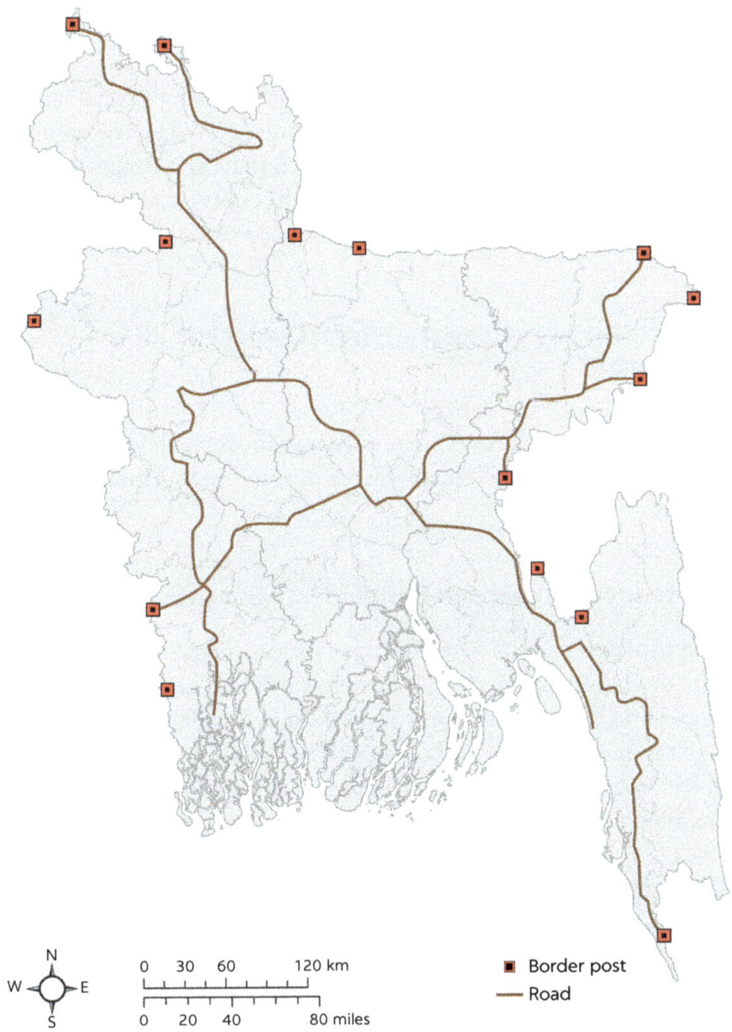

Source: World Bank.

This scenario assumes that transloading is no longer required, although it is an option (some shippers might still prefer to transload cargo), and some other border frictions are removed, leading to a border crossing time of 55 hours at any of the border posts on the corridors. In the remaining border posts, cargo can cross the border, but it has to be transloaded; the total crossing time remains 138 hours, as in the baseline. Removing frictions at the border, including the need to transload cargo, reduces the transport costs for bilateral trade between some locations. The new transit routes reduce travel times and transport costs for freight moving between the northeast states and some other states in India, particularly states in the center and south of the country.

Efficient MVA. The second scenario is similar to the first, except that it assumes that additional frictions at the border are removed so that Indian trucks transiting through Bangladesh do not need to stop at the border and trucks carrying bilateral trade spend only 10 hours at the border. If Indian trucks transiting through Bangladesh use electronic locks, as in the trial runs done so far, the border times would be similar to times at the most efficient border crossing points outside a customs union, which tend to be up to 3 hours. Given the cumbersome customs clearance process currently in place, this scenario assumes that not all frictions will be removed for bilateral trade and that the border crossing time will be slightly more than three times that in the most efficient border crossing points outside a customs union.

Full integration. The third scenario assumes complete regional integration, with no restrictions on foreign truck movements. This scenario assumes that trucks do not need to stop at the border between India and Bangladesh and that trucks can use any border posts and roads in both countries. As a result, transport costs in this scenario are the lowest of the three scenarios.

ECONOMIC GAINS FROM THE MOTOR VEHICLES AGREEMENT

This section presents the results of the economic model for both MVA scenarios. It starts with the aggregate results for each country and then discusses the spatial effects.

Aggregate income gains in Bangladesh and India

The opening of new transit routes for Indian trucks traveling to and from northeast India through Bangladesh and the removal of border frictions for bilateral trade would bring significant economic benefits to Bangladesh and India.

Under the inefficient MVA scenario, income is estimated to increase by 3.4 percent in Bangladesh and 1.4 percent in India; under the efficient MVA scenario, income is estimated to increase by 11.3 percent in Bangladesh and 5.6 percent in India (table 3.1). The MVA would lead to reductions in travel time and transport costs for freight, with their extent varying between the inefficient and efficient MVA scenarios, which explains the differences in income gains between the two scenarios. The reduction in transport times and costs reduces the prices of intermediate and final goods.

Lower prices of final goods increase the purchasing power of consumers, and cheaper input prices make producers more competitive. The locations

TABLE 3.1 **Percentage changes in income in Bangladesh and India as a result of the Motor Vehicles Agreement**

SCENARIO	BANGLADESH	INDIA
Inefficient MVA	3.5	1.4
Efficient MVA	11.3	5.6

Source: World Bank analysis.

experiencing the largest decreases in prices become more competitive, attracting more workers and increasing their economic activity. The reductions in prices, the relocation of economic activity, and potential increases in wages lead to the increase in aggregate income in Bangladesh and India.

The effects of regional integration differ between countries because of differences in the magnitude and nature of the economic shocks on Bangladesh and India. Bangladeshi districts benefit from improved access to Indian markets. Indian states experience both an improvement in access to Bangladeshi markets and a decrease in trade costs to reach other Indian markets, with the former more important than the latter.[2] The gains from regional integration are much larger for Bangladesh than for India, because Bangladeshi markets are relatively small for India and Indian markets are large for Bangladesh. Small countries tend to gain more from regional integration if they remain competitive enough to export to foreign markets.

Uneven spatial effects within countries

Both new transit routes and improved connectivity for bilateral trade will reduce spatial inequality across states in India; it will increase it across districts in Bangladesh. Improvement in the connectivity of northeast Indian states with the rest of India and the increase in competitiveness of the states close to Bangladesh will lead to a relocation of economic activity across the country—and therefore a reduction in wage dispersion across states (figure 3.2). The MVA leads to a marginal increase in the wage dispersion across Bangladeshi districts,

FIGURE 3.2
Spatial inequality in wages in Bangladesh and India

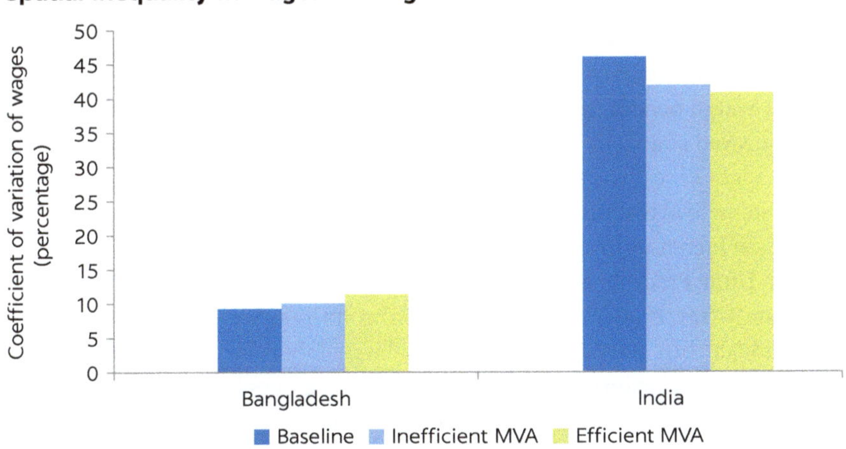

Source: World Bank analysis.
Note: Spatial inequality is measured using the coefficient of variation (the ratio of the standard deviation to the mean).

because of the significant comparative advantage of Dhaka and Chattogram districts. The rest of this subsection discusses in detail the spatial effects under the efficient MVA only, as the spatial patterns under the inefficient MVA are the same, with only the magnitude of the impacts changing.

By lowering transport and trade costs to and from the northeast Indian states and Bangladesh, the MVA will increase the competitiveness of some states in India more than others. The decrease in transport and trade costs leads to reductions in the prices of goods and inputs consumed in the states, with the states closer to Bangladesh seeing the largest reductions in percentage terms; as the distance from Bangladesh increases, the reductions become smaller. The decrease in transport and trade costs also leads to increases in the price net of transport costs that firms receive for their exports (to Bangladesh and other states), which together with the lower costs of inputs leads to an increase in the competitiveness of those states.

The increase in competitiveness of states leads to increases in wages in those states, as firms in more competitive states can pay more to attract workers. The increases in wages and decreases in prices across states lead to relocation of workers and economic activity toward those states. Higher wages and the inflow of workers leads to an increase in demand for final goods and inputs in those states and therefore increases in prices. The increase in wages leads to increases in the cost and therefore price of inputs exported to other states and Bangladesh, which then leads to increases in production costs and therefore the prices of final goods and inputs in other states.

As a result of all these forces, prices decrease in the states closer to Bangladesh and increase slightly in more distant states (map 3.2). States close to Bangladesh–such as West Bengal, Odisha, Mizoram, Tripura, Meghalaya, and Assam–experience relatively large reductions in prices, because the direct effect of the reduction in transport and trade costs dominates the effect of higher demand and production costs on prices. Prices increase slightly in more distant states because the latter effect dominates.

The changes in wages and prices triggered by the MVA will lead to improved standards of living in almost all Indian states. Real wages will increase by as much as 11 percent in most states, with a median change of 4.5 percent. Some states in the northwest and the more eastern states, such as Arunachal Pradesh and Nagaland, will experience small reductions in real wages (map 3.3). West Bengal, which borders Bangladesh in the west, experiences the largest increase in real wages. In the northeast, Assam, Mizoram, and Tripura are among the top third of states in terms of real wage increases.

The overall benefit from the opening of new transit routes for Indian trucks and improved connectivity for bilateral trade will be spread across the country. The changes in real wages and the relocation of people and economic activities across states lead to changes in real income (map 3.4). The states expected to see the largest increases in real income are to the west of Bangladesh, such as West Bengal, Uttar Pradesh, and Maharashtra. West Bengal benefits from its prime location. Uttar Pradesh also benefits from its relatively short distance to Bangladesh, but particularly from its large labor force and low wages. Maharashtra, the main industrial state in India, leverages its comparative advantage to enjoy significant benefits from better trade opportunities with the northeast (because of shorter routes) and Bangladesh.

In northeast India, the overall benefits from integration are largest in Assam, Meghalaya, Mizoram, and Tripura. These states are among the top 11 in terms of

MAP 3.2

Predicted percentage changes in prices in Bangladesh and India as a result of the efficient Motor Vehicles Agreement

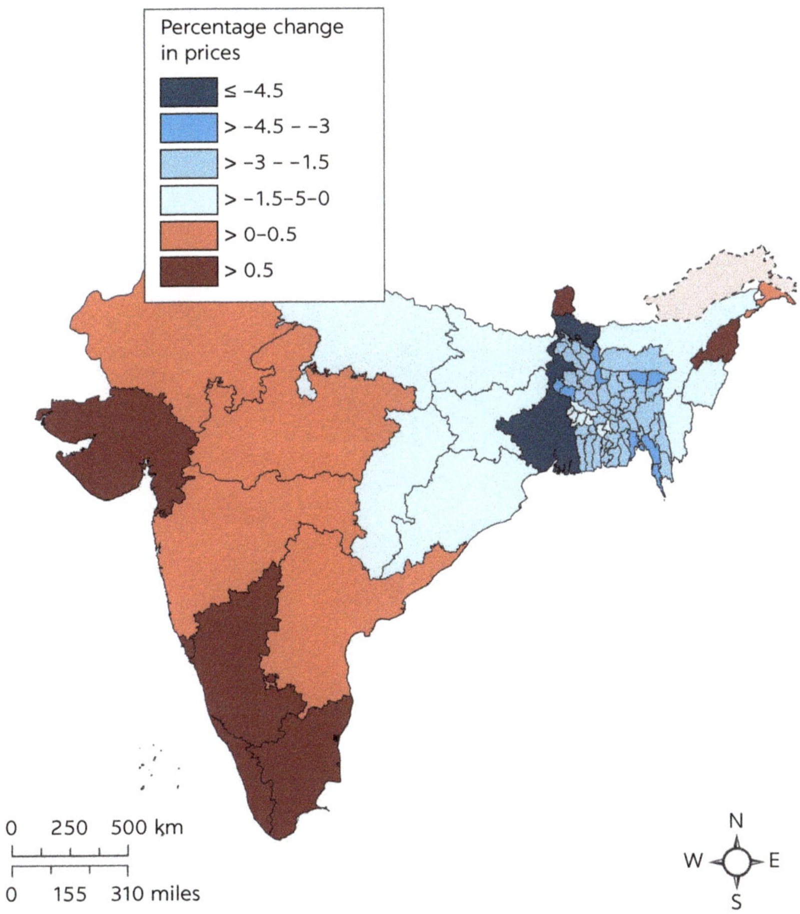

Source: World Bank analysis.

real income gains. Assam, the largest economy in the northeast, has a comparative advantage that it leverages to benefit from integration. Meghalaya, Mizoram, and Tripura take advantage of their location to benefit from integration. All these states attract workers and economic activity from other states, particularly from their eastern neighbors. The isolation of the northeast is a curse, but it also isolates the northeast states from competition from other Indian states and Bangladesh. After implementation of the MVA, Arunachal Pradesh, Nagaland, and Manipur, the easternmost states, lose that advantage, leading to losses in real wages, economic activity, and real income (map 3.4).

As a result of the reductions in transport and trade costs to India, all districts in Bangladesh benefit in the efficient MVA scenario. All Bangladeshi districts experience reductions in the prices of final goods and intermediate inputs (see map 3.2), becoming more competitive. Integration with India improves access to Indian markets for Bangladeshi exports and to cheaper imports from India. Access to cheaper inputs from India and higher prices (net of transport costs) for their exports increase profit margins for producers, who can then offer higher wages to attract workers; they also boost economic activities.

MAP 3.3

Predicted percentage changes in real wages in Bangladesh and India as a result of the efficient Motor Vehicles Agreement

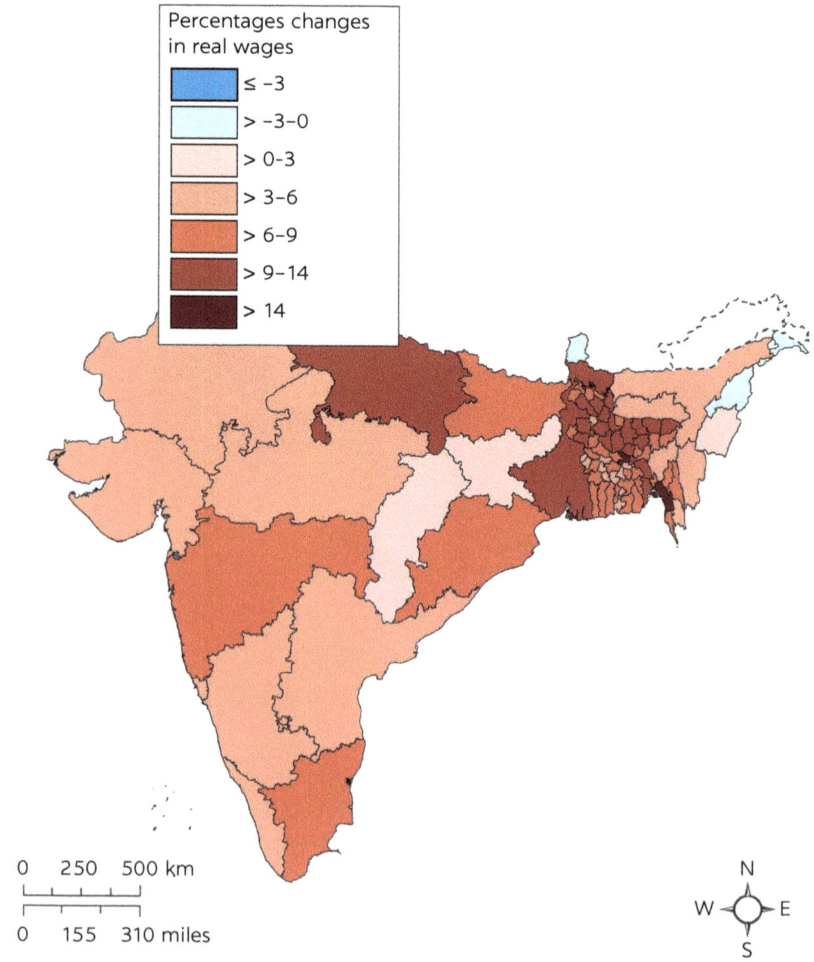

Source: World Bank analysis.

Increased trade opportunities lead to higher standards of living and economic activity across the entire country. Districts on the southeast-northwest axis, particularly Dhaka and Chattogram, enjoy the largest gains in real wages, where real wages increase by as much as 24 percent (see map 3.3). These districts benefit most because of their comparative advantage, which leads workers in the southwest and southeast to migrate to Dhaka, Chattogram, and other districts on the southeast-northwest axis, further concentrating employment and economic activity. Real income increases by as much as 40 percent in Dhaka and 28 percent in Chattogram, with a median increase of 8 percent (see map 3.4).

ECONOMIC GAINS FROM FULL REGIONAL INTEGRATION

Removing all border frictions to the movement of trucks between Bangladesh and India would reduce trade costs between Bangladesh and India further and yield greater benefits to both countries. Full transport integration between both countries would allow Indian trucks to transit through Bangladesh and to deliver

MAP 3.4

Percentage changes in real income in Bangladesh and India as a result of the efficient Motor Vehicles Agreement

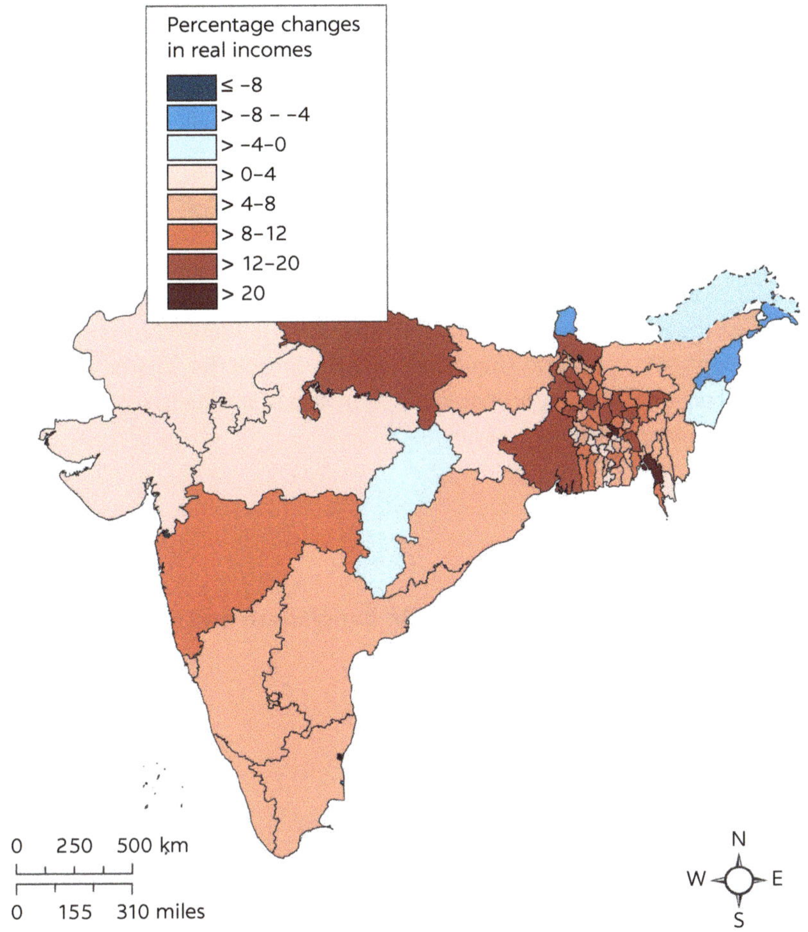

Source: World Bank analysis.

exports and pick up imports anywhere in Bangladesh and Bangladeshi trucks to deliver exports and pick up imports anywhere in India using any border post. India's national real income would increase 7.6 percent over the baseline case—35 percent more than in the efficient MVA scenario. National real income in Bangladesh would rise by 16.6 percent—48 percent higher than in the efficient MVA scenario. The additional gains are driven by the fact that trucks transporting bilateral trade would not need to stop at the border and would be able to use any road and border post, allowing them to use the lowest-cost routes.

The further reduction in transport costs under full integration intensifies the spatial patterns observed under the efficient MVA scenario, particularly in Bangladesh. In all districts in Bangladesh, the percentage gains in real income are higher under full integration than under the MVA (map 3.5 and figure 3.3). The districts along the northwest–southeast axis and those in the northeast enjoy larger gains in real incomes, because of further improvements in their competitiveness and the relocation of workers from the southwest and southeast (except Chattogram) to the rest of the country. Under both full integration and the MVA, Dhaka district enjoys the largest gains in real income, followed by

Chattogram district. However, under the efficient MVA, real income gains in Dhaka and Chattogram will be 67 percent and 59 percent, respectively, of the gains under full integration. In India, all states that enjoy gains in real income under the efficient MVA also gain under full integration, and they tend to gain more (map 3.5 and figure 3.3). For example, gains in real income in West Bengal and Meghalaya under full integration will be about two-thirds larger than under the efficient MVA; in Assam, Mizoram, Nagaland, and Tripura, they will be 22–43 percent larger.

Full integration leads to larger increases in economic activity across both countries, with a higher concentration of economic activity in the leading districts in Bangladesh. The changes in economic activity are driven partly by internal migration in response to changes in wages across districts and states. In both countries, the wage dispersion under full integration is almost the same as under the efficient MVA scenario (figure 3.4), which means that spatial inequality under full regional integration marginally increases in Bangladesh and decreases in India compared with the baseline.

MAP 3.5

Percentage changes in real income in Bangladesh and India under full regional integration

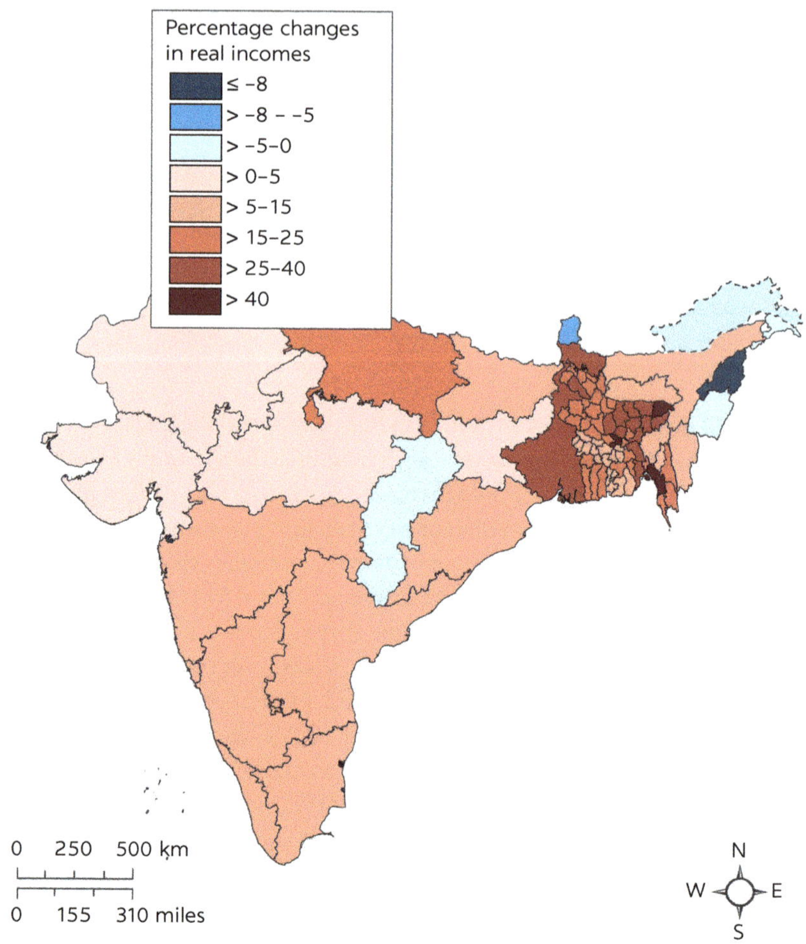

Source: World Bank analysis.

FIGURE 3.3

Correlations between real income gains in Bangladesh and India under full integration and the Motor Vehicles Agreement, by district and state

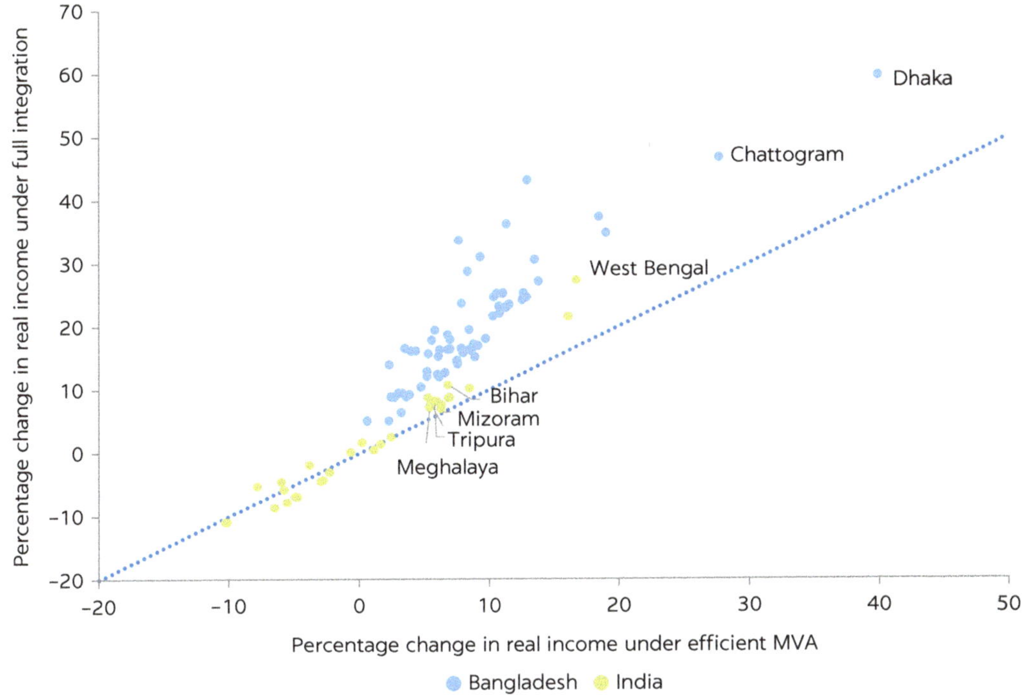

Source: World Bank analysis.

FIGURE 3.4

Spatial inequality in wages in Bangladesh and India

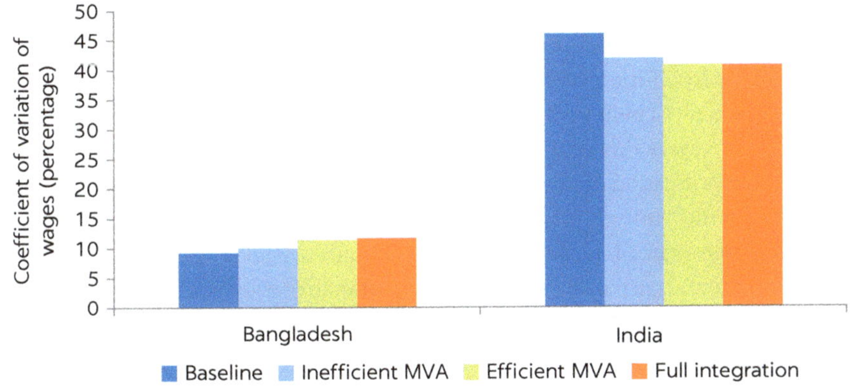

Source: World Bank analysis.
Note: Spatial inequality is measured using the coefficient of variation (the ratio of the standard deviation to the mean).

GAINS FROM REGIONAL INTEGRATION AND LABOR MOBILITY

The gains from regional integration depend on workers being able to relocate within their countries. Barriers to domestic mobility can emerge when housing prices are too high, deterring workers from moving, or regulations or informal labor market barriers limit the ability of migrating workers to quickly find jobs and be integrated in a new location. Lack of good education and health services—and a low level of overall livability—can also create barriers to domestic mobility. In addition to reducing national income, high barriers can increase inequality if workers are forced to remain in poorer areas that do not benefit from increase in competitiveness through better connectivity and trade opportunities.

The findings presented so far were estimated assuming low labor mobility in Bangladesh and India. Allen and Donaldson (2018) estimate that the migration elasticity in the United States decreased from 8.5 in 1850 to 4.5 in 2000. Historically, the United States has been a country with high labor mobility (although it has decreased over time). The migration elasticities estimated by Allen and Donaldson are much higher than the 1.5 migration elasticity used in the calibration of the model, which better represents the level of labor mobility in Bangladesh and India.

Complementary policies that increase labor mobility in Bangladesh and India would increase the gains from regional integration. The efficient MVA scenario was simulated assuming a migration elasticity of 4.5, the same as in the United States in 2000. Relative to the baseline, national real income would increase 6.2 percent in India (11 percent more than in the efficient MVA scenario with low labor mobility) and 14.5 percent in Bangladesh (28 percent more). These gains are smaller than the gains under full integration and low labor mobility, highlighting the significant potential of full integration. If trucks are allowed to cross the border at certain border posts and most border frictions are removed, going the extra mile by allowing trucks to use any border post and removing all border frictions should be easier to implement than an array of policies to increase labor mobility and should also deliver higher benefits.

SUMMARY AND CONCLUDING REMARKS

Quantitative spatial models improve the understanding of the determinants of the spatial distribution of economic activity and allow quantification of the potential impact of policy interventions. These models capture, in an empirically meaningful way, reality on the ground through observed data, thereby permitting the quantification of key mechanisms and the evaluation of counterfactual effects of policy interventions. The insights from these models include the empirical relevance of market access, the strength of agglomeration and dispersion forces within urban areas, and the importance of the dynamic forces shaping the evolution of the spatial distribution of economic activity over time (Redding and Rossi-Hansberg 2017).

A criticism of quantitative spatial general equilibrium models is that to generate reasonable simulation predictions, they need to correctly capture the factual transmission mechanisms and underlying functional forms when linking policy interventions to outcomes. Some researchers (such as Baum-Snow and others 2020) prefer an approach based on reduced-form modeling, which first estimates a reduced-form relationship and then uses this estimated relationship to conduct simulations. An empirical strategy would not be useful in predicting the impact of transport integration between Bangladesh and India, as no similar event has happened in the past. Once Bangladesh and India integrate and the benefits of integration are realized, an ex post empirical analysis could shed light on the mechanisms at play. Until then, to ensure that the context of both countries is captured in the analysis of counterfactuals presented in this chapter, the model relies on calibrated parameters from both countries, including actual speed on the roads (see annex 3A).

Allowing trucks from Bangladesh and India to ply the roads of both countries would remove inefficiencies in the movement of freight across Bangladesh and India and bring economic benefits to both countries. It would reduce costs by obviating the need to transload cargo at the border and take longer routes through the Siliguri corridor. The reduction in transport and trade costs would increase income in both Bangladesh and India by reducing the prices of final goods and intermediate inputs. By increasing the competitiveness of some states and districts more than others, it would increase economic activity in some areas, where firms would have to pay higher wages to attract enough workers to take advantage of the improved competitiveness and access to markets. The relocation of economic activity would lead to reductions in spatial wage inequality in India and a marginal increase in Bangladesh.

Competition in trucking services is required for the benefits of integrating road transport services predicted by the model to fully materialize. Without it, reductions in trade costs would be limited and captured by trucking service providers instead of shippers. Opening the borders to regional transport services can affect competition in regional transport service markets and potentially competition in domestic transport service markets, because truckers might decide to focus on one of the markets. Assessing such implications requires modeling the behavior of trucking service providers, but doing it in a sound manner requires data that are not publicly available. Further work needs to be conducted to understand the effect on prices of trucking services. Even without such work, however, it is clear that policies to increase competition in the trucking sectors are required. In Bangladesh, for example, the interference of agents linked to unions and associations, which determine trucking rates, distorts trucking services markets (Herrera Dappe, Kunaka, and others 2020). The Bangladesh Competition Commission needs to become functional and independent, as established by the Competition Act, and enforce competition regulation in transport service markets to let market forces determine prices.

The analysis presented in this chapter assumes that speeds on Indian and Bangladeshi roads, which are low, would not change as a result of the changes in traffic patterns. This assumption implies that investments and policies to increase the effective capacity of roads would have to be implemented. In Bangladesh, Herrera Dappe and others (2020) highlight the need to maintain roads, promote inland containerization, and coordinate the development of transport infrastructure to remove bottlenecks.

Subnational gains from regional integration depend on economic activity being able to expand in response to reductions in transport costs. Inadequate access to skilled labor, capital, and land can constrain economic activity. Barriers to acquiring and developing land for industrial use can limit the ability of existing firms to expand their production capacity and new firms from starting operations in states and districts that become more competitive and enjoy increased market access. Complementary policies to ensure functioning land and capital markets and the provision of basic infrastructure are needed to realize the gains.

ANNEX 3.A: MODEL AND CALIBRATION

The Model

The model uses tools found in the literature on quantitative spatial economics, summarized by Redding and Rossi-Hansberg (2017), Eaton and Kortum (2002), and Anderson and van Wincoop (2003). The setting allows for multiple regions—districts in Bangladesh and states in India—that trade differentiated products while facing bilateral trade costs. The model follows Allen and Arkolakis (2014) in having the trade costs proportional to the least-cost route connecting any pair of locations given the road networks of both countries.

The economy of each country consists of a set N of regions indexed by n. Each location is endowed with an exogenous amount of effective land, which is used in productive activities or for housing, and a number of workers, where each worker has one unit of labor that is supplied inelastically with zero disutility. Workers are imperfectly mobile across locations. Locations also differ by their level of amenities and productivity in the tradable sector. Amenities represent exogenous characteristics that are valued by individuals, such as good weather. Regions are connected by a bilateral transport network that can be used to ship goods subject to symmetric iceberg trade costs, such that $\tau_{ni} = \tau_{in} > 1$ units must be shipped from region i in order for one unit to arrive in region n (or vice versa).

There are two types of agents in the economy, mobile workers and immobile capital (land) owners. Workers earn a wage in the location where they live and work; landowners earn the total returns to land in the region where they live. The model is static; workers and capital owners therefore spend all income in the region where they live.

Consumer Preferences

Workers are imperfectly mobile across locations within a country and choose the location that maximizes their utility. Their preferences are defined over consumption of goods of varieties produced in all locations and residential land use. The utility of each individual worker i in region n is given by the product of a common component, v_n^W, from living and working in location n, and an idiosyncratic shock, e_n^i, defining the preference of individual i to be in that location.

The common component of workers' (W) utility depends on amenities from location n, U_n, and consumption of traded goods, c_n^W, and housing, h_n^W:

$$v_n^W = U_n \left(c_n^W\right)^{\alpha_C^W} \left(h_n^W\right)^{1-\alpha_C^W}$$

subject to the budget constraint, $P_n c_n^W + R_n h_n^W = w_n$, with P_n the aggregate price of the final good in location n, R_n the land rent, and w_n the wage in location n.

The random component e_n^i is assumed to be independent and identically distributed Fréchet with the parameter ε_w. As a result, the fraction of workers that choose to live in n is

$$\frac{L_n}{L} = \left(\frac{v_n^W}{v^W}\right)^{\varepsilon_W}$$

where v^W is worker welfare in the country.

Production

In each location n, there are M_n firms that produce tradable goods that can be either consumed as final goods, used as intermediate inputs by other firms in the same location, or exported to other locations. Varieties of the tradable goods are produced under conditions of monopolistic competition and increasing returns to scale. To produce a variety, a firm must incur a fixed cost of F units of an intermediate bundle and a constant variable cost in terms of intermediate inputs that depends on a location's productivity. The total number of firms is pinned down by a free-entry condition, such that firms continue to enter until there are no profits.

The total output q_n of each firm at location n is sold in all locations l subject to transport costs τ_{ln}; hence:

$$q_n = \sum_l \tau_{ln} q_{ln}$$

where q_{ln} is the quantity exported by each firm from n to l. Assuming that firms are monopolistically competitive, they set prices equal to

$$P_{ln} = \tau_{ln} p_{nn}$$

where p_{nn} is the domestic price equal to $p_{nn} = \frac{\sigma}{\sigma - 1} p_n^X$ with p_n^X the cost of a bundle of factors and intermediate inputs used in production, and σ the elasticity of substitution between all varieties.

The intermediate bundle X_n used by the M_n monopolistic firms is produced by local perfectly competitive firms using labor, capital, and tradable goods from domestic and foreign firms through a Cobb-Douglas production function:

$$X_n = A_n\left(L_n\right) L_n^{\beta_L} K_n^{\beta_K} I_n^{1-\beta_L-\beta_K}$$

The productivity shifter of each location A_n may be endogenous through an agglomeration externality,

$$A_n\left(L_n\right) = A_n^0 L_n^\gamma$$

where γ is the aggregate total factor productivity (TFP) elasticity of the economy. The price of the bundle of intermediate inputs in location n equals its marginal cost.

Equilibrium in Relative Changes

The equilibrium is defined in changes comparing the counterfactuals with the baseline situation. The counterfactuals consider shocks to trade costs $\hat{\tau}_{ni}$, where $\hat{x}$ denotes the value of variable x in the counterfactual equilibrium relative to the initial equilibrium. Following standard steps (Redding and Rossi-Hansberg 2017), the equilibrium in changes is defined for employment, price indexes, and wages $\{\hat{L}_n, \hat{P}_n, \hat{w}_n\}$,; and the welfare of workers $\hat{v}^W$ is defined as a function of calibrated parameters and data.

Calibration

Table 3A.1 presents the values of the parameters used in the calibration and their sources. The elasticity of substitution between traded varieties is assumed to be $\sigma = 5$, as given by Head and Mayer (2014). The aggregate TFP elasticity is calibrated to 0.05, following Ciccone and Hall (1996). The Cobb-Douglas share of

TABLE 3A.1 **Summary of calibration parameters of the model**

PARAMETER	VALUE	SOURCE
σ	5	Head and Mayer (2014)
γ	0.05	Ciccone and Hall (1996)
β_L	0.39 (India)	KLEMS
	0.46 (Bangladesh)	WITS
β_K	0.49 (India)	KLEMS
	0.26 (Bangladesh)	WITS
$1-\alpha_C^W$	0.44 (India)	UN data
	0.35 (Bangladesh)	UN data
ε_W	1.5	Fajgelbaum and others (2015)

labor, β_L, is set to 0.39, and the share of private capital, β_k, to 0.49, using data from KLEMS for India, and to 0.46 and 0.26, respectively, for Bangladesh, using data from the World Integrated Trade Solution database (WITS). The share of housing expenditures $1-\alpha_C^W$ is set to 0.35 for Bangladesh and 0.44 for India, using the share of household consumption expenditures in total expenditures from UN data. Following Fajgelbaum and others (2015), the calibrated shape parameter of the random component of utility, ε_W, is chosen to be 1.5. For robustness, other values for ε_W are considered to study how the results vary with workers mobility.

NOTES

1. The selection of corridors and border posts is based on Road Transport and Highways Division (2016).
2. A scenario with no border time for transit and 55 hours of border time for bilateral freight (that is, a scenario in between the inefficient and efficient MVA scenarios) yields a 1.6 percent gain in income in India relative to the baseline. Even if all those gains were attributed to transit, which is unlikely, improved access to Bangladeshi markets would account for 71 percent of the income gains under the efficient MVA scenario.

REFERENCES

ADB (Asian Development Bank), DFID (Department for International Development), JICA (Japan International Cooperation Agency), and World Bank. 2018. *The Web of Transport Corridors in South Asia.* Washington, DC: World Bank.

Ahlfeldt, G. M., S. J. Redding, D. M. Sturm, and N. Wolf. 2015. "The Economics of Density: Evidence from the Berlin Wall." *Econometrica* 83 (6): 2127–89.

Allen, T., and C. Arkolakis. 2014. "Trade and the Topography of the Spatial Economy." *Quarterly Journal of Economics* 129 (3): 1085–139.

Allen, T., and D. Donaldson. 2018. "The Geography of Path Dependence." Working paper.

Anderson, J. E., and E. van Wincoop. 2003. "Gravity with Gravitas: A Solution to the Border Puzzle." *American Economic Review* 93 (1): 170–92.

Balboni, C. 2019. "In Harm's Way? Infrastructure Investments and the Persistence of Coastal Cities." Department of Economics, Massachusetts Institute of Technology, Cambridge, MA. https://www.dropbox.com/s/16p58q2psl8sscm/Clare%20Balboni%20Living%20on%20the%20edge.pdf?dl=0.

Baum-Snow, N., J. V. Henderson, M. A. Turner, Q. Zhang, and L. Brandt. 2020. "Does Investment in National Highways Help or Hurt Hinterland City Growth?" *Journal of Urban Economics* 115: 103–14.

Ciccone, A., and R. E. Hall. 1996. "Productivity and the Density of Economic Activity." American Economic Review 86 (1): 54–70.

Donaldson, D. 2018. "Railroads of the Raj: Estimating the Impact of Transportation Infrastructure." *American Economic Review* 108 (4–5): 899–934.

Eaton, J., and S. Kortum. 2002. "Technology, Geography, and Trade." *Econometrica* 70 (5): 1741–79.

Fajgelbaum, P., and S. J. Redding. 2014. "External Integration, Structural Transformation and Economic Development: Evidence from Argentina." CEP Discussion Paper 1273, Centre for Economic Performance, London School of Economics and Political Science.

Fajgelbaum, P. D., E. Morales, J. C. Suarez Serrato, and O. M. Zidar. 2015. *State Taxes and Spatial Misallocation.* Technical report, National Bureau of Economic Research, Cambridge, MA.

Head, K., and T. Mayer. 2006. "Regional Wage and Employment Responses to Market Potential in the EU." *Regional Science and Urban Economics* 36 (5): 573–95.

Herrera Dappe, M., C. Kunaka, M. Lebrand, and N. Weisskopf. 2020. *Moving Forward: Connectivity and Logistics to Sustain Bangladesh's Success.* Washington, DC: World Bank.

Herrera Dappe, M., and M. Lebrand. 2020. "The Spatial Effects of Logistics Cost Reductions in Bangladesh." Working paper, World Bank, Washington, DC.

Herrera Dappe, M., M. Lebrand, and D. Van Patten. 2021. "Bridging Bangladesh and India: Cross-Border Trade and the Motor Vehicles Agreement." Working paper, World Bank, Washington, DC.

Krishna, P., and E. Van Leemput. 2018. "Quantifying the Sources of Internal Barriers to Trade in India: Evidence from Indian Truck GPS Data." Unpublished paper, Washington, DC.

Lall, S., and M. Lebrand. 2019. "Who Wins, Who Loses? Understanding the Spatially Differentiated Effects of the Belt and Road Initiative." Policy Research Working Paper 8806, World Bank, Washington, DC.

Redding, S. J., and E. A. Rossi-Hansberg. 2017. "Quantitative Spatial Economics." *Annual Review of Economics* 9 (1): 21–58.

Road Transport and Highways Division. 2016. *Regional Road Connectivity Bangladesh Perspective.* Ministry of Road Transport and Bridges, Government of the People's Republic of Bangladesh, Dhaka.

4 Maximizing Rural Spillovers of Regional Corridors

A CASE STUDY OF BANGLADESH

CHARLES KUNAKA, NIKLAS SIEBER, AND ROMAN CONSTANTIN SKORZUS

Regional trade and transport integration initiatives in South Asia are based on the designation of corridors through which trade flows or is expected to flow. Many major corridors need better infrastructure, policies, and procedures to facilitate trade; other interventions are needed as well. The huge amount of resources typically invested in corridors makes it imperative to broaden the regional effects as much as possible. Extending the benefits of corridors at the local level cannot be achieved without integrating rural development into the design of regional transport corridors.

Empirical evidence shows that improving corridors increases intercountry connectivity and spurs development of the regions through which corridors pass (Alam and others 2018; Roberts and others 2019). However, the impacts have often been assessed only at an aggregate level, which does not capture the mechanisms or nature of interventions that may be needed to maximize them. This chapter argues that an important mechanism for reducing poverty is enhancement of the connectivity of local produce markets to corridors.

The extent and depth of the local impacts of corridors depends on the ability of local communities to access improved transport and logistics services to markets located across the border. Increased regional integration can yield meaningful local benefits—but only if economic agents located along corridors can take advantage of improved connectivity. As small and medium farmers and enterprises are the ones that typically suffer from inefficiencies (because of the high unit costs of their shipments), they are likely to benefit most from improved market access. The challenges faced by small and medium enterprises (SMEs) are greatest in rural areas, where economic activities are dominated by agriculture and small-scale production, most of which is led by women.

This chapter explores how the local impacts of corridor projects can be enhanced by improving markets along a corridor. It proposes an approach to determining a package of improvements for rural roads and local markets that would help maximize the impacts of improvements to core regional trade corridors. The chapter proposes a generic methodology that can be adapted to different situations to plan investments in ways that deepen the local impacts of regional corridors.

The chapter uses a case study—of Jessore district, in Western Bangladesh—to illustrate how the local impacts of a regional corridor could be maximized. A regional corridor connecting western Bangladesh to India passes through the district; the district also has an extensive network of rural roads and markets. The government of Bangladesh has designated the corridor a priority for improvement. The district therefore meets the prerequisites for identifying a combination of local roads and markets that would best leverage the proposed improvements to the corridor.

REGIONAL AND LOCAL DIMENSIONS OF CONNECTIVITY

Regional corridors, local transport networks, and associated services are components of the integrated transport networks in a country or region. However, the development impact of networks is often considered in a partial manner, as corridors are examined separately from the network of secondary and tertiary roads. This classical approach does not capture the manner in which goods flow, especially in economies where agriculture is the dominant sector. Goods and people pass through rural and urban nodes that are connected by transport and logistics services. Produce, for instance, may pass from the farm through a market town, where it is consolidated with the produce of other farmers; be loaded onto a vehicle with larger carrying capacity; and use a regional or national corridor to reach major consumption centers in the country or a gateway for export to another country. There is limited treatment in the literature of how transport and logistics networks can be integrated for more holistic planning and strategy development. This chapter develops and tests a conceptual approach that could be adopted to fill this gap.

The literature addresses the contribution of trade and transport corridors to development. It almost takes for granted that the development of corridors has positive outcomes. Corridors have increasing returns to scale in transport services, as they can handle large volumes of traffic at lower unit costs than surrounding networks. Roberts and others (2019) provide a comprehensive review of the literature on the development impact of corridors. Alam and others (2018) assess which design and implementation characteristics of transport corridors and country characteristics could help maximize the wider economic benefits from transport corridors. The two papers conclude that investing in corridors contributes to structural changes in districts on or near highways. They find that economic benefits as measured by household expenditure and poverty rates are maximized when investments are complemented with supporting policies and institutions. These conclusions are largely consistent with received knowledge that transport corridors increase market access and trade between connected locations. It is the local dimension that leads to the need to consider how rural communities connect to markets.

Different approaches can be used to model the interaction between local access and regional networks for trade and transport. One approach is to model accessibility at the local level, to optimize the placement of rural roads so as to maximize accessibility to key services. Such modeling takes into account population and the location of key services, such as health centers and schools; through simulation, it identifies the road improvements that would minimize travel time within a budget constraint for the improvements. The approach can also be used to determine optimal locations for economic infrastructure at the local level (Heyns and van Vuuren 2018). These spatio-analytical approaches seek to optimize investments across geographical space in order to achieve intended outcomes. They are ideal for local development, especially in regions where agriculture is a dominant economic activity.

Alternative approaches focus more on access to markets, especially in large agglomerations. They focus more on the topology of rural supply chains and how producers can minimize costs to reach markets, especially in large urban centers. It is this second school of modeling that this chapter is based on, as its approaches can more explicitly integrate the impact of improvements at the local level and the development of regional corridors.

Rural communities connect to markets through a cascade of rural market centers, market towns, and secondary and tertiary networks of roads that link to larger markets, either directly or via regional and national corridors (figure 4.1). Rural roads and rural markets are the two main elements of rural trade and transport connectivity infrastructure.

Improved rural connectivity enhances access to economic opportunities and increases welfare (Jacoby 2000; Fafchamps and Shilpi 2009). Sieber and Allen (2016) identify two mechanisms of impact. First, rural roads induce market-led local development, via agricultural marketing and increased incomes from farming. Second, rural roads increase revenues from nonfarming activities, by spurring a shift from subsistence agricultural to commercial agriculture or nonfarm activities (Khandker, and Koolwal 2011; Gertler and others 2014; Gachassin, Najman, and Raballand 2015; Herrera Dappe, Andres, and Alam 2020).

Investing in infrastructure enhances efficiency in production, consumption, and distribution and increases productivity, which raises income levels.

FIGURE 4.1

Analytical framework for corridors and local connectivity

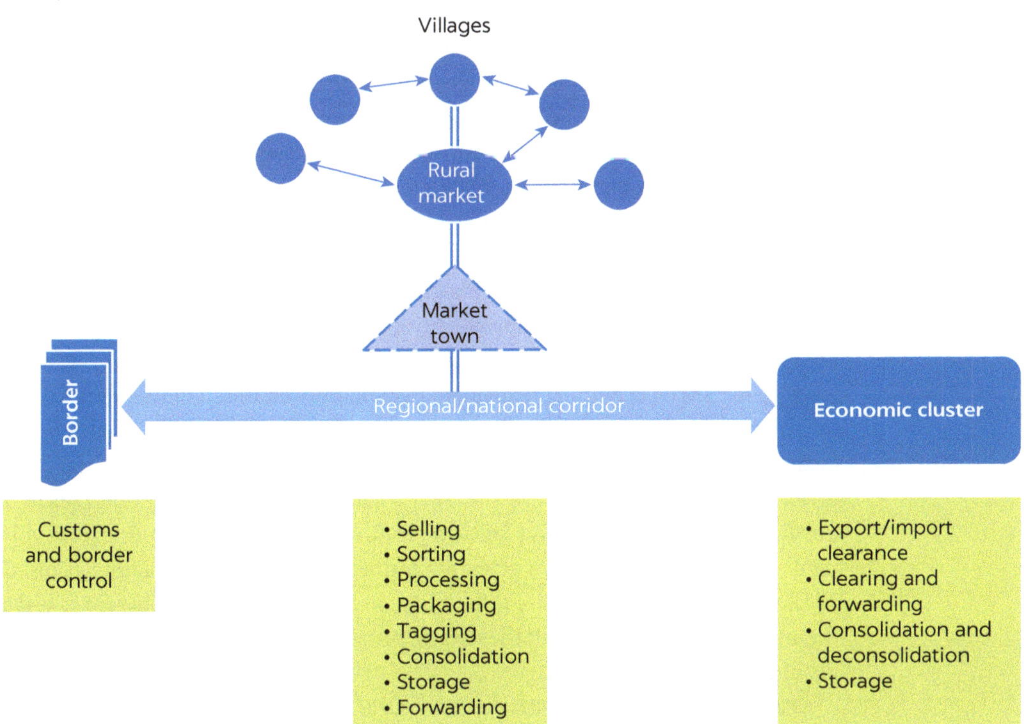

Source: World Bank.

Khandker and Samad (2016) examine the linkages between infrastructure endowments and household consumption and income growth in Bangladesh. They find that infrastructure development can be transformative in a rural economy, by helping villages and households increase and diversify incomes and consumption. Nonfarm income typically increases more than farm income.

Bradbury and others (2017) observe that good road access and transport services can enable people to diversify their income to nonagricultural and more profitable enterprise or employment. Mu and van de Walle (2008, 23) find "that rural roads had a positive impact on the presence and frequency of markets" in Vietnam. Better transport allowed farmers to export their produce and increased the inward flows of goods, knowledge, and ideas. Mu and van de Walle maintain that small road improvements have significant impacts on local development when they target areas that were poorly served with markets and are bundled with other social development policies (such as adult literacy). In theory, producer prices should rise after road rehabilitation, because of lower transport costs, which are transmitted to local producers in a competitive transport market.

Fan and Chan-Kang (2005) and Banjo, Gordon, and Riverson (2012) argue that rural roads should be improved where poverty is most severe and improved access to markets would provide opportunities for subsistence farmers to integrate into the market economy and thus increase farm production, marketing, and agricultural incomes. Based on a review of several studies, Starkey and Hine (2014, 4) maintain that "building roads (and/or trails and footbridges) to connect rural communities to the road network provides numerous benefits and reduces the numbers of people in extreme poverty. Trails and roads enable safer and faster access to markets and services."

Many studies of rural transport emphasize the importance of markets as a key component of rural connectivity. The development of markets is often an integral part of the development of rural road and transport networks. Tracey-White (1995) argues that enhancing access to markets can stimulate growth in agricultural production. The impacts are most pronounced for smallholders, who may rely on markets as their sole or main outlet for products. Exposure to more competitive conditions in large economic centers, especially cities, can force small-scale producers to upgrade their products through on-farm grading and packing and direct sales to consumers. Table 4.1 summarizes the benefits of markets for rural communities.

Raising standards in markets is likely to provide a means by which small-scale producers in rural areas can improve the efficiency of their marketing in order to compete in the sale of greater quantities of cheaper produce. In addition, a growing role for SMEs is helping transform rural supply chains. There are instances in which SMEs have become primary markets for rural producers, enabling the aggregation of volumes and the processing of produce to take place at the local level. Integration of producers and SMEs can be formalized through contract farming. The main impacts on logistics are through increases in per capita volumes and a reduction in unit costs of shipments to market, transformation of products to add value or prolong shelf life, and changes in the allocation of risks for any postharvest losses. All these factors can affect the topology of rural supply chains.

Other influences on the structure of rural supply chains occur through the adoption of digital applications and platforms. By accessing almost real-time information on market conditions, producers and traders are able to

TABLE 4.1 **Benefits of markets for rural communities**

BENEFIT	EFFECT
Reductions in crop losses	• Quicker and better handling reduces crop losses. • Provision of covered stalls, better storage, and end to flooding of markets in rainy season reduce postharvest losses. • Improved security reduces theft.
Improved efficiency of market operations	• Market operators enjoy substantial savings. • Potential for greater throughput increases. • Rents and charges increase.
Public health benefits	• Better sanitary conditions for the slaughter of poultry and the sale of meat and fish, provision of public toilets and hand-washing facilities, adoption of better market-cleaning and solid-waste disposal practices, and adequate paving and drainage reduce food contamination.
Amenity and aesthetic benefits	• Better stalls provide greater protection from sun and rain. • Produce is cleaner and more attractively displayed.
Time savings	• Waiting times for delivering and collecting produce are shorter. • Relocation of markets away from main road reduces travel time for nonmarket visitors.
Impact on agricultural production	• Greater access to market opportunities arising from demographic and income changes increases growth of agricultural production. • Efficiency of marketing for small and medium enterprises increases agricultural production. • More sophisticated techniques, such as on-farm grading and packing and direct sales to supermarkets, are used.
Other effects	• Income from additional services increases. • Public funds are generated.

Source: Tracey-White 1995.

continuously modify their behavior and patterns of shipments to access the markets that offer them the highest returns. The evidence of the impact of digital apps on costs of rural logistics is mixed, however. In some cases, the apps encourage fragmentation of volumes.

The decision of which markets producers choose to access has implications for the quality of the connecting road infrastructure and the range of services offered at different marketplaces. The theoretical background for the location of markets and how they are connected to each other is the concept of central locations, developed by Christaller in 1933. According to Christaller's model, marketplaces form a three-level hierarchy of central locations, distributed on a hexagonal grid. Each level of the hierarchy provides specific goods and services to its catchment area. The quality and capacity of connecting transport infrastructure are influenced by the position in the hierarchy of the centers being connected. Low-level centers are usually connected with tertiary links, for example; higher-level centers usually have higher-quality and–capacity links.

The hierarchy of markets typically reflects the function a market serves in an area. Tracey-White (2005) identifies four main types of markets (leaving out supermarkets):

- *Rural primary markets.* Trade at rural primary markets is characterized by direct sales of small quantities of produce by producers to village traders and by retail sales to rural consumers. Rural markets normally form part of a local trade network and are usually arranged on a periodic basis, on specific weekdays. They are usually organized at a central place in a village or district center or beside a village's access road. In some instances, provincial and district-level markets serve this function, as well as providing an assembly function (by combining produce in larger quantities for onward sale to outside buyers).

- *Assembly markets*. Assembly markets are rural markets at which larger quantities of produce are traded, by producers or traders. They are often combined with local rural or town markets and are normally situated on main highways near local transport interchange points. Traders, product consolidators, and commission agents acting on behalf of urban wholesalers are the main buyers of produce at these markets.
- *Wholesale markets*. Terminal wholesale and semi-wholesale markets are located in or near major cities. They may be supplied by purchasing/assembly centers in rural areas or directly from farms, particularly farms in peri-urban areas. Agents, traders, and farmers themselves supply these markets.
- *Retail markets*. Retail markets serve consumers directly. In many countries, small retail shops (often called "comer" shops) and roadside stands sell produce close to consumers' homes. These retailers usually purchase their produce from wholesale markets. In some cities, hawkers operating from bicycles or small carts provide retailers with small quantities of produce or sell directly to consumers. Although primarily retail, these markets may have a semi-wholesale function, particularly if they allow farmers to trade in them. In this case, they are often called *farmers markets*.

For connectivity to corridors, assembly markets are most relevant, as they are where locally produced goods are marketed in larger quantities for onward sale to outside buyers. The main market functions are exchange of goods and consolidation of large quantities for transport. Instead of farmers carrying small quantities of produce to the wholesale market, traders use large vehicles, which reduces transport costs. With a growing volume of local production, the quantities marketed and transported soar and truck loads increase. For this reason, good access to assembly markets is essential.

Although physical markets remain the dominant facilities for market exchanges in rural areas, other mechanisms can also help facilitate trade. They include producer cooperatives, in which groups of farmers coordinate to supply products to consumers or traders, and information technology–based solutions, especially mobile phone–based applications, which link producers and consumers and even facilitate payment. Ultimately, however, regardless of the mechanism used to organize rural supply chains—physical, organizational, or virtual mechanisms—the challenges of optimizing logistics and minimizing unit costs are the same.

Accessibility

Access to markets is a *sine qua non* condition for rural development. A World Bank (2016) study finds that agricultural production is highly correlated with travel time to urban markets. The highest productivity, at 45 percent of production potential, is within four hours of an urban market; the lowest, at 5 percent, is eight hours away. However, when population distribution is included in the analysis, 45 percent of the population in low-income countries is within one hour of the nearest market (World Bank 2016). Secondary and tertiary road networks and the placement of market infrastructure are critical in terms of the time it takes to get to market. In fact, larger markets, especially assembly markets, are often important junctions or located at major junctions in transport networks.

Based on their work in Bangladesh, Gautam and Faruqee (2016) argue that continued investments in infrastructure will remain a high priority given the role roads play in raising productivity, promoting diversification, and creating employment opportunities for rural communities. Traders identify poor road conditions and roadblocks, limited access to and the high cost of financing, and the lack of shop or storage space as constraints (figure 4.2). More than half of the traders they surveyed viewed poor road conditions and roadblocks as major or severe problems; another fourth rated them as minor or moderate problems.

Market access needs to be considered from the perspectives of both farmers and traders. Farmers need to transport their products on the "first mile" (from the field or homestead to the market). They use market access roads—the roads, paths, and tracks within the catchment area needed to reach the market. Traders need to transport goods to and from the market. They use market feeder roads—roads that connect markets to the main road network.

Rural goods are transported on paths, trails, tracks, footbridges, pontoons, and earth and sealed roads. On-farm transport is mainly along paths belonging to the farm estate. The remaining part of the first mile is conducted on infrastructure owned by the community. Local and regional transport is mainly on tracks and roads managed by district or provincial authorities. Rural roads usually account for the largest proportion of road network length in many countries, although they may carry only a small proportion of motorized traffic.

FIGURE 4.2

Traders' perceptions of obstacles to business operation in Bangladesh

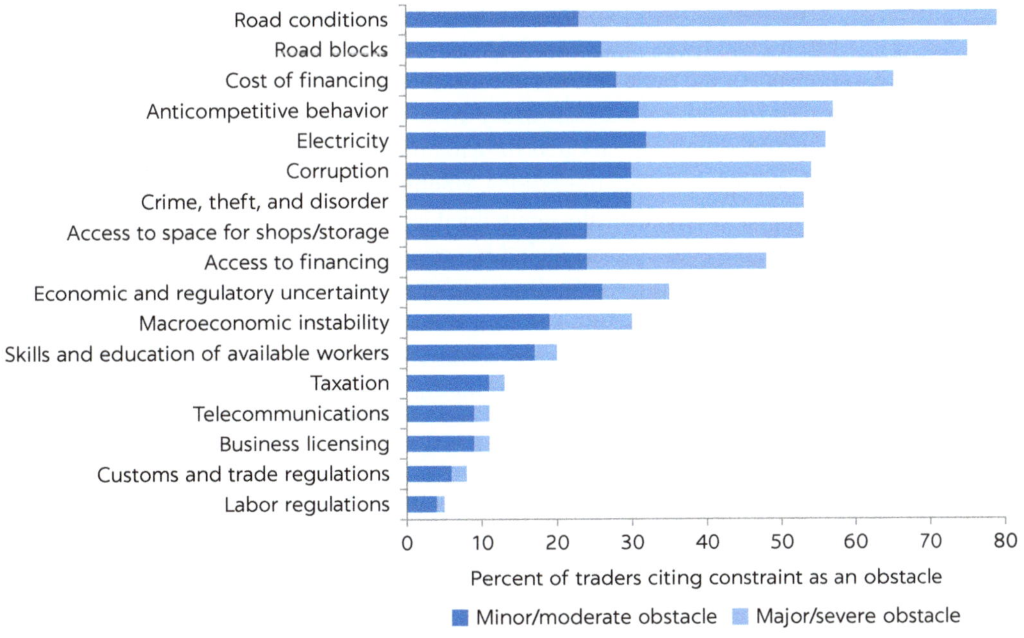

Source: Gautam and Faruqee 2016.

On the first mile, goods are transported by "intermediate means of transport" (IMT)—nonmotorized transport, animal traction, motorcycles, and other means of transport that fall between walking and four-wheel vehicles—which is more cost-efficient than motorized transport and has far lower infrastructure requirements. Innovations in IMT technology, especially the introduction of electric, solar powered vehicles, is rapidly transforming the rural transport landscape, especially in South and East Asia. From fields and plantations, produce is transported to buying points, village storage facilities, and local markets or directly to rural hubs, using infrastructure that is inexpensive to build and can be maintained by local manpower. From buying points or rural hubs, goods are transshipped onto light or heavy goods vehicles, which operate on market feeder roads, allowing higher speeds at lower costs.

All-weather accessibility is essential for the marketing of agricultural produce year round. Therefore, a low-cost approach for road improvements is recommended. Instead of upgrading main roads to higher standards, priority is given to upgrading a larger network to an all-weather standard. Only if the capacities of roads are largely exceeded can upgrading to wider standards be justified.

Market infrastructure

Different types of markets have different endowments of infrastructure, facilities, and associated services. A major concern is usually the susceptibility of products to losses during handling and storage. Bradbury and others (2017) show that several factors contribute to postharvest crop, "including the age of the produce, handling during harvesting, loading and unloading, and quality of transport and storage." They find that in Tanzania, initial transport costs and crop losses reduce the net income from the sale of potatoes and pineapples by 30–40 percent. In Bangladesh nearly 30 percent of aubergine traders and 26 percent of chicken traders experienced product damage or loss over a three-month period (Gautam and Faruqee 2016). Transport caused 21 percent of aubergine losses and 44 percent of chicken losses.

Because of their perishability, most high-value agricultural products require careful handling; special facilities (packhouses, cold storage, and refrigerated transport); and rapid delivery to consumers to maintain quality and reduce physical and nutritional losses. In order to satisfy demand from customers and adhere to quality standards, products have to undergo a number of processes, including precooling, pack line operations, ripening, degreening, and labeling. A well-equipped and hygienically maintained infrastructural asset base is a pivotal element of the chain. Assets include storage and handling capacity, transportation equipment and related facilities, processing machinery, and financial capital (Reardon and others 2009). Recent studies of agricultural food value chains and market infrastructure in several countries reveal significant investment in all of these areas in rapidly transforming food systems (Reardon 2007; Tschirley, Reardon, and others 2015).

The goal of the exercise was to maximize the benefits generated by the corridor by improving the endowment of markets with logistic and market facilities, market feeder roads connecting the market with the corridor, and the market access road within the catchment area of the market. The approach seeks to optimize investments under a given budget in order to maximize impact. Because of data limitations, which are common in rural areas, the approach was made as simple as possible.

ENHANCING LOCAL CONNECTIVITY: A CASE STUDY

Jessore district is located in the southwestern region of Bangladesh. It borders India to the west and other districts in Bangladesh to the north, east, and south. It is predominantly an agricultural district, producing primarily cereals and vegetables.

The district produces various agricultural products all year round, making all-weather connectivity imperative. Trade with India is mainly through the Benapole land customs station, Bangladesh's largest land border crossing point with India. The border post sits at one end of a major corridor that leads to Dhaka and other important economic centers in Bangladesh as well as the northeast states of India. Jessore is also a major junction on Bangladesh's railway network, with links to the Indian network in the west and the rest of the broad gauge-based network of Bangladesh to the east. Jessore district was selected for the case study because it is an agricultural economy with a major corridor that is about to be developed, a network of rural markets, and a dense network of rural feeder roads.

The analysis identified the improvements needed to enhance the performance of and grow specific value chains. The requirements for modern supply chains differ for each product. Significant potential may exist to increase the marketing of traditional products, for example. As estimates of the increase cannot be made without local knowledge, stakeholder participation is crucial. Investments in logistic facilities can be identified only through discussions with local and regional stakeholders, such as market committees, local and regional councils, government officials, and possible private investors.

The methodology for the analysis included three stages: identifying the set of interconnected markets in the district; classifying the road network, especially the rural road network; and identifying a package of interconnected roads and markets that determine the spatial extent of the corridor hinterland. Each stage is described below; annex 4.A outlines the data needed for the analysis.

Identifying a market cluster

The first step in designing the package is to select the markets that should be part of the assessment procedure. Only assembly markets are relevant for this analysis; other markets are excluded, because they either serve only local demand (rural primary markets, retail markets) or supply large towns with agricultural goods (wholesale markets, supermarkets).

The catchment area of a market is needed to identify market access roads and the number of inhabitants potentially affected by the market. The markets of interest in the district are identified using the principles of the Christaller model. The flat plane assumption of Christaller is relaxed and markets are identified by their spatial distribution patterns and later the existence of connecting road links. The catchment area and population of a market may be defined as follows:

$$cam = \frac{3}{2} * dm^2 * \tan(30°)$$

$$in = \sum_{1}^{n} cam_n * pd_n$$

where

cam_n = catchment area of market n
dm = average distance between neighboring markets
in_n = number of inhabitants in market n
pd_n = population density of ward where market n is located.

The distance between neighboring markets, dm, can be derived empirically from GIS data by calculating the average distance to the neighboring assembly market.

Two official data sets provided information on the locations and sizes of rural markets in Jessore district. Between them, they provide information on the name and class, location, and lease values of the markets. The lease values are the rental fees charged by the local authorities to users of the markets. The values evolve to reflect the intensity of use of each market. They are used as a proxy for the size of each market. Based on the data sets, the markets within the corridor were extracted, given unique market identifiers, and used for the analysis.

Based on annual lease values (a proxy for turnover), 38 markets were identified as having large enough turnover for inclusion in the analysis (table 4.2 presents the top 10 markets). The markets included in the analysis account for more than 95 percent of total lease values of all markets in Jessore. One market (Market 51) accounts for almost two-thirds of the turnover of all markets within the corridor buffer. It is an important hub for the district's trade with Dhaka; as it is located near the border with India, it also has potential for trade with India. Markets 64, 70, and 67 have lease values of about Tk 3 million each. Because of their high turnover, these four markets were categorized as Tier 1 markets and the rural hubs for trade in Jessore. The next-largest markets have annual turnover of about Tk 1 million each. They are categorized as Tier 2 markets.

Tier 3+ markets are the starting point for this analysis. However, the starting level in each case depends on the peculiarities of the supply chains that are most dominant. On the first mile, which provides access to these markets, goods are typically transported by IMT or head loading. Although the first mile is an essential part of the network, accounting for a large share of

TABLE 4.2 **Lease values of large markets within 10 kilometers of corridor**

MARKET ID NUMBER	LEASE VALUE (THOUSAND TK)	SHARE OF LEASE VALUE OF THE 38 MARKETS IDENTIFIED (PERCENT)	CUMULATIVE SHARE (PERCENT)	TIER
51	36,893	65.8	65.8	1
64	3,178	5.7	71.5	1
70	2,925	5.2	76.7	1
67	3,333	5.9	82.6	1
69	1,442	2.6	85.2	2
82	1,689	3.0	88.2	2
48	994	1.8	90.0	2
71	1,170	2.1	92.1	2
50	974	1.7	93.8	2
81	957	1.7	95.5	2

Source: World Bank estimates based on data from the Local Government Engineering Department, Bangladesh.

transport costs, it was not taken into account, because analyzing the first mile would require the location of each household and a large number of village roads and tracks to connect to the road network.

Hub-and-spokes systems optimize the flow of goods and the use of transport infrastructure. Not every market need be connected to the main corridor; some markets can be linked to the closest larger market near the corridor, which then distributes goods to smaller markets. Consumers and vendors need not interact with larger markets; instead, they can access smaller markets, based on their needs. Some markets share access ways; investment in some routes could make more than one market accessible.

Classifying the road network

The classification of road networks is an important step in the design, financing, construction, maintenance, and management of networks. Traditional approaches emphasize the volume of traffic carried or likely to be carried by a road when determining its class. Modern approaches focus on the function of the road.

A functional approach allows the class of a road to be revised depending on patterns of spatial development in an area or region. In the case of local connectivity to regional corridors, the class of roads is as much a function of its place in the wider network of roads as it is of the market centers it connects. Recent research on economic corridors suggests that the depth of their impacts is in part defined by the density of surrounding lower-order roads. Ghani, Goswami, and Kerr (2016) find that in India the economic impact and benefits of corridor investments are concentrated within 10 kilometers of the transport corridor. For the analysis in Bangladesh, a 10-kilometer zone around the transport corridor was used to identify the roads that provide access to the corridor while at the same time connecting high-order market centers (map 4.1). The roads and markets were classified based on the criteria used by the road agencies in Bangladesh. As the function of each road is deemed most important, the local roads included both secondary and tertiary roads, as classified by the agency responsible for rural roads.

Identifying a package of interconnected markets and roads

The concept of basic accessibility (Lebo and Schelling 2001) argues for providing reliable access to as many rural residents as possible. Instead of providing high-capacity roads for a few farmers, the principle provides for low-cost access to a larger production area. All-year access is provided on low-cost roads for motor vehicles and paths and tracks that serve as IMT. Investment in nonmotorized infrastructures may reap returns on investment that are comparable to returns on traditional roads (Sieber 1996). Priority should be placed on market access roads, which connect lower-hierarchy markets to major markets. The first mile, which connects the farmstead with the local market, should also be taken into account. Costs can be particularly high over the first mile, as there are limited opportunities to scale up volumes.

A network analysis was performed to evaluate the spatial relationship between Tier 1 and Tier 2 markets. Each Tier 2 market was assigned to a Tier 1 market based on the shortest travel time within the network. Map 4.2 shows the

MAP 4.1

Main transport corridors passing through Jessore district and 10-kilometer impact area

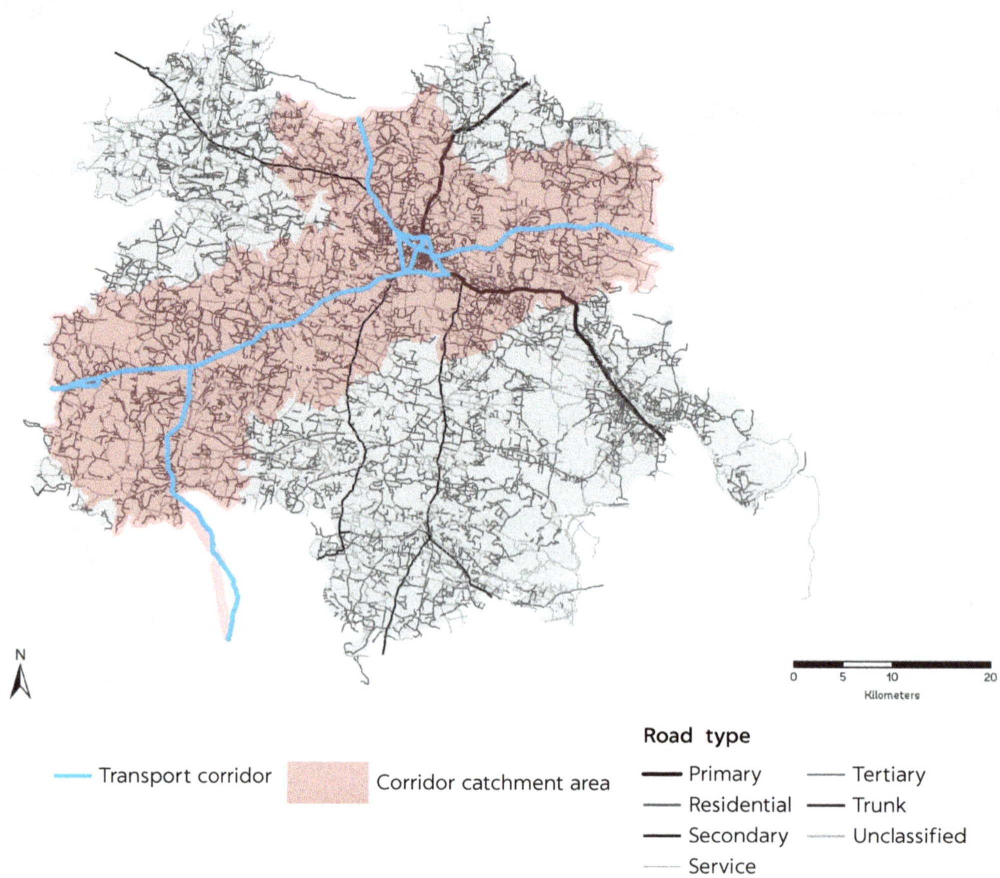

Source: World Bank.

Tier 1 and Tier 2 markets in Jessore district, the shortest routes between them, and the first two layers of the hub-and-spoke system. The location of the Tier 1 and 2 markets along the existing corridor may explain their high turnover values.

For road improvements, the following principles should be considered:

1. Improve only roads within the catchment area of small markets.

2. Minimize distance. As all-year accessibility is critical for marketing agricultural products, elasticity to travel time tends to be low, which means that some farmers may take large detours when roads are not passable.

3. Adopt a low-cost approach. Instead of improving a few roads to a high standard, perform spot improvement on a larger number of paths, tracks, trails, and roads that allow for year-round passability.

4. Consider widening or upgrading of roads only when warranted by traffic and the need to deploy larger vehicles.

Estimates of the impact of rural roads are subject to much uncertainty. It is particularly difficult to predict how agricultural output will change or traffic levels develop. Where benefits can be monetized, planners can adopt a producer

MAP 4.2
Location of Tier 1, Tier 2, and Tier 3+ markets in Jessore district

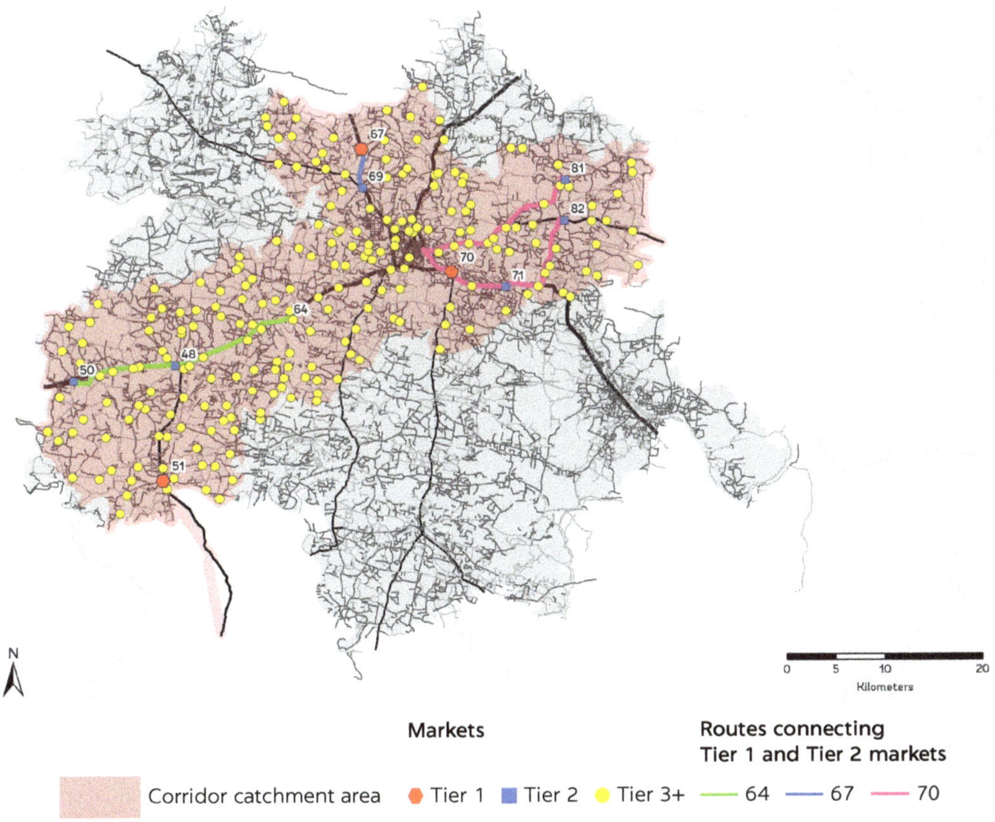

Source: World Bank.

surplus approach (Carnemark, Biderman, and Bovet 1976), which assumes an increase in agricultural production.

When benefits cannot easily be quantified in monetary terms, as in the case of roads with very low volumes, cost-effectiveness should be used (see Liu 2000; Lebo and Schelling 2001). The easiest approach is to compare the cost per inhabitant within the catchment area of the market, where the costs of improving a package of markets and roads is the sum of the costs of investing in and maintaining markets and feeder and access roads. Consequently, and consistent with the functional approach described above, the selection of roads to be included in a package has to be based on a participatory and iterative process involving local stakeholders, especially farmers and traders.

The selection of the investment packages is determined by the project's budget for market and rural road improvements. The costs of the ranked investment packages are cumulated until the budget is reached. The clusters that would have the most impact included Tier 1 and Tier 2 markets (map 4.3). All other markets (Tier 3 and beyond) either had very low turnover values or no data were available on them. These markets benefit from the network effects of connecting to a higher-order center.

All routes in the Jessore district were identified in terms of their relationship with the four Tier 1 hubs, resulting in four hub-and-spokes subsystems (map 4.4). The potential catchment area of each cluster of markets was then obtained, with each point assigned to the nearest market.

MAP 4.3

Shortest routes between Tier 1 and Tier 2 markets in Jessore district

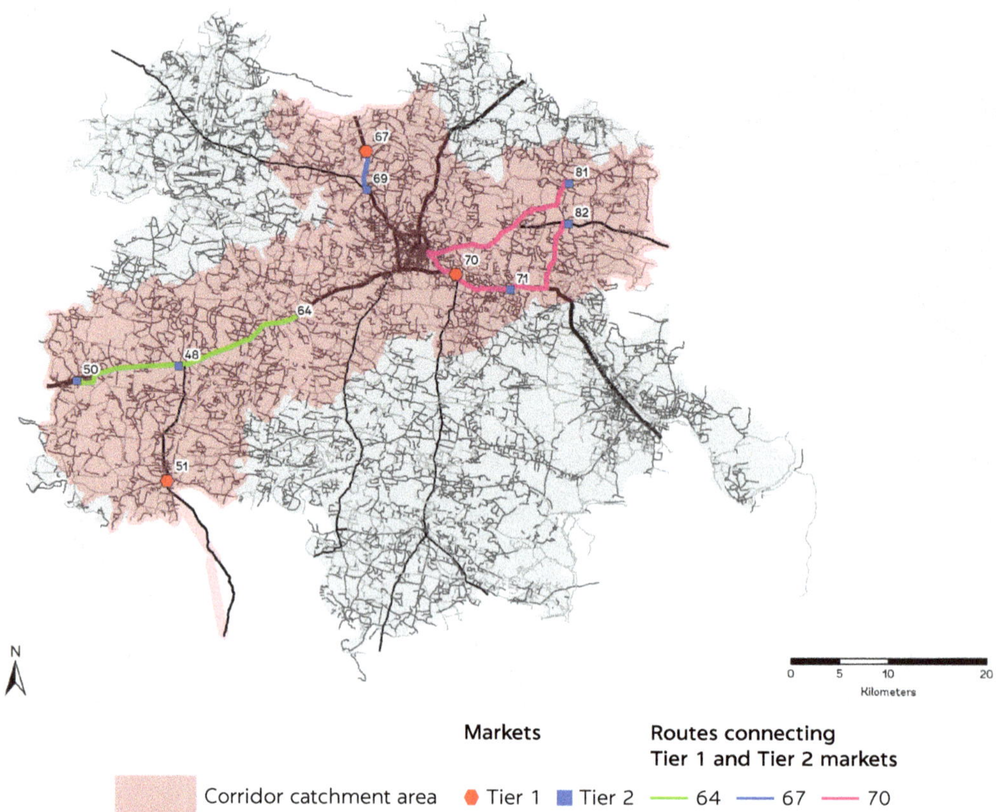

Source: World Bank.

The length of the roads that connect small markets with the hubs was calculated within the newly generated catchment areas of the clusters (table 4.3).

SUMMARY AND CONCLUDING REMARKS

Corridors are high-capacity systems that are most efficient when they facilitate the unimpeded movement of large volumes of traffic. Large-scale investments in trade corridors are especially important for long-distance access to major markets. A development challenge is that most rural producers, including in territories through which corridors pass, generate small and irregular volumes of marketable produce. There is a need to consolidate these traffic volumes, so that producers can benefit from the economies of scale that corridors offer.

In general, although a corridor may enhance access, doing so often does not imply that economic impacts spread automatically and equally across a region. Additional investments in rural roads and markets are needed to maximize the local benefits of corridor improvements.

Investments in rural transport have been proven to be critical to accessibility to markets. Many studies confirm that rural roads spur market-led local development, via agricultural marketing and increased income from farming. The effect of improved access can be enhanced by investing in facilities such as markets. By enhancing opportunities to sell produce, the development of markets

MAP 4.4

Clusters of markets and shortest routes between Tier 3+ and Tier 1 and 2 markets in the catchment area of the corridor in Jessore district

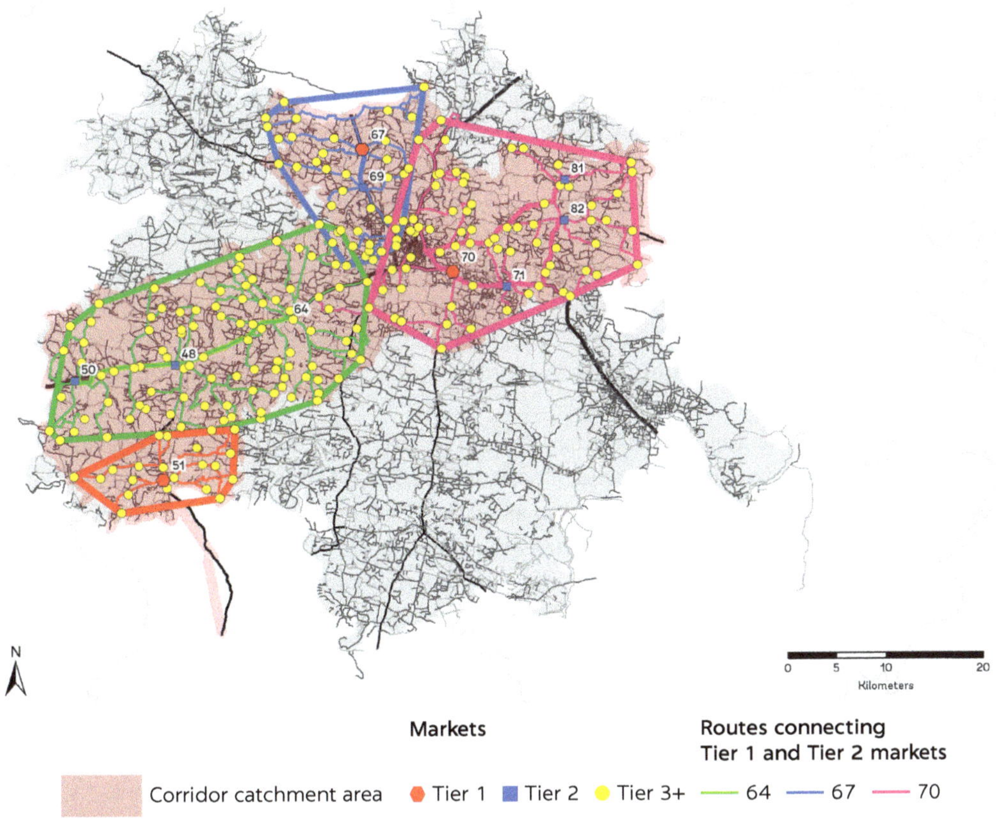

Source: World Bank.

TABLE 4.3 **Lengths of target roads to improve market access in Jessore district**

TARGET ROAD	CLUSTER NUMBER			
Road type	70	51	67	64
Primary	27.3	4.5	0	5.3
Residential	29.4	13.5	26.6	52.2
Secondary	13.4	0	8.6	2.0
Service	0	0	0	0.7
Tertiary	29.9	13.8	2.4	18.9
Trunk	53.9	0	15.2	60.6
Unclassified	81.4	23.8	51.6	152.9
Total	235.2	55.6	104.2	292.7

Source: World Bank.

stimulates agricultural production, especially for smallholder farmers, who are highly dependent on local markets to sell their produce. In order to participate in marketable chains, farmers need to transport their products over the "first mile" (from the field or homestead to the next small market) and from there to a major hub. They do so over market access roads—the roads, paths, and tracks within the catchment area needed to reach the market.

Many developing countries pursue investments in regional corridors, feeder roads, and markets separately. While often this may be effective if not convenient from a project design and implementation perspective, it can result in suboptimal outcomes.

Using an empirical approach, the chapter lays out a methodology that can be adopted to identify a package of roads and markets that could leverage investments in regional corridors in order to extend the scale effects of a corridor into surrounding rural regions. The approach, based on a case study of a district in Bangladesh, shows that it is possible to identify clusters of rural markets and their connecting transport infrastructure that would expand the zone of influence of a corridor into predominantly rural areas. The approach solves two simultaneous equations, one that describes a corridor as a limited access system with only a few points of entry and another that describes numerous small-scale producers whose traffic has to be consolidated in order to reach faraway markets with minimal product losses.

The approach has three steps. The first is to identify a cluster of rural markets that are co-dependent, either as origins of shipments or as assembly markets where shipments from small facilities are consolidated. The second step involves classifying the links that make up the connecting transports system depending on the volume of traffic that they carry. The third step integrates the results of the first two steps, in order to identify a package of markets and roads that maximizes returns for rural producers within a budget constraint for infrastructure. The solution provides the minimum set of markets, in hierarchy and length of roads, needed to integrate the cluster.

Improving local connectivity to corridors is important to strengthen the economies of lagging regions and reduce economic inequalities. As South Asian countries invest in large-scale corridors for regional integration, it is important that they pay special attention to local connectivity, which is particularly important in a region that is still predominantly rural and based on agriculture.

ANNEX 4.A: DATA REQUIREMENTS FOR IMPLEMENTING THE ANALYTICAL MODEL

TABLE 4A.1 **Data requirements for implementing the analytical model**

DATA	DESCRIPTION
Administration	
Administrative units	Shape files of administrative units Area of units
Population	
Inhabitants	Number of people within administrative units
Markets	
Location	Coordinates or shapefiles
Function	Rural primary market, assembly market, wholesale market
Turnover	Annual turnover or lease value

table continues on next page

TABLE 4A.1, *continued*

Facilities	Availability and condition of following facilities:
	Cooling house
	Deep freezer
	Warehouse
	Packaging facilities
	Processing facilities
	Sanitary facilities: Water supply, tanks, toilets
	Social facilities: Training room, women's corner
	Transport facilities: Parking, bus, loading and unloading facilities
	Technical facilities: Electricity, Internet, telecommunication, mill
	Multistory building
Roads	
Location	Shape files
Road type	National, regional, etc.
Design	Road design of section according to design standard
Length	Length of road section
Surface	Surface of road section
Road condition	Very good, good, average, bad, very bad or International Roughness Index
Speed	Average speed on road section
Traffic volume	Past and present annual average daily traffic
Design standards	National standards for width, maximum speed, traffic volumes
Investment costs	
Market facilities	Investment costs for market facilities (as given above)
	Annual maintenance costs
Road works	Regular maintenance costs per kilometer
	Periodic maintenance costs per kilometer
	Rehabilitation costs per kilometer
Road improvement	Costs per kilometer of upgrading to next design standard
	Standard costs per kilometer of upgrading from earth to sealed
	Costs per kilometer of widening of road

Source: World Bank.

REFERENCES

Alam, M., M. Herrera Dappe, M. Melecky, and R. Goldblatt. 2018. "Wider Economic Benefits of Transport Corridors: Evidence from International Development Organizations." Policy Research Working Paper 9057, World Bank, Washington, DC.

Banjo, G. A., H. F. Gordon, and J. Riverson. 2012. "Rural Transport: Improving Its Contribution to Growth and Poverty Reduction in Sub-Saharan Africa." SSATP Working Paper 93, World Bank, Sub-Saharan Africa Transport Policy Program, Washington, DC.

Bradbury, A., J. Hine, P. Njenga, A. Otto, G. Muhia, and S. Willilo. 2017. *Evaluation of the Effect of Road Condition on the Quality of Agricultural Produce*. Phase 2 Report, TRL Limited, International Forum for Rural Transport and Development.

Carnemark, C., J. Biderman, and D. Bovet. 1976. "The Economic Analysis of Rural Road Projects." Working Paper 241, World Bank, Washington DC.

Christaller, W. 1933. *Central Places in Southern Germany*. Englewood Cliffs, NJ: Prentice Hall.

Fafchamps, M., and F. Shilpi. 2009. "Isolation and Subjective Welfare: Evidence from South Asia." *Economic Development and Cultural Change* 57 (4): 641–83.

Fan, S., and C. Chan-Kang. 2005. *Road Development, Economic Growth and Poverty Reduction in China*. Research Report 138, International Food Policy Research Institute (IFPRI), Washington, DC.

Gachassin, M., B. Najman, and G. Raballand. 2015. "Roads and Diversification of Activities in Rural Areas: A Cameroon Case Study." *Development Policy Review* 33 (3): 355–72.

Ghani, E., A. G. Goswami, and W. R. Kerr. 2016. "Highway to Success: The Impact of the Golden Quadrilateral Project for the Location and Performance of Indian Manufacturing." *Economic Journal* 126: 317–57.

Gautam, M., and R. Faruqee. 2016. *Dynamics of Rural Growth in Bangladesh: Sustaining Poverty Reduction*. Washington, DC: World Bank.

Gertler, P. J., M. Gonzalez-Navarro, T. Gracner, and A. D. Rothenberg. 2014. "The Role of Road Quality Investments on Economic Activity and Welfare: Evidence from Indonesia's Highways." Unpublished manuscript. http://sites.bu.edu/neudc/files/2014/10/paper_250.pdf.

Heyns, A. M. and J. H. van Vuuren. 2018. "Multi-Type, Multi-Zone Facility Location." *Geographical Analysis* 50: 3–31.

Herrera Dappe, M., L. Andres, and M. Alam. 2020. *Impact Evaluation of Pradhan Mantri Gram Sadak Yojana (PMGSY)*. Washington, DC: World Bank.

Jacoby, H. G. 2000. "Access to Markets and the Benefits of Rural Roads." *Economic Journal* 110: 713–37.

Khandker, S. R., and G. Koolwal. 2011. "Estimating the Long-Term Impacts of Rural Roads: A Dynamic Panel Approach." Policy Research Working Paper 5867, World Bank, Washington, DC.

Khandker, S. R., and H. A. Samad. 2016. "Transformation of Rural Bangladesh: Role of Infrastructure and Financial Institutions." Working Paper 128, JICA Research Institute, Tokyo. https://www.jica.go.jp/jica-ri/publication/workingpaper/jrft3q00000027sa-att/JICA-RI_WP_No.128.pdf.

Lebo, J., and D. Schelling. 2001. *Design and Appraisal of Rural Transport Infrastructure: Ensuring Basic Access for Rural Communities*. Technical Paper 496, World Bank, Washington, DC.

Liu, Z. 2000. "Economic Analysis of a Rural Basic Access Road Project: The Case of Andhra Pradesh, India." Infrastructure Notes, Transport Sector RT-5. World Bank, Washington, DC.

Mu, R., and D. v. d. Walle. 2008. "Rural Roads and Market Development in Viet Nam." Policy Research Working Paper 4340, World Bank, Development Research Group, Washington, DC.

Reardon, T. 2007. "Transformation of Markets for Agricultural Output in Developing Countries since 1950: How Has Thinking Changed?" In *Handbook of Agricultural Economics*, vol. 3, 2808–55. Amsterdam: Elsevier.

Reardon, T., C. B. Barrett, Julio A. Berdegué, and Johan F. M. Swinnen. 2009. "Agrifood Industry Transformation and Small Farmers in Developing Countries." *World Development* 37 (11): 1717–27.

Roberts, M., M. Melecky, T. Bougna, and Y. Xu. 2019. "Transport Corridors and Their Wider Economic Benefits: A Critical Review of the Literature." *Journal of Regional Science* 60 (2): 1–42.

Sieber, N. 1996. *Rural Transport and Regional Development: The Case of Makete District, Tanzania*. Baden-Baden: Nomos Verlag.

Sieber, N., and H. Allen. 2016. "Impacts of Rural Roads on Poverty and Equity." *Transport and Communications Bulletin for Asia and the Pacific* 86: 23–40.

Starkey, P., and J. Hine. 2014. *Poverty and Sustainable Transport: How Transport Affects Poor People with Policy Implications for Poverty Reduction—A Literature Review*. London: Overseas Development Institute.

Tracey-White, J. D. 1995. "Retail Markets Planning." *Agricultural Services Bulletin* 121 (Food and Agriculture Organization, Rome).

Tracey-White, J. D. 2005. *Rural–Urban Marketing Linkages*. Rome: Food and Agriculture Organization.

Tschirley, D., T. Reardon, M. Dolislager, and J. Snyder 2015. "The Rise of a Middle Class in Urban and Rural East and Southern Africa: Implications for Food System Transformation." *Journal of International Development* 27 (5): 628–46.

World Bank. 2016. *Measuring Rural Access: Using New Technologies*. Washington, DC: World Bank.

5 Enhancing Women's Opportunities in Export-Oriented Agricultural Value Chains in Bangladesh

MUNEEZA MEHMOOD ALAM, URSULA CASABONNE, BARBARA COELLO, AND GAIA HATZFELDT

Trade liberalization and market-oriented reforms have enabled Bangladesh to take advantage of emerging global market opportunities in recent years. These changes have led to extraordinary growth of exports since the early 1990s and have allowed Bangladesh to become a leading exporter of apparel (Rahman 2014). Expansion of global trade has opened up employment opportunities for millions of women. Indeed, women represented 55 percent of the 3.6 million workers employed in the export-oriented, ready-made garment industry, which accounted for 84 percent of export earnings in fiscal year 2018/19 (Solotaroff and others 2019; Moazzem and Ahmad Radia 2018). Increased employment opportunities for women in manufacturing in urban areas has helped narrow the gender gap in labor force participation (Farole and others 2017), although women's labor force participation rate is still substantially lower (36 percent in 2019) than that of men (81 percent in 2019) (World Bank 2020). Women also have less access to paid jobs than men, with 39 percent of working women in unpaid work, as opposed to 5 percent of working men (Farole and others 2017).

Intraregional trade accounts for a little more than 5 percent of South Asia's total trade—a much smaller share than in East Asia and the Pacific (50 percent) or Sub-Saharan Africa (22 percent) (Kathuria 2018). The government of Bangladesh recently enacted trade facilitation measures to increase the untapped economic opportunity of intraregional trade. The Bangladesh-Bhutan-India-Nepal Motor Vehicles Agreement (BBIN MVA), enacted in 2015, is expected to increase intraregional trade within South Asia by 60 percent (Chaudhury and others 2015).[1]

Increased regional integration can yield meaningful local benefits—but only if economic agents located along corridors can take advantage of improved connectivity. Rural women in Bangladesh are disadvantaged by restrictive socioreligious norms, including *purdah*.[2] These norms confine women to their homesteads, limiting their participation in public spaces; their access to economic resources and assets (such as land, credit, and productive inputs); and broad social interactions (Paul 1992; Kabeer 2011; Bridges, Lawson, and Begum 2011). Women in Bangladesh are 29 percentage points less likely than men to have a bank account, and men are twice as likely as women to have access to both mobile phone and the Internet (Demirgüç-Kunt and others 2018).

Studies have consistently shown that improving women's access to paid employment enhances economic growth and productivity and improves outcomes for the next generation (World Bank 2012). Efforts to revitalize the rural economy in Bangladesh can create an enabling environment for women to participate in export-oriented agricultural value chains and help weaken gender norms that constrain their employment.

PURPOSE, METHODOLOGY, AND CONCEPTUAL FRAMEWORK

This chapter identifies the constraints women face in Bangladesh in different export-/regional trade–oriented agricultural value chains and proposes interventions to remove them. It reports on research conducted in the districts of Jashore, Jhenaidah, and Chuadanga in southwestern Bangladesh on three export-oriented agricultural value chains that have a strong potential for women's participation: cut flowers, mangoes, and fisheries. Separate focus group discussions with male and female workers in the sector and key informant interviews with local actors, including representatives of farmer/producer associations, women's groups, cooperatives, the government, women's affairs agencies, nongovernmental organizations (NGOs), and the private sector shed light on the barriers and challenges women face. The semistructured questionnaires used covered production and packaging, product transport, marketing and pricing, gender roles in the production process, and problems associated with inequitable systems and structures. Twelve focus group discussions (122 participants) and six key informant interviews were conducted (table 5.1). The research instruments were prepared with input from sectoral and value chain experts from the World Bank, then field-tested, revised, finalized, and translated into Bangla.

The chapter also examines opportunities for women as vendors at border *haats* (cross-border markets). Table 5.2 describes the sample for that part of the research.

The chapter adopts an ecological framework to help conceptualize, identify, and integrate the constraints on women's participation in agricultural value chains in terms of three broad levels of societal constraints: (table 5.3):

- The macro, or national, enabling environment (societal level) encompasses the normative, policy, and legal context that can impose constraints or facilitate women's market employment.
- The meso, or local, enabling environment (community level) encompasses institutions and local or community-level factors. Institutions include workplaces, cooperatives, cross-border trade organizations, occupational networks, and business associations that have formal rules and regulations as well as informal culture and norms that influence women's positioning and role within these organizations. Local or community-level factors include market and job opportunities; community norms; and the activities

TABLE 5.1 **Research sample for study of women as producers in agricultural value chains**

ITEM	AREA	GROUP	NUMBER OF PARTICIPANTS
Focus groups			
Cut flowers	Jhikargacha, Jashore	Men	12
		Women	10
	Jibonnagar, Chuadanga	Women	10
	Kaligonj, Jhenaidah	Women	10
Mangoes	Chowgacha, Jashore	Men	10
		Women	10
	Jibonnagar, Chuadanga	Women	10
	Kaligonj, Jhenaidah	Women	10
Fish	Sadar, Jashore	Women	10
	Sharsa, Jashore	Men	10
	Jibonnagar, Chuadanga	Women	10
	Kotchandpur, Jhenaidah	Women	10
Key informant interviews			
Female entrepreneur	Jashore	Woman	1
President, Bangladesh Flower Society	Jashore	Man	1
Representative of local transport company	Chuadanga	Man	1
Fisheries officer	Chuadanga	Man	1
Agriculture officer	Jhenaidah	Man	1
NGO worker	Jhenaidah	Man	1
Total			128

Source: World Bank.

TABLE 5.2 **Research sample for the study of women vendors at border *haats***

AREA/TOOL/CATEGORY	NUMBER OF PARTICIPANTS
Tarapur (Brahmanbaria district, Bangladesh)–Kamalasagar (Sipahijala district, Tripura, India)	
Focus group discussions	
Female vendors and work assistants	6
Male vendors	10
Key informant interview	
Border *haat* management committee members (UNO)	2
Mayor-Kasba Municipality	
Purba Madhugram and Middle Sagaria (Feni district, Bangladesh)–Srinagar (West Tripura, India)	
Focus group discussion	
Male vendors	10
Key informant interview	
Member of border *haat* management committee members (a local government representative)	1
President of border *haat* vendors association	1
Total	30

Source: World Bank.

TABLE 5.3 **Analytical framework for identifying barriers to and facilitators of women's participation in agricultural value chains**

MACRO	MESO	MICRO
Normative environment: • Unwritten rules of conduct and behavior, consisting of norms, values, societal roles, family values, religious beliefs, traditional attitudes, stereotyping, and roles ascribed to men and women Economic/business environment: • Economic growth • Favorable economic policies Legal environment: • Labor laws that restrict women from participating in certain jobs • Laws restricting women from engaging in entrepreneurship (for example, restrictions on opening up a bank account, taking out a loan) • Laws restricting women from owning land, property and other productive assets, including customary laws	Institutional level: • Organizational structures that are gender-segregated or do not allow for women's participation in leadership positions • Infrastructure/facilities that are unfit for women • Lack of codes of conduct, antiharassment policies, and grievance redress mechanisms • Policies and procedures that are not gender sensitive • Lack of staff training/sensitization on gender issues (organizational culture is hostile to women) Community level: • Stigmatization of women who work outside the home • Market opportunities and job opportunities enabled by improved trade policies/promotion and business environment • Networks and support organizations	Access to productive resources: • Capital assets (land ownership, capital, equipment, and inputs) • Financial services and networks • Technology and information • Agricultural services Power and agency: • Capabilities: Limited vocational, technical, and business development skills; Lower educational attainment; Limited skills/experience outside traditional or female sectors • Self-confidence: Lack of confidence needed to exercise agency • Decision-making power: Lack of decision-making power, lack of control over income Other limiting factors: • Lack of childcare and higher burden of household/care responsibilities • Social norms such as permission, safety, trust, and mobility

Sources: Brush, de Bruin, and Welter 2009; Terrillon 2010; FAO 2018; Senders and others 2012.

of government agencies, private firms, and support organizations, such as business development services, financial business services, and NGOs.

- Micro, or individual-level factors, are personal characteristics, such as access to productive resources (assets like access to land and equipment, technology and information, agricultural services, and financial services) and power and agency (capabilities, self-confidence, and decision-making).

This framework helps identify and separate the factors that affect women's participation, placing all of them in a common interconnected framework. Some of these factors and barriers are formal, put in place by laws and institutional policies. Others run deeper and are the product of long-held cultural and gender norms and beliefs, which are often more challenging to overcome. The multiple factors at various levels often overlap, influence, interact, and reinforce one another, producing cumulative effects. Depending on the scope of the project intervention, the framework helps prioritize actions and strategies to strengthen women's participation as producers in agricultural value chains. Solutions presented at the end of this chapter suggest a way forward for creating a more inclusive trade environment for women, one that addresses barriers at different levels using synergistic approaches.

WOMEN'S PARTICIPATION IN EXPORT-ORIENTED AGRICULTURAL VALUE CHAINS

The agricultural sector (crops, animal farming, forests, and fishing) contributes 15 percent to Bangladesh's GDP and employs almost half of all workers (World Bank 2015). The sector experiences labor force shortages, especially in peak seasons, because many men have left agriculture for nonfarm occupations (Rahman 2017).

In 2016, Bangladesh had a high prevalence of unpaid work in rural areas, most of which was driven by women in agriculture (Farole and others 2017). Cultural norms governing women's seclusion and mobility constraints are one of the causes of women's overrepresentation in unpaid work. These norms are more prevalent in rural areas, where 70 percent of women work at or close to home; in urban areas the figure is 42 percent (Farole and others 2017).

Improving the performance of and expanding women's participation in export-oriented agricultural value chains can generate spillover benefits for their households and communities (Quisumbing and McClafferty 2006). Changes in women's productive roles and earnings capacity may also lead to shifts in the balance of decision-making power within households and increase their access to and control over income (Rubin and Manfre 2014).

Agricultural value chains encompass the entire range of activities that take place at the farm or rural level, including input supply, handling, processing, storage, packaging, and distribution. As products move through the various stages, transactions take place between multiple stakeholders, money changes hands, information is exchanged, and value is added. The value chain environment includes macroeconomic conditions; trade facilitation policies; and standards, regulations, and institutional support services (communications, research, innovation, finance, business development, and so forth). It has a critical effect on the performance of value chains. Analysis of value chains sheds light on the interactions between small and medium farmers and firms with markets—domestic or global—and identifies areas and activities that will benefit from changes that profitability improve the flow of products to endusers.

Gender relations are a primary component of the social and economic context that shapes the functioning of value chains at all levels. These relations affect the types of jobs available to men and women, differences in remuneration, and the qualitative nature of individuals' productive roles in the value chain (for example, time use, adoption of labor-saving technologies, and participation in decision-making) (Senders and others 2012). A gender value chain analysis examines chain-based and contextual factors that define men's and women's roles as well as the challenges they face in participating in value chains. The goal of this analysis is the establishment of an environment in which women and men can fully participate in and benefit from market opportunities.

CHARACTERISTICS OF THE CUT FLOWER, MANGO, AND FISH-FARMING VALUE CHAINS

Cut flowers

Export earnings from cut flowers rose by a factor of almost 20, rising from \$200,000 in 2017/18 to \$3.98 million in 2018/19, according to the Export Promotion Bureau (*Independent* 2019). The increase reflects increasing demand, land under flower cultivation, and yield of flowers (Rakibuzzaman and others 2018). Flower and floral products are exported to Britain,

Denmark, France, Germany, India, Italy, Japan, Pakistan, the Philippines, Portugal, the Republic of Korea, Saudi Arabia, Singapore, and the United States. In 2018/19, the local market for flowers and cut foliage reached $141.5 million, an increase of 10 percent over the previous year, according to the Dhaka Chamber of Commerce and Industry (*Dhaka Tribune* 2019). The higher disposable income of Bangladesh's growing middle class—along with the rise of corporate businesses and the widespread use of flowers to celebrate Western holidays such as Valentine's Day and Mother's Day and iconic cultural events such as Pohela Boishakh and Pohela Falgun—have accelerated the growth of the flower business in Bangladesh (Hossain Ovi and Mahmud 2018).The end market for cut flowers is the wholesale market in Dhaka and the Chattogram, although district and other retailers are linked with local wholesale markets as well (figure 5.1). Farmers cultivate cut flowers throughout the year, although production peaks between October and March. According to the president of the Bangladesh Flower Society, about 25,000 families are directly engaged in cut flower farming, and about 200,000 people either directly or indirectly depend on this sector (*Dhaka Tribune* 2019). The main center of cut flower production is Godkhali, Jashore, where six types of flowers (marigolds, tuberoses, hybrid tuberoses, gerberas, gladiolus, and roses) are commercially cultivated.

According to focus group discussion participants, cut flowers represent the main income source for farmers in Jashore district. In contrast, in the Chuadanga and Jhenaidah districts, cut flower farmers also produce alternative agricultural vegetables, rice, jute, and other products. According to the president of the Bangladesh Flower Society, in the districts surveyed for this

FIGURE 5.1

Cut flower value chain in Bangladesh

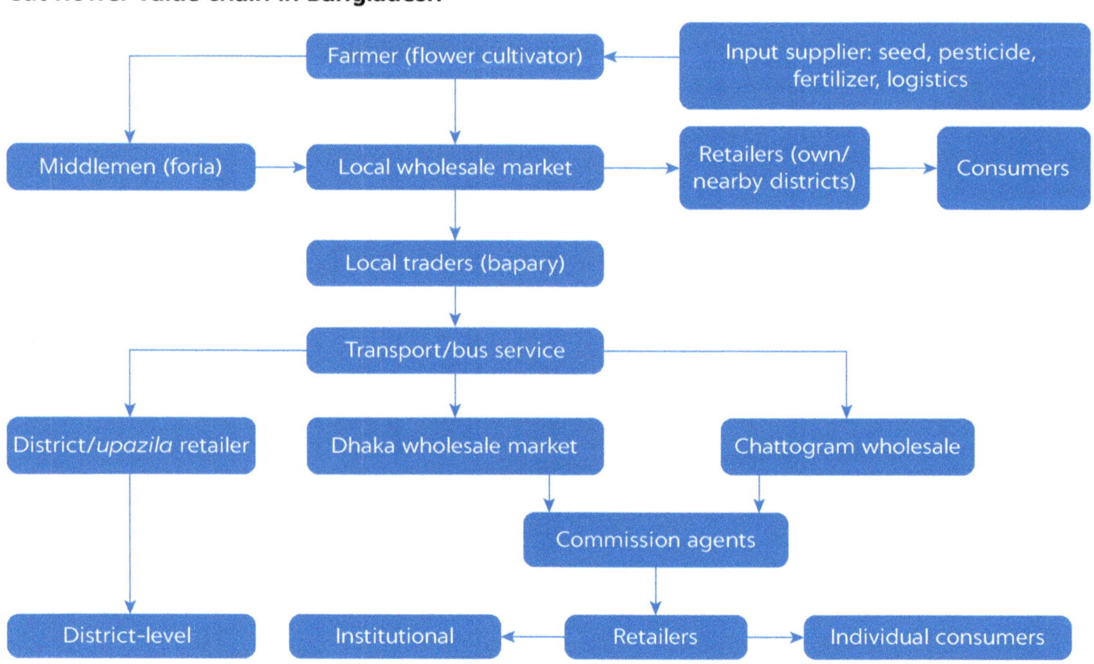

Source: World Bank.

study, about 100 women are actively engaged in cut flower farming and about 400–500 women are engaged in harvesting, sorting, grading, and stringing garlands. Another 6,000 female family members are engaged with cut flower farming in some form or another. Women in the sector earn the equivalent of about \$1.90–\$2.40 day; men earn \$3.00–\$3.50, according to the president of the Bangladesh Flower Society interviewed for this study.

Mangoes

Bangladesh is the world's ninth-large producer of mangoes (Pariona 2018). In the districts surveyed, mango production is an important income source for both commercial and small-scale farmers. Mango trees yield 10–15 years of production with very little nursing. During the first three years after planting mangoes, farmers can cultivate other crops inside the mango garden, including vegetables, nuts, and pulses. The mango season lasts three months (May–July). Income from the sale of mangoes is a key source of savings for farmers; money for daily expenses comes from the sale of other products. Figure 5.2 presents the mango value chain.

Fish farming

Bangladesh is the world's fifth-largest aquaculture producer (FAO 2018). It employs about 17.8 million people (11 percent of the population), of which 1.4 million (about 8 percent) are women. Fish farmers in Jashore have developed a complete value chain, including hatcheries, nurseries, transport, and

FIGURE 5.2

Mango value chain in Bangladesh

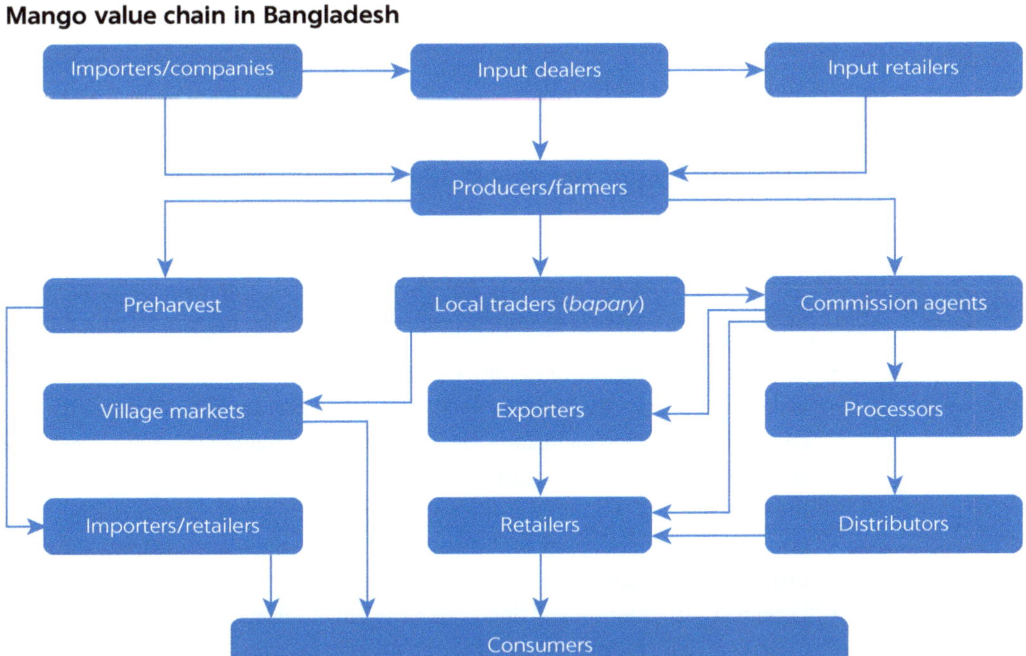

Source: World Bank.

FIGURE 5.3
Fish-farming value chain in Bangladesh

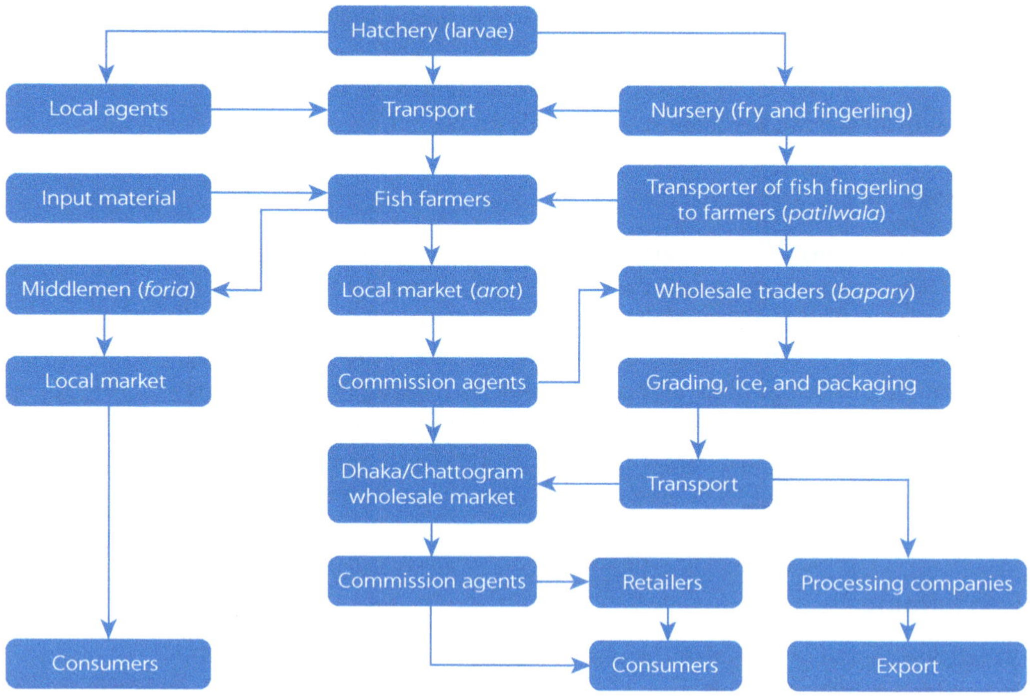

Source: World Bank.

fry trading, and wholesale markets (figure 5.3). The hatchery industry in Jashore created employment opportunities for people in Chasra, Jeshore (the largest fish seed trading marketplace in Bangladesh), where thousands of households are engaged in fish farming and fingerling production. According to respondents in the sector in the Jashore and Jhenaidah districts, most of their household income contribution comes from fish nursery farming and the commercial cultivation of fish.

CHALLENGES FACED BY PRODUCERS

Focus group discussions and key informant interviews revealed several challenges at different nodes of the cut flower, mango, and fish-farming value chains (table 5.4). The most salient issues identified included the following:

- lack of pest management know-how
- lack of infrastructure facilities from farm to market (cold chain capacity and adequate packaging materials) for cut flowers and mangoes, which is responsible for large postharvest losses
- the high price of seeds and fish feed, which affects small-scale farmers
- poor transport and road infrastructure, which makes it difficult to bring products to market
- large price fluctuation and delays in payments to farmers.

TABLE 5.4 **Key challenges in the cut flower, mango, and fish-farming value chains**

VALUE CHAIN NODE	CUT FLOWERS	MANGOES	FISH FARMING
Production	• Most flower farms are traditionally managed and lack access to modern technologies and support (for the construction of greenhouses/ polyhouses, for example).[a] • Lacking cold storage facilities for seeds, farmers store seeds in cold storage facilities used for preserving potatoes, which are not cool enough. • Changing temperature and precipitation patterns because of climate change adversely affects the quality of flowers. • The capital investment required to grow gerbera, lilium, eustoma, and other types of flowers is high. • Farmers lack good-quality input materials for shed construction, such as high-quality polythene. • Sourcing good-quality seed for gerbera flowers and other new types of flowers is expensive. Farmers are highly dependent on imported seeds from India. • Research and technical support for production (soil testing systems, equipment, flower disease control, introduction of new species and technology) is lacking.	• Technology and knowledge of disease management is inadequate (few farmers have spray machines, for example). • Changing temperature and precipitation patterns (hailstorms, fog) affect product quality.	• Technology is not used. • Sourcing good-quality fish feed is challenging. • Inputs, especially fish feed, are expensive. • Knowledge of managing ponds and monitoring fish growth is inadequate.
Harvesting and postharvesting	• No cold chain system exists for postharvest management of cut flowers (sorting, grading, packaging, and storing). • A standard packaging and transport system (material support, technical knowledge) is lacking, reducing the quality of flowers and increasing wastage. • Farmers do not use cartons or baskets for packaging gerbera. • The packaging system often fails to ensure proper ventilation around the flowers. • A collection center, including a cold chain, is lacking. • Supporting materials for grading, packaging, and transporting flowers are not available. • Logistics (good packaging material, flower-specific paper cartons, grading and sorting trays, trolleys) are inadequate. • Sourcing the logistics for cut flowers is expensive.	• Postharvest infrastructure logistics (such as trimming net, crates, packinghouses, precooling units, and cold chain units) are inadequate. • Collection centers where harvested mangoes are washed, sorted, graded, and packaged, do not exist.	• Harvesting costs are high, and traditional technology is used to harvest fish fry and fingerlings. • Packaging materials and transport of fresh fish (plastic drams, special jars for carrying live fish, oxygen support system facilities in truck, and so forth) are inadequate. • Ice sourcing points are far away.

continued

TABLE 5.4, *continued*

VALUE CHAIN NODE	CUT FLOWERS	MANGOES	FISH FARMING
Transport	• The Daulatdia–Paturia–Dhaka route is challenging, because of the uncertainty of crossing the Padma River (because of rough weather or traffic jams). • No back-up plan exists for transporting flowers during the winter or the rainy season. • Temperature, humidity, and ethylene production during transport affect the quality of cut flowers, as the journey is about 10–12 hours. • Facilities and logistics for loading and unloading flowers are inadequate. • No cold chain transport system has been developed to ensure the quality of cut flowers.	• The Daulatdia–Paturia–Dhaka route is challenging, because of the uncertainty of crossing the Padma River in the mango (rainy) season. • Transport costs are high, because bribes need to paid to use roads and the ferry *ghat* (port). • Inadequate facilities and logistics for loading and unloading mangoes in the local market leads to product damage. • Connecting roads (including bridges and culverts) are in poor condition	• Vehicles that lack road permits are used to carry fish to the local market; when they police intercept them, the fish go bad. • Road infrastructure from the fish farm to the local market is poor. • Specialized vehicles used to carry perishable items to far away markets or second-tier wholesale markets are not used. • The cost of transporting fish to wholesale markets (in Dhaka and Chattogram) is high, because of the long distance and the ferry *ghat* fee. • Roads are in poor condition, especially during the rainy season/ • No back-up plan exists for transporting fish during the winter or rainy season.
Commercialization	• The market for premium quality flowers has not been explored. • Updated market information is not available. • Prices fluctuate erratically. • Delayed payments subject farmers to uncertainty. • The price of flowers is cut in half because of damage. • Farmers feel they do not get a fair price because they sell to monopoly traders in the wholesale market.	• A formal market structure for the mango value chain is lacking; most farmers sell to local seasonal businessmen. • Farmers lack direct links to the wholesale market. • Farmers lack price and updated market information. • No network with mango pulp- or/juice-producing companies exists. • Farmers lack knowledge of the green mango market. • The price of mangoes falls in the peak season, as mangoes ripen simultaneously all over the country, flooding the market. • No customer hub exists for premium products.	• Price and updated market information are not available. • Market facilities where farmers can sell their fish locally are inadequate.

Source: World Bank analysis.
Note: a. A polyhouse is a type of greenhouse in which polyethylene is used as the cover.

MAPPING WOMEN'S PARTICIPATION IN THREE VALUE CHAINS

Women are involved in various processes of the cut flowers, mango, and fish-farming value chains (table 5.5). Their participation is greatest in the cut flower value chain, where they work in production, harvesting, and postharvesting. In the mango and fish-farming value chains, women work only in a few nodes, and even there their participation is minor. Women are entirely absent from the transport and commercialization nodes, except for the small number of women who sell cut flowers in markets.

Cut flowers

Men dominate the production, transport, and marketing of cut flowers. Women are partially engaged in postharvest nursing, grading, and packaging within their homestead. They pick the flowers from the gardens, string the flowers into garlands, package the garlands, grade and preserve seeds, and assist their husbands with pest management. Women also make garlands out of marigolds. Women who work in the cut flowers sector perceive floriculture primarily as men's work, viewing their own roles as "supportive." Few women are involved in the commercialization phase (table 5.6).

TABLE 5.5 **Mapping of the roles of men and women in the cut flower, mango, and fish-farming value chains in Bangladesh**

VALUE CHAIN NODE	PHASE	CUT FLOWERS	MANGOES	FISH FARMING
Production	Production	Mostly men, few women	Men only	Both men and women
	Harvesting	Mostly men, few women	Men only	Men only
Harvesting and postharvesting	Postharvesting	Mostly women, few men	Mostly men, few women	Mostly men, few women
	Carry product to house	Mostly men, few women	Men only	Not applicable
	Sorting and grading	Mostly men, few women	Mostly men, few women	Men only
	Packaging	Mostly men, few women	Mostly men, few women	Men only
Transportation	Farmers to the local market	Men only	Men only	Men only
	Local to the wholesale market	Men only	Men only	Men only
	Wholesale to retailer	Men only	Men only	Men only
Commercialization	Local traders	Men only	Men only	Men only
	Wholesale traders	Mostly men, few women	Men only	Men only
	Retail traders	Mostly men, few women	Men only	Men only

KEY

- Men only
- Women only
- Mostly men, few women
- Mostly women, few men
- Both men and women
- Not applicable

Source: World Bank analysis.

TABLE 5.6 **Activities performed by men and women in the cut flower value chain in Bangladesh**

VALUE CHAIN NODE / TYPE OF ACTIVITY	PERFORMED BY	
	MEN	WOMEN
Production		
Cold storing seeds	Yes	No
Preserving seeds	No	Yes
Collecting inputs	Yes	Yes
Preparing the land for cultivation	Yes	No
Building the shed	Yes	No
Planting or seeding	Yes	No
Nursing (weeding, watering, fertilizing)	Yes	Yes
Harvesting and postharvesting		
Harvesting	Yes	Yes
Carrying to home	Yes	Yes
Bundling, packing, and storing	No	Yes
Stringing garlands of marigolds	No	Yes
Transportation and commercialization		
Carrying to local market and wholesale market	Yes	No
Selling at local market / wholesale market	Yes	No
Selling to retail customers	Yes	Yes

Source: World Bank analysis

Mangoes

The mango value chain includes five steps: gardening, harvesting, grading and packaging, transporting, and marketing. Focus group discussions with men and women revealed that women have little scope to engage in the mango value chain because of the nature of the production and marketing system. In most cases, men perform production-related activities (purchasing mango seedlings; grafting mangoes; preparing fields, hiring workers; watering, manuring, and nursing the trees; checking for symptoms of diseases and taking necessary actions, harvesting mangoes, negotiating prices with buyers, and so forth). Men also perform the postharvest nursing of trees to prepare for further production, including cutting the mature green shoots, spraying pesticides to protect the new shoots from insects, watering, applying fertilizer to the soil, and so forth. Women are sometimes involved in the postharvest stage, trimming, grading, sorting, cleaning, packaging, and storing mangoes. They also assist their husbands with pest management and the preparation of fertilizer at home. Some women prepare ketchup from green mangoes as well as bars from ripe mangoes for own consumption (table 5.7).

Fish farming

Men and women perform different activities in the fish-farming value chain. Women are engaged in the nursery and during production; men are engaged in hatchery, transport, and marketing (table 5.8).

TABLE 5.7 **Activities performed by men and women in the mango value chain in Bangladesh**

	PERFORMED BY	
VALUE CHAIN NODE / TYPE OF ACTIVITY	MEN	WOMEN
Production		
Preparing land for cultivation	Yes	No
Souring quality pen for plantation	Yes	No
Planting	Yes	No
Nursing (weeding, watering, fertilizing)	Yes	No
Spraying pesticide per schedule (three to four times)	Yes	No
Harvesting and postharvesting		
Harvesting from tree	Yes	No
Trimming	Yes	Yes
Sorting and grading; packaging at garden	Yes	No
Sorting grading and packaging at local market	Yes	No
Grading and sorting; storing at home	No	Yes
Transportation and commercialization		
Loading and carrying to local market	Yes	No
Transporting to home or local market	Yes	No
Transporting to wholesale market	Yes	No
Unloading from truck	Yes	No
Selling at local market	Yes	No
Selling at wholesale and retail markets	Yes	No

Source: World Bank analysis.

TABLE 5.8 **Activities performed by men and women in the fish-farming value chain in Bangladesh**

	PERFORMED BY	
VALUE CHAIN NODE / TYPE OF ACTIVITY	MEN	WOMEN
Production		
Pond preparation	Yes	No
Collecting eggs (larvae) from hatchery	Yes	No
Collecting fry/ fingerlings from nursery	Yes	No
Transporting fish larvae, fry/fingerlings	Yes	No
Sourcing and preparing feed	Yes	Yes
Feeding	Yes	Yes
Monitoring growth at pond	Yes	Yes
Checking water quality, PH, oxygen level	Yes	Yes
Cleaning wastage feed and mono carbon gas	Yes	No
Harvesting (capturing)	Yes	No
Transportation and commercialization		
Carrying to local market	Yes	No
Selling to wholesale market	Yes	No
Selling to consumers	Yes	No

Source: World Bank analysis.

FACTORS LIMITING WOMEN'S PARTICIPATION IN VALUE CHAINS

Women participate mainly in production and postharvest processing, where their participation is constrained by *purdah* norms that restrict their ability to leave the homestead. They participate only as employees in home-based and informal activities that typically generate low value and low returns and little income for themselves. Women's limited mobility also reduces their agency and ability to access financial, technical, and business development services that could help them form small and medium enterprises and engage in the most profitable stages of the value chain—transformation and commercialization.

Barriers at the (macro) societal level

Focus group discussions revealed that the main factor limiting women's participation in agricultural value chains is the strongly embedded social norm of *purdah*, which prohibits women from leaving the boundaries of their homestead unaccompanied by their husbands or male relatives. This norm is upheld by strong social sanctions from family and community members if women break the norm. As two women in focus group discussions in Kaligonj, Jhenaidah stated:

> *The women of this locality do not go to the field or to the market. Men don't let women go. They say that while we are alive, why would you go? The women from other localities can go. But in our locality, this thing doesn't happen.*

> *If the flower field is beside the house, the woman may go for plucking and bring them to the house and make garlands. But if it's far away from the home, they won't go there. It's a matter of prestige.*

Focus group discussions revealed that the proper behavior of women as sheltered people is an important source of the socioeconomic status of their husbands/fathers. Women's behavior is also important in terms of the honor and pride of the extended family. Seclusion is expected of women of good social status. Women accept their seclusion for the sake of their own prestige and the maintenance of social distance.

> *No, there is no barrier. Women do not go [to the field] because of their own will. If we need anything, we tell our husband and they do that. If we need anything from the market, we send our children to bring that.*
>
> —*Woman in Kaligonj, Jhenaidah*

> *A woman who has a good man, he will tell her not to work. But [a woman] who has a bad man will tell her to work.*
>
> —*Woman in Chowgacha, Jashore*

> *The women in my society won't go fishing with the men. None of us would go. All of us are someone's wives. We all come from prestigious families. Going fishing would be absurd.*
>
> —*Woman in Kotchandpur, Jhenaidah*

In keeping with distinctions of class, status, and position, the focus group discussions revealed that the observance and saliency of *purdah* varies among village women. This variability reflects and exemplifies a family's social status and strengthens class relations.

> *Moderator: For women, what are the obstacles in this business?*
>
> *Respondent: There are no obstacles now. But in our country, there is a social obstacle that women shouldn't work in a field. People in our country think women have to be in the house. Why would they be in the field? Poor women can work in the fields. The family that is capable, its women will not work in a field.*
>
> *—Man in Jhikargacha, Jashore*

> *The women of the city can do all the work. But in the village, this doesn't happen. The women of Muchi (a cobbler community) can do all the work. They also go to the market.*
>
> *—Woman in Kaligonj, Jhenaidah*

Interviews revealed that the *purdah* norm is allowed to be bent in special circumstances and situations, such as when a husband works away from home or is disabled or a woman is widowed. In such circumstances, women leave the homestead, usually escorted by a family member or friend. The focus group discussions revealed a consensus that constructively engaging men, particularly husbands, is key to opening doors to women's increased participation in agricultural value chains. Participants emphasized that without the involvement of men, the norm of women's seclusion will not change. Sensitizing men and communities about the economic benefits of women's participation in value chains, particularly in value-adding activities that could generate higher income for households, might help change attitudes. New opportunities for women may be generated by introducing new technologies and marketing tactics.

> *I think the men of our society should change their views. There should be workshops for men to change their views. There should take training for this.*
>
> *—Woman in Jhikargacha, Jashore*

Barriers at the meso (value chain/community) level

Women's work is informal and goes unacknowledged. Their roles in value chains lack visibility, as they are seen as supporting and helping out their husbands rather than being key players. Gender norms and attitudes are also apparent in the recognition of women's contributions and their self-perceptions of their contributions. When society does not perceive that women have the right to participate in paid work outside the household, women themselves may fail to recognize their contribution in the value chain.

> *Moderator: If your husband were asked what you did, what would he say first?*
>
> *Respondent: Nothing. These jobs have no value.*
>
> *—Woman in Chowgacha, Jashore*

Women are expected to fulfill reproductive roles and responsibilities, such as household management, food preparation, and homestead farming tasks. The focus group discussion revealed that women's workload is a constraint to their increased involvement in productive activities in the value chain.

> *We face some problems. Like while we do flower knotting, we can't do cooking properly. We can't feed our children properly or can't send them to school.*
>
> *—Woman in Kaligonj, Jhenaidah*

Lack of access to training and equipment

Women's confinement to the home affects their access to equipment and other inputs (seed, feed, fertilizers) as well as information, knowledge, skills, and training. Several women described the social sanctions they faced for taking part in training in cut flower production.

> *We face difficulties at every step. We cannot sell the products locally in the market. People will laugh pointing at us. . . . We had to answer many questions before going to the training [in India for training on flowers]. Many people said we were going to India for prostitution.*
>
> *—Woman in Jhikargacha, Jashore*

Female focus group participants in all three value chains said they needed training, information, and equipment to improve their contribution to production. Women in the cut flower value chain said they needed training in preservation, seed storage, and marketing their products using information and communications technology (ICT). Women in the mango value chain said they needed training in pest management and the commercialization of mango pickles and bars. Women in the fish-farming value chain said they needed training in breeding and equipment for feed preparation.

Lack of access to credit

Focus group discussions revealed that value chain producers have difficulty accessing loans. As women are the primary targets of microcredit programs, they are used as conduits to, rather than endusers of, credit. Female focus group participants said they often take out loans because their husbands order them to do so. Women indicated that they felt saddled with the credit risk but did not profit directly benefit from the income generated by the productive investment from loans. If a man fails to repay the loan, his wife bears the pressure from the microcredit organization. Women are not allowed to take out loans for their own productive purposes without their husband's permission.

Lack of markets and spaces to commercialize women's products

Woman indicated that they lacked venues and opportunities to market their products (mango pickles, mango bars, and cut flowers). The social norms of women's seclusion limit women's own expectations and prospects of being able to sell in marketplaces.

Barriers at the micro (household/individual) level

Lack of control over income and assets

The focus group discussions revealed women's lack of control over income derived from their participation in agricultural value chains. Women may own certain types of livestock (cows, chickens, and ducks), but their lack of decision-making power at the household level sometimes precludes them from using the profits from the sale of their assets for their own production purposes.

Lack access to land/property ownership

Lack of land and property ownership translates into a lack of access to collateral-based formal credit and loans.[3]

> *If we want to borrow money from the bank, our husbands might not agree to include the land as collateral.*
>
> —*Woman in Jhikargacha, Jashore*

OPPORTUNITIES FOR WOMEN IN CROSS-BORDER TRADE

New trading opportunities are arising from improved regional connectivity, including for women. Although only small numbers of women currently participate in border *haat* trade, their presence represents a change in the status quo of men traditionally dominating regional trade. Qualitative data were collected through 3 focus group discussions with 26 male and female *haat* vendors, as well as through key informant interviews in two border *haats* along the India–Bangladesh border (see table 5.2). Box 5.1 summarizes the key findings and recommendations from this data-gathering exercise.

BOX 5.1

Opening up opportunities for women as cross-border traders

Since 2011 the governments of India and Bangladesh have established a number of *haats* along the border between the two countries. The 2010 Memorandum of Understanding between the governments placed restrictions on the number of license holder vendors and the types of products that can be sold. It limited buyers to people living within a 5-kilometer radius of the border, limited market days to two days a week, and set daily purchasing limits on buyers.

Border *haats* contribute only a negligible amount to the overall trade between Bangladesh and India: The number of traders, vendees, and stakeholders involved in trade in these *haats* represent less than 1 percent of Bangladesh's export. Border *haats* have had a positive welfare impact on the communities near them, however (Kathuria 2018). Border *haats* accounted for 32 percent of total household income for vendors from Bangladesh and 73 percent of total household income for vendors from India vendors; they accounted for

continued

Box 5.1, *continued*

16 percent of income of Bangladeshi laborers and 27 percent of the income of Bangladeshi transporters (CUTS International 2019). Border *haats* have also helped restore family ties that were disconnected by political barriers and create new bonds and friendships with people residing across the border. Of the two border *haats* visited as part of the study—Srinagar (Tripura)–Chagalnaiya (Chittagong) and Kamalasagar (Tripura)–Kasba (Chittagong)—one had no female participants and the other had only a few female Bangladeshi vendors. Male vendors sell a more diversified and more profitable range of products than women. Most women vendors sell products that have a female customer base—such as dresses, toys, cosmetics, and toiletries—because they prefer to interact mainly with female customers. Male vendors' income is higher than that of female vendors, because of the type of products sold. Despite their lower earnings, women vendors appreciate the livelihood opportunities offered by the border *haat*, given the limited job opportunities for women. Focus group discussions and key informant interviews yielded insights into the multiple and overlapping challenges and barriers women face as vendors at border *haats*. At the societal level, the main barrier is the social norm of *purdah*. Women vendors reported facing constant criticism from friends, relatives, and community members. Women are stigmatized when working on their own in public places and risk ostracism from friends and acquaintances. At the institutional level, women vendors cited various constraints, including the following:

- Female-friendly facilities—such as separate toilets with doors that close, disposal bins for sanitary pads, and water for handwashing—are lacking.
- The border *haat* has a single gate for each country, with no separate or priority lines for women and children, making it very difficult for them to enter and exit the *haat* when it gets crowded with shoppers.
- Product checking and screening are not automated. Border Guards of Bangladesh (BGBs) open boxes to check products, creating delays. All of the guards are men.
- Vendors are required to unload their products at the BGB check post and carry products to and from the *haat* back to the gate when the market closes. Doing so is particularly difficult for women, who may lack the strength to carry the boxes or the monetary means to hire helpers. These difficulties reinforce the idea that border *haat* trading is not a suitable occupation for women.
- The lack of banking and currency exchange facilities puts female traders in a vulnerable position, as it forces them to use informal networks for foreign currency transactions, which men control.
- Border *haat* vendors are reportedly selected in a nontransparent manner, in which personal connections and political affiliation play roles. As women lack these connections, they are less likely than men to obtain a vendor's license.
- The costs of cross-border trade (in the form of customs duties and taxes) are high.
- Male border management officials (district administrators, customs officers, local police, border security agents) create an intimidating environment.

At the individual level, constraints on women's participation include their lack of business experience and business networks. Women participants noted that most male vendors had previous business experience, particularly as merchants at the local market; business capital and merchandise to sell; networks of suppliers; and no mobility restrictions. Women's participation in cross-border trade can be enhanced by multifaceted efforts that focus primarily on institutional-level barriers but also include complementary efforts at the societal, community, and individual levels. Institutional-level changes include both infrastructure adaptations and policies. They could include the following:

- creating separate bathrooms for women and providing menstrual hygiene management kits

continued

Box 5.1, *continued*

- creating separate lines for women and children, at entrance staffed by female checkers
- establishing a common area in which buyers can mingle, with earmarked sitting for women and children
- designating stall space for female vendors, to accommodate the *purdah*
- creating storage space for women inside the border *haat* for their merchandise
- establishing quotas for the number of women granted vendor licenses
- reducing the fees and taxes paid by female vendors
- educating female entrepreneurs on border *haat* vendor policies and incentives for female vendors
- adopting codes of conduct to address sexual harassment and sexual extortion by border *haat* personnel, accompanied by awareness-raising, training, a clear accountability structure, and effective grievance redress procedures.

At the societal level, efforts to mainstream gender in trade facilitation policy frameworks could include policy directives to incentivize the participation of women as cross-border traders as well as the establishment of a network of women traders and entrepreneurs, to facilitate information exchange and showcase female role models in trade. At the community level, communication campaigns to change behavior could help reduce the stigma of women's participation in income-earning opportunities at the border *haat*. At the individual level, interventions could include improving women's business development skills, access to credit, and business networks.

POLICY CONSIDERATIONS

Bangladesh has enormous potential to increase its exports of agriculture commodities, which could improve livelihood opportunities in rural areas. Realizing this potential requires targeted trade facilitation measures that help move the country farther up the value chain as well as measures that foster women's participation. Collaboration by stakeholders in the supply chain and strategic support from the government, the private sector, and international organizations are necessary to optimize the agricultural value chain in Bangladesh. This section describes key areas of intervention.

Trade facilitation measures to improve export-oriented value chains

Trade facilitation and logistics measures aim to identify and remove administrative, logistical, and procedural obstacles to the movement of goods and services across borders. Measures can be grouped into two categories: behind-the-border and gateway interventions. Behind-the-border interventions reduce transactions costs within Bangladesh, by, for example, improving the quality and reducing the costs of transport infrastructure, logistical support (such as warehousing facilities), and other measure to optimize the agriculture value chain, including the following:

- At the production stage, training in efficient production practices and pest management and easier access to new technologies and input materials, such as feed fish, flower seeds, and fertilizers, are needed.

- At the harvesting and postharvesting stages, access needs to be provided to modern packaging and transport materials that add value to flowers, mangoes, and fish.
- At the transport and commercialization stage, cold chains need to be developed to reduce losses and waste, transport infrastructure needs to be improved to cut transport costs and postharvest losses, better loading and unloading facilities for produce need to be built, delays and illicit crossing charges at ferry *ghats* need to be reduced, financial services for farmers that allow them to obtain agricultural loans to finance needed investment need to be expanded, and producers' knowledge of cut flower and mango exports and value addition needs to be increased.

Gateway interventions facilitate trade at the border. They include improving customs and other border formalities, information efficiency, the transparency of regulations, the efficacy and logistical capability of ports and border crossings, and the cost and quality of international transport linkages (Ahmed, Kelegama, and Ghani 2010). Strategic thinking and action planning require the coordination of the activities of multiple actors and support organizations, including national and international organizations, such as the World Bank and the Food and Agricultural Organization. Policies to support organizing food producers into groups or associations should be encouraged, in order to facilitate investment and the dissemination of technologies and information, improve handling at the production level, and consolidate the volume of raw material needed to supply the chain and justify large-scale infrastructure and process investments. Other measures include the formation of farmers' marketing groups; the development of a marketing information system for cut flower, mango, and fish-farming producers; efforts to increase access to affordable ICT; and promotion activities, such as branding Bangladeshi products.

Measures to improve women's participation in export-oriented agricultural value chains

Lack of freedom of movement and confinement to home-based work limit the ability of Bangladeshi women to upgrade their participation in agricultural value chains.[4] *Purdah* norms exclude their participation in cultivation, direct negotiation in the market for labor and other inputs, and trading. Men tend to perform activities that would take women away from the household and prevent them from performing reproductive and domestic work. Strategies need to be grounded in the realities of women's lives and the fact that gender norms change only gradually and slowly. The most effective strategies are the ones that are applied to value chain products and processes in nodes in which women are already participating. Removing blockages to adding value at these nodes and increasing women's control of income over benefits can have direct impacts on returns to female value chain participants and be used as to incrementally facilitate behavior and norms change. In designing these strategies, care should be exercised to ensure that they do not lead to an increase in violence toward them (engaging in community dialogue and working with men can help reduce the likelihood of violence). Upgrading is more likely to occur when men and women have the desire to change and are shown the monetary rewards of doing so. Strategies for upgrading women's participation therefore need to be supplemented by communication and advocacy strategies directed primarily at men on the benefits of women's economic empowerment and efforts to make women's roles in the agricultural value chain visible. At the macro (policy) level, governments can conduct mass and multimedia campaigns describing the importance of empowering women economically by increasing their access to productive employment and showing that doing so increases their prestige and the purchasing power of the household. Governments can also pass legislation that encourages the formation of women-led cooperative organizations and helps spearhead partnerships with aid organizations to catalyze the development of agricultural value chains and strategic plans that include a strong emphasis on women's participation. Governments also need to prioritize women when developing economic policies or subsidy schemes.

At the mesolevel, several actions can be implemented to facilitate women's economic opportunities in agricultural value chains. Technical assistance can help form women-driven cooperatives and SMEs. Such assistance is currently missing in the cut flower, mango, and fish-farming value chains, according to focus group participants. A growing body of literature shows that women-led cooperatives improve women's social and economic capacities and participation in agricultural value chains (Amaza, Kwagbe, and Amos 1999; World Bank and FAO 2009; Jones, Smith, and Wills 2012; Datta and Gailey 2012). Technical support can be provided to mobilize the group; identify and formulate viable businesses; establish linkages downstream and upstream of the value chain; and explore venues to access finance, equipment, and technical training. Women-led cooperatives can target niche markets and corporate social responsibility. For example, women-only coffee cooperatives such as Café Femenino in Peru and Las Hermanas in Honduras are supplying large coffee retailers eager to meet consumer interest in social responsibility (Rubin and Manfre 2014). The formation of women-led cooperatives ensures that women benefit from their work, maintain control over their income, and expand their businesses. As part of SME development and technical assistance, training modules for women can address women's identity, the social construction of gender, gender discrimination, and women's self-confidence and self-esteem in a culturally grounded manner. Strategies to encourage women's control over income and financial inclusion can foster behavioral change by increasing women's economic autonomy. They include the following:

- Providing access to individual savings and credit products that are designed to meet the needs and preferences of women can improve women's control over investment decisions and rewards related to upgrading.
- Providing a low-cost alternative to conventional collateral through well-designed financial services such as group-based delivery channels for credit and savings can allow women to gain access to loans even if they do not own assets.
- Improving women's knowledge of financial service options and how to use them to their advantage can help women accumulate and control lump sums for future investment in their production enterprise.
- Bringing rural banking agents closer to prospective clients can address the mobility constraints women face and facilitate women's money management.
- Using mobile banking can increase women's access to financial services.
- Establishing direct payment systems and facilitating electronic payments for products women produce can make it more difficult for their husbands to control their earnings, giving women more decision-making power over

their income (Blackden and Makambo 2014). In Kenya, for example, payments to sweet potato farmers are made through M-Pesa, the cell phone money transfer service. Interviews suggest that using M-Pesa creates an opportunity for women to increase their control over income (Sebstad and Manfre 2011). Where payment is delivered to bank accounts, it is important to ensure that both women and men have access to those accounts, either through the use of joint bank accounts or by ensuring that women have access to an individual account without interference from spouses. "Choice architecture" can be used that allows the default decision to route payments to the female producer (while allowing farmers to opt out of this arrangement) (Chetty and others 2018).[5]

At the community level, projects could create advocacy groups that seek to mobilize male opinion leaders—religious leaders, teachers, government officials, politicians—to advocate for changes in women's status. Advocacy campaigns using community radio stations could help work to increase women's economic opportunities and empowerment. Such campaigns were launched in Rwanda as part of a USAID project that sought to educate citizens about the new gender-equal legal framework for land governance. To ensure that the messages were effective and targeted to men, the project conducted a baseline survey to assess local knowledge, attitudes, and beliefs about gender-equal land rights. The project partnered with a community radio station to launch a 10-month communications campaign across several districts with tailored messages (Chemonics n.d.). At the household level, training and sensitization of men—and women—needs to work toward moving away from the local cultural norm of *purdah*. Value chain projects could provide training to small-scale farming families on adopting a "farming as a family business" approach that fosters more cooperative efforts between men and women in planning and managing family farm enterprises to maximize household profits. Topics addressed include individual time and task allocation, family management and budgeting, and conflict resolution (USAID 2012). These workshops helped raise awareness of women's contributions to the family business, producer organizations, and value chains. The farming-as-a-family-business approach can also facilitate the delivery of agricultural extension services, capacity development, technology transfer, and access to productive inputs for women producers.

SUMMARY AND CONCLUDING REMARKS

This chapter presents the findings of a qualitative assessment of the challenges and constraints of three export-oriented agricultural value chains in Bangladesh, with a focus on barriers to women's participation. The value chain analysis identifies critical needs for increasing farmers' technical know-how on cut flower and mango cultivation, and pest management; improving the procurement of adequate packing materials and feed fish; developing cold chain capacity; and improving road infrastructure, among other actions to add value and access markets. Trade facilitation and value chain support measures that address these constraints can help strengthen livelihoods by increasing the prices farmers receive for their outputs. Restrictive gender norms, particularly *purdah*, constrain women's participation in agricultural value chains. Actions and strategies to address the problem need to be grounded in local sociocultural dynamics, especially in environments like Bangladesh, where interventions cause resentment and anger among men that could lead to an increase in gender-based violence.

By helping spur growth, trade facilitation measures may spur changes in social norms, customs, and behavior that could be accelerated through meso-level measures to open up employment and entrepreneurial opportunities for women. Slowly, a community's exposure to more women in respected roles in the workforce can help shift thinking, increase women's space in the public sphere, and improve women's status in the family and the community. Measures need to engage both women and men. Some measures can be taken quickly (and are low-hanging fruit); others will take time to implement but yield longer-term impacts. Men possess the power to remove obstacles to women's employment and access to productive resources, such as training, technology, and capital. A key component of interventions is to change the behavior and mind-sets of men and help them understand the benefits and prestige they—as well as their families—could gain by supporting employment opportunities for women outside of their households.

NOTES

1. The agreement lifts past restrictions on cross-border road transit for vehicles, passengers, and cargo across the territories of the countries.
2. *Purdah* means "curtain," implying female seclusion.
3. Islamic law allows women to own and inherit property, but it stipulates that sisters inherit half the share of their brothers. In practice, women face other constraints on owning land. Husbands may acquire property in their wives' names, and women may be encouraged to relinquish inheritance claims to their brothers (Sproule and others 2015).
4. Upgrading involves changes within a value chain to respond to changing market conditions and new market opportunities. In agricultural value chains, upgrading may include (a) process upgrading (an increase in the efficiency of production processes, resulting in reduced unit costs, which can involve improved organization of the production process or improved technology); (b) product upgrading (improvement in the quality of a product or variety that increases its value to consumers); (c) functional upgrading (entry into a new function in the value chain that generates higher returns); and (d) channel upgrading (entry into a marketing channel that leads to a new end market in the value chain, for example, from the domestic to the export market for the same product) (Sebstad and Manfre 2011).
5. Choice architecture refers to way in which alternatives are presented to prospective customers. Selecting an opt-in rather than an opt-out default affects the decisions people make (Chetty and others 2018).

REFERENCES

Ahmed, S., S. Kelegama, and E. Ghani. 2010. *Promoting Economic Cooperation in South Asia: Beyond SAFTA*. New Delhi: SAGE.

Amaza, P. S., P. V. Kwagbe, and A. A. Amos. 1999. "Analysis of Women's Participation in Agricultural Cooperatives: Case Study of Borno State, Nigeria." *Annals of Borno* 15: 187–96.

Blackden, M., and M. Makambo. 2014. *The Fruit of Her Labor: Promoting Gender-Equitable Agribusiness in Papua New Guinea*. Washington, DC: World Bank and International Finance Corporation.

Bridges, S., D. Lawson, and S. Begum. 2011. "Labour Market Outcomes in Bangladesh: The Role of Poverty and Gender." *European Journal of Development Research* 23 (3): 459–87.

Brush, C. G., A. de Bruin, and F. Welter. 2009. "A Gender-Aware Framework for Women's Entrepreneurship." *International Journal of Gender and Entrepreneurship* 1 (1): 8–24.

Chaudhury, A. B. R., M. Bhonsale, and P. Basu. 2015. *Driving across the South Asian Borders: The Motor Vehicle Agreement between Bhutan, Bangladesh, India and Nepal.* ORF Occasional Paper, Observer Research Foundation, New Delhi.

Chemonics. n.d. "From Policy to Practice: Exercising Gender-Equal Land Rights in Rwanda." https://chemonics.com/impact-story/policy-practice-exercising-gender-equal-land-rights-rwanda/.

Chetty, R., L. D. Villiers, B. Duda, and H. Smit. 2018. *What Can Behavioural Science Tell Us about the Financial Decisions of Women? Evidence from a Systematic Review of Behavioural Interventions.* Ottawa: International Development Research Centre (IDRC).

CUTS International. 2019. *Bordering on Happiness: An Assessment of Socio-Economic Impacts of Bangladesh-India Border* Haats. Jaipur.

Datta, P., and R. Gailey. 2012. "Empowering Women through Social Entrepreneurship: Case Study of a Women's Cooperative in India." *Entrepreneurship Theory and Practice* 36 (3): 569–87.

Demirgüç-Kunt, A., L. Klapper, D. Singer, S. Ansar, and J. Hess. 2018. *The Global Findex Database 2017: Measuring Financial Inclusion and the Fintech Revolution.* Washington, DC: World Bank. doi:10.1596/978-1-4648-1259-0. License: Creative Commons Attribution CC BY 3.0 IGO.

Dhaka Tribune. 2019. "Floriculture Business Showing Robust Growth." February 24. https://www.dhakatribune.com/business/2019/02/24/floriculture-business-showing-robust-growth.

FAO (Food and Agriculture Organization). 2018. *The State of World Fisheries and Aquaculture 2018.* Rome.

Farole, T., Y. Cho, L. L. Y. Bossavie, and R. Aterido. 2017. *Bangladesh Jobs Diagnostic.* Jobs Series, Issue 9, World Bank, Washington, DC.

Hossain Ovi, I., and N. Mahmud. 2018. "Bangladesh Flower Market Reaches Tk1, 200cr, Expanding at 10% Rate." *Dhaka Tribune,* December 4.

Independent. 2019. "Cut Flower Export on the Rise." March 1. http://www.theindependentbd.com/post/189677.

Jones, E., S. Smith, and C. Wills. 2012. "Women Producers and the Benefits of Collective Forms of Enterprise." *Gender and Development* 20 (1): 13–32.

Kabeer, N. 2011. "Between Affiliation and Autonomy: Navigating Pathways of Women's Empowerment and Gender Justice in Rural Bangladesh." *Development and Change* 42 (2): 499–528.

Kathuria, S. 2018. *A Glass Half Full: The Promise of Regional Trade in South Asia.* South Asia Development Forum. Washington, DC: World Bank.

Moazzem, K. G., and M. A. Radia. 2018. *Data Universe of Bangladesh's RMG Enterprises: Key Features and Limitations.* Dhaka: Centre for Policy Dialogue.

Pariona, A. 2018. "The Top Mango Producing Countries in the World." *WorldAtlas.* worldatlas.com/articles/the-top-mango-producing-countries-in-the-world.html.

Paul, B. 1992. "Female Activity Space in Rural Bangladesh." *Geographical Review* 82 (1): 1–12.

Quisumbing, A., and B. McClafferty. 2006. *Using Gender Research in Development.* Food Security in Practice Technical Guide Series. Washington, DC: International Food Policy Research Institute.

Rahman, M. 2014. "Trade Benefits for Least Developed Countries: The Bangladesh Case Market Access Initiatives, Limitations and Policy Recommendations." Committee for Development Policy (CDP) Background Paper 18, Department of Economic and Social Affairs, United Nations, New York.

Rahman, T. 2017. "Role of Agriculture in Bangladesh Economy: Uncovering the Problems and Challenges." *International Journal of Business and Management Invention* 6 (7): 36–46.

Rakibuzzaman, M., S. Rahul, M. R. Jahan, M. I. Ifaz, and A. J. Uddin. 2018. "Flower Industry in Bangladesh." *International Journal of Business, Social and Scientific Research* 7 (1): 50–56.

Rubin, D., and C. Manfre. 2014. "Promoting Gender-Equitable Agricultural Value Chains." In *Gender in Agriculture: Closing the Knowledge Gap*, ed. Agnes Q., T. Meinzen-Dick, T. Raney, A. Croppenstedt, J. Behrman, and A. Peterman, 287–314. Rome: Springer and International Food Policy Research Institute.

Sebstad, J., and C. Manfre. 2011. *Behavior Change Perspective on Gender and Value Chain Development*. Washington, DC: US Agency for International Development (USAID).

Senders, A., A. Lentink, M. Vanderschaeghe, and J. Terrillon. 2012. *Gender in Value Chains: Practical Toolkit to Integrate a Gender Perspective in Agricultural Value Chain Development*. Agri-ProFocus. https://agriprofocus.com/upload/ToolkitENGender_in_Value_ChainsJan2014compressed1415203230.pdf.

Solotaroff, J., A. Kotikula, T. Lonnberg, S. Ali, R. P. Pande, and F. Jahan. 2019. *Voices to Choices: Bangladesh's Journey in Women's Economic Empowerment*. Washington, DC: World Bank.

Sproule, K., C. Kieran, A. Quisumbing, and D. Cheryl. 2015. *Gender, Headship, and the Life Cycle: Land Ownership in Four Asian Countries*. IFPRI Discussion Paper 01481, International Food Policy Research Institute, Washington DC.

Terrillon, J. 2010. *Gender Mainstreaming in Value Chain Development: Practical Guidelines and Tools*. The Hague: Corporate Network Agriculture SNV.

USAID (US Agency for International Development). 2012. *Farming as a Family Business: Training Manual*. Washington, DC. http://pdf.usaid.gov/pdf_docs/PA00JRZQ.pdf.

World Bank. 2012. *World Development Report 2012: Gender and Development*. Washington, DC.

World Bank. 2015. *Bangladesh: More and Better Jobs to Accelerate Shared Growth and End Extreme Poverty*. Systematic Country Diagnostic. Washington, DC.

World Bank. 2020. *World Development Indicators*. Washington, DC.

World Bank and FAO (Food and Agriculture Organization). 2009. *Gender in Agriculture Sourcebook*. Washington, DC: World Bank.

www.ingramcontent.com/pod-product-compliance
Ingram Content Group UK Ltd.
Pitfield, Milton Keynes, MK11 3LW, UK
UKHW050036060726
472907UK00008B/293

9 781464 816352